INSTRUCTOR'S BIG BOOK OF

HOLIDAY WORD PUZZLES

Over 400 reproducible
skill-builders for
130 year-round celebrations!

Rebuses, crosswords, unscramblers, wordfinds,
brainteasers, magic squares — a calendar collection
to help you highlight seasons and special occasions
throughout the year; teach fun facts; and strengthen skills
in reading, thinking, logic, and language arts!

Diane Hellriegel

SCHOLASTIC INC., 2931 East McCarty Street, Jefferson City, MO 65102
Or call (800) 325-6149 between 7:30 a.m. and 5 p.m. Central Time. In Missouri, call (800) 392-2179.

INSTRUCTOR RESOURCE SERIES

Big Idea Book — 750 best classroom do-its and use-its from Instructor magazine. 49000.
Big Basics Book — 55 master plans for teaching the basics, with over 100 reproducibles. 49001.
Big Holiday Book — Seasonal songs, stories, poems, plays, and art, plus an activities calendar. 49002.
Big Seasonal Arts & Crafts Book — Over 300 projects for special days and seasons. 49003.
Big Language Arts Book for Primary Grades — 136 reading and language skills reproducibles. 49004.
Big Math Book for Primary Grades — 135 reproducibles on number concepts and processes. 49005.
Big Book of Teacher Savers — Class lists, letters to parents, record-keeping forms, calendars, maps, writing forms, and more. 49006.
Synonyms, Sentences, and Spelling Bees: Language Skills Book A — 140 reproducibles. 49007.
Periods, Paragraphs, and Prepositions: Language Skills Book B — Over 140 reproducibles. 49008.
Big Book of Reading Ideas — Teacher-tested reading ideas for use with any reading system. 49009.
Teacher's Activity Calendar — Red letter days, ideas, units for the school year. 49010.
Early Education Almanac — Hundreds of activities for kindergarten and beyond. 49011.
Paper, Pen, and Think — Ideas galore for developing a sequential writing program. 49012.
Beating the Bulletin Board Blues — Step-by-step ways to bulletin board learning centers. 49013.
Success with Sticky Subjects — Books A and B together offer over 240 reproducible worksheets for classroom drill in problem areas of the curriculum. **Book A** — 49014 **Book B** — 49015.
Foolproof, Failsafe Seasonal Science — Units, experiments, and quick activities. 49016.
Poetry Place Anthology — 605 favorite poems from Instructor, organized for instant access. 49017.
Big Book of Plays — 82 original, reproducible plays for all occasions and levels. 49018.
Artfully Easy! — "How-to" workshops on teaching art basics, group projects, and more! 49019.
Big Book of Study Skills — Techniques and activities for the basic subject areas. 49020.
Big Book of Study Skills Reproducibles — Over 125 classroom-tested worksheets for all levels. 49021.
Big Book of Computer Activities — A hands-on guide for using computers in every subject. 49022.
Read-Aloud Anthology — 98 stories for all grades and all occasions. 49023.
Page-a-Day Pursuits — Over 300 reproducibles on famous days, birthdays, and events. 49024.
Big Book of Holiday Word Puzzles — 400 skill-builders for 130 year 'round celebrations. 49025.
Big Book of Health and Safety — Reproducible activities to shape up the health curriculum. 49026.
Teacher Savers Two — Reproducible awards, contracts, letters, sanity-keepers galore. 49027.
Celebrate America — Over 200 reproducible activities about the symbols, the land, the people of the U.S.A. Maps, graphs, timelines, folklore, and more. Eight pull-out posters. 49028.
Big Book of Absolutely Everything — 1001 ideas to take you through the school year. 49029.
Language Unlimited — 160 reproducibles sharpen reading, writing, speaking, listening skills. 49030.
Children and Media — Activities help kids learn from TV, radio, film, videotape, print. 49031.
Blockbuster Bulletin Boards — 366 teacher originals for all grades, subjects, and seasons. 49032.
Hey Gang! Let's Put On A Show — 50 original skits, choral readings, plays for all ages. 49033.
Puzzle Pals — Mazes, decoders, wordsearches, hidden objects and more. 49034.
Hands-On Science — Jam-packed with facts and activities to develop young scientists, K-8. 49035.
21st Century Discipline — Practical strategies to teach students responsibility and self-control. 49036.
Learning to Teach — A blend of research on teaching with the practical insights of experienced teachers. 49037.
Loving Literature — Literature selections and accompanying activities that encourage kids to laugh, cry, wonder, and keep on reading. 49038.
Teaching Kids to Care — 156 activities to help young children cooperate, share, and learn together. 49039.
Games, Giggles, and Giant Steps — 250 games for children ages 2-8; no equipment needed. 49040.
Everybody Sing and Dance — 80 hands-on, shoes-off song, dance, rhythm, and creative movement experiences. 49041.
Toward Tomorrow — Reproducible activities that challenge students to focus on and believe in the future. 49070.

INSTRUCTOR'S BIG BOOK OF HOLIDAY WORD PUZZLES

12 11 10 9 8 7 6 5 4 3 2 1 9/8 0 1 2 3 4/9
Printed in the U.S.A.
First Scholastic printing, December 1989

Author, Diane Hellriegel; artist, Michelle Berg. Cover design by Regina Vorgang. The author would like to thank her family, Vivian Padmore and her fourth grade class, and Ruth Moench, sixth grade teacher, for testing the puzzles in this book.

ISBN 0-590-49025-7

CONTENTS

Introduction 5

September 7
Labor Day ● First Day of School ● Grandparents'
Day ● Mayflower Day ● Citizenship Day ● Mickey
Mouse's Birthday ● Autumn ● Tet Trung-Thu ●
Rosh Hashanah ● Succot

October 22
Launch of Sputnik I ● Fire Prevention Week ●
Columbus Day ● Alaska Day Festival ● First
National Horse Show ● United Nations Day ●
Dedication of Statue of Liberty ● Halloween ●
National Magic Week ● Diwali

November 38
Daniel Boone's Birthday ● Election Day ●
Veterans Day ● Frederick Banting's Birthday ●
National Children's Book Week ● National
Family Week ● Thanksgiving ● Mark Twain's
Birthday ● Advent

December 50
St. Nicholas Day ● Human Rights Day ● Santa
Lucia Day ● Wright Brothers Day ● Winter ●
Pilgrims' Day ● Hanukkah ● Christmas ● Clara
Barton's Birthday ● Boxing Day ● New Year's
Eve

January 66
New Year's Day ● National Hobby Month ● Jakob
Grimm's Birthday ● Louis Braille's Birthday ●
George Washington Carver ● Twelfth Night ●
Epiphany ● John A. MacDonald's Birthday ●
Charles Perrault's Birthday ● Martin Luther
King's Birthday ● Benjamin Franklin's
Birthday ● Inauguration Day ● First Basketball
Game ● Australia Day ● Wayne Gretsky's Birthday ●
Anna Pavlova's Day ● Chinese New Year

February 86
Black History Month ● Groundhog Day ● Candlemas ●
Elizabeth Blackwell's Birthday ● Babe Ruth's
Birthday ● Boy Scouts Founded ● Thomas
Edison's Birthday ● Abraham Lincoln's Birthday ●
Judy Blume's Birthday ● Valentine's Day ●
Canada's Maple Leaf Flag ● Susan B. Anthony's Birthday ●
Heritage Day ● George Washington's Birthday ●
Leap Year ● Lent

March 108
Alexander Graham Bell's Birthday ● Hina
Matsuri ● Knute Rockne's Birthday ● Girl
Scouts Founded ● National Wildlife Week ●
St. Patrick's Day ● Purim ● Spring ● Earth Day ●
Noruz ● Passover ● Easter

April 127
National Humor Month ● April Fool's Day ●
Hans Christian Andersen ● First
Modern Olympic Games ● Buddha's Birthday ●
Be Kind to Animals Week ● Arbor Day ●
Beverly Cleary's Birthday ● National Library
Week ● William Shakespeare's Birthday ● Bird
Day ● Samuel F. B. Morse's Birthday

May 143
Older Americans' Month ● May Day ● Law Day ●
Tango-no-Sekku ● Cinco de Mayo ● Native
American Day ● Florence Nightingale's
Birthday ● Mother's Day ● International
Pickle Week ● Armed Forces Day ● Victoria
Day ● Sally Ride's Birthday ● Memorial Day

June 158
Jefferson Davis's Birthday ● Kamehameha Day ●
Flag Day ● Children's Day ● Father's Day ●
Summer ● Midsummer's Day ● Helen Keller's
Birthday ● Green Corn Celebration

July 171
Canada Day ● First Regular TV Telecasts ●
Independence Day ● P.T. Barnum's Birthday ●
Bastille Day ● U.S. Landing on the Moon ● Puerto
Rico's Constitution Day

August 182
First America's Cup Race ● 19th Amendment

Your Birthday 184

Answer Key 187

INTRODUCTION

What child doesn't look forward to the special celebrations that holidays bring? With *Instructor's Big Book of Holiday Word Puzzles,* you can turn that enthusiasm into meaningful classroom activities. Each page deals with one of 125 different holidays, birthdays of famous men and women, anniversaries, festivals, and seasonal events. The holidays are those most commonly celebrated in the United States and Canada, plus lesser-known ones representing many different cultures and nationalities. They appear chronologically according to the school calendar, beginning with September's Labor Day.

Answering the questions and solving the puzzles will help pupils improve or reinforce their language arts skills. The puzzles will:

- expand vocabularies with puzzles involving synonyms, antonyms, and homonyms.
- improve spelling and grammar skills.
- give practice in basic reading skills and in following directions.
- sharpen reasoning abilities.
- stretch imaginations.

And while building these skills, pupils will also learn the historical origins of many holidays and events as well as some of the customs and traditions evolving from them.

The puzzles touch on other curriculum areas, too. Social studies is represented in the accounts of historical events (from Columbus to moon landings) and in puzzles that deal with geography and map skills. Famous scientists (Edison, Carver) and some of their important discoveries are recognized. Sports is featured prominently from the first Olympic Games to America's Cup Race.

The number and variety of puzzles guarantees a year full of stimulating, challenging holidays. There are over 400 activities designed especially for the abilities and interests of middle graders. The baker's dozen types include:

1. Unscrambling letters to form words and messages.
2. Making small words from the letters in a larger word. Pupils may not be able to make all the words asked for, but suggest they see who can find the most. They may find different words from those listed in the answer key.
3. Finding words hidden in sentences. The hidden word will usually be found as part of one or more words in the sentence.
4. Building words from letters and word parts.
5. Making word pyramids by adding, subtracting, or scrambling letters.
6. Completing word chains. Pupils should be reminded to change only one letter in each word in order to form the final word.
7. Completing word squares. A word square is a crossword-type puzzle in which each answer reads the same across and down.

8. Fitting words into a blank puzzle grid.

9. Solving crossword puzzles. The bigger or more challenging crosswords also include a word bank which lists all the words used in the puzzle. More skilled or older pupils might try to complete the puzzle on their own before checking the word bank.

10. Solving word-search puzzles. These are also called *word finds* or *word hunts.* The hidden words may appear forward or backward when written vertically or horizontally, but only appear forward when written diagonally.

11. Translating rebuses. A rebus is a way of writing a word or phrase by using pictures to suggest the word or its syllables. Pupils must be careful to subtract any letters in the correct order. When told to subtract the letter N, for example, they must be sure to drop the first N in the answer.

12. Solving codes, ciphers, and cryptograms. To solve a shift cipher, pupils should draw a line and print the letters of the alphabet from A to Z above it. These are the answer letters. For a three-shift cipher, a second alphabet is written directly under the top letters, starting with X, Y, Z, so that A falls under the D of the top line. These are the code letters. To solve a puzzle, pupils match letters in the code line with the letters in the answer line. The code word MRWWIB in a three-shift cipher equals PUZZLE.

13. Answering riddles, brainteasers, and matching games.

Each puzzle activity is complete in itself, requiring no additional materials or information in order to be solved. A solid line across a puzzle page means that the puzzles can be used separately. When there is only time for a brief activity, the page can be cut in half and distributed individually. Answers are included at the end of the book. For those puzzles with more than one possible answer, some, but not all, variations are given.

Keep this book handy. You will find its pages a perfect way to:

● Introduce a lesson.
● Serve as a catalyst for a class discussion or debate.
● Act as a warm-up exercise to start the day.
● Provide a take-home activity to share with parents. (The last 20 pages or so would be a good end-of-school gift for families to complete over the summer.)
● Use as a time filler for the pupil who has finished an assignment early.
● Serve, on occasion, as an entertaining alternative to traditional homework.
● Provide independent seatwork or group activity (depending on pupils' ability and special class needs).

A note about dates. Many of the feast days of certain cultures are kept according to ancient calendars. The dates on which they are celebrated do not always fall on the same date in our calendar, or the same day each year. These holidays are listed at the time of year when they occur (Rosh Hashanah—September/October). Movable holidays (Thanksgiving) are listed for the day or week they occur (fourth Thursday in November). Holidays now legally celebrated on a Monday are listed on either their original dates or as a movable holiday.

Job Hunting

On Labor Day, we honor working people. Take a look at the sentences below. Hidden in each one is the name of a job or career. Can you find them all? (The first one is done.)

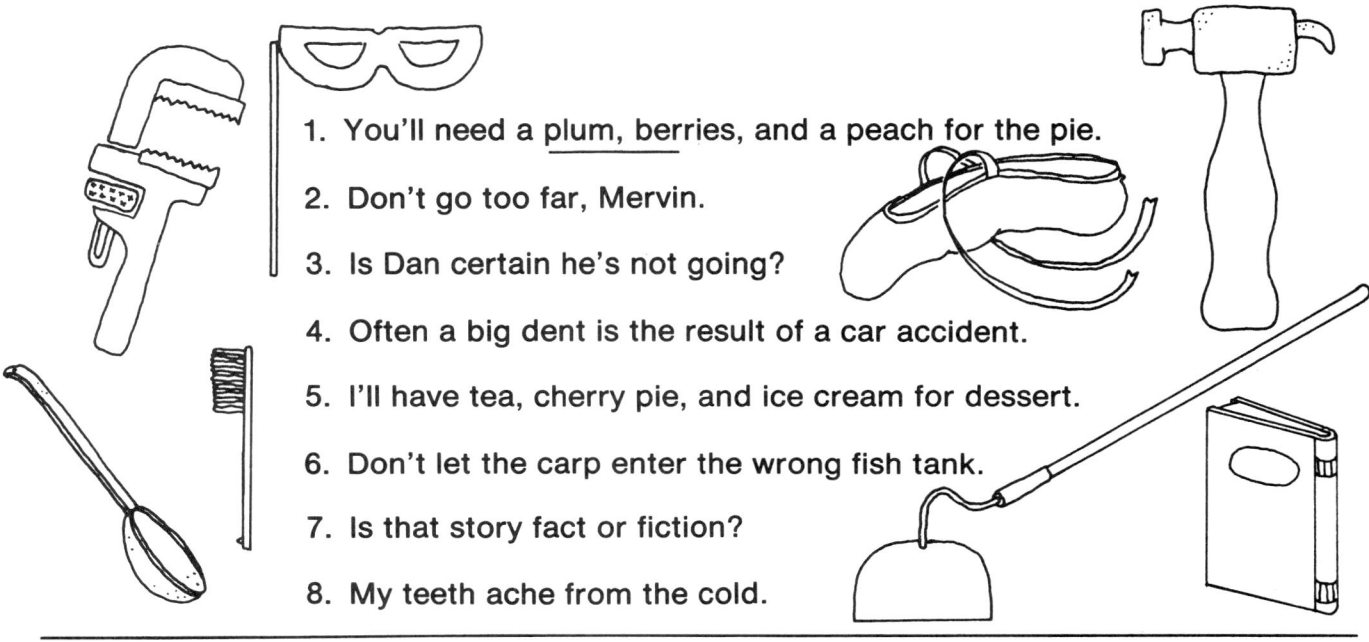

1. You'll need a plum, berries, and a peach for the pie.

2. Don't go too far, Mervin.

3. Is Dan certain he's not going?

4. Often a big dent is the result of a car accident.

5. I'll have tea, cherry pie, and ice cream for dessert.

6. Don't let the carp enter the wrong fish tank.

7. Is that story fact or fiction?

8. My teeth ache from the cold.

Take a Break

In the United States, Labor Day marks the end of summer vacation. **Here's your last chance to do some of your favorite summer activities. Unscramble the words below and write them correctly in the spaces provided.**

When you've unscrambled them all, print the circled letters in order in the space below and see what you get for all your trouble!

SEABLALB _ ◯ _ _ _ _ _ _

LSIA _ _ ◯ _

LEORLR—KASET _ ◯ _ _ _ — _ _ _ ◯ _

PMAC TOU _ _ _ _ ◯ _ _

SFIH ◯ _ _ _

FSRU _ _ ◯ _

NSUAHBET _ ◯ _ _ _ _ _ _

NCIPCI _ _ _ ◯ _ _

_ _ _ _ _ _ _ _ _ _!

7

Name: _____

FIRST DAY OF SCHOOL

"The Good Ole Days"

Take a peek inside a one-room frontier schoolhouse.

The teacher's desk usually held a bell and a ruler. There was a stove in the center of the room for heat. Many of the students sat on a long, wooden bench. Each child took turns reading from the Bible, a speller, and a reader. They wrote on a slate with pieces of chalk. Many children had to walk more than a mile across the prairie to get to the school.

See how good a pioneer pupil you would be by filling in the puzzle grid opposite with the words underlined in the paragraph above.

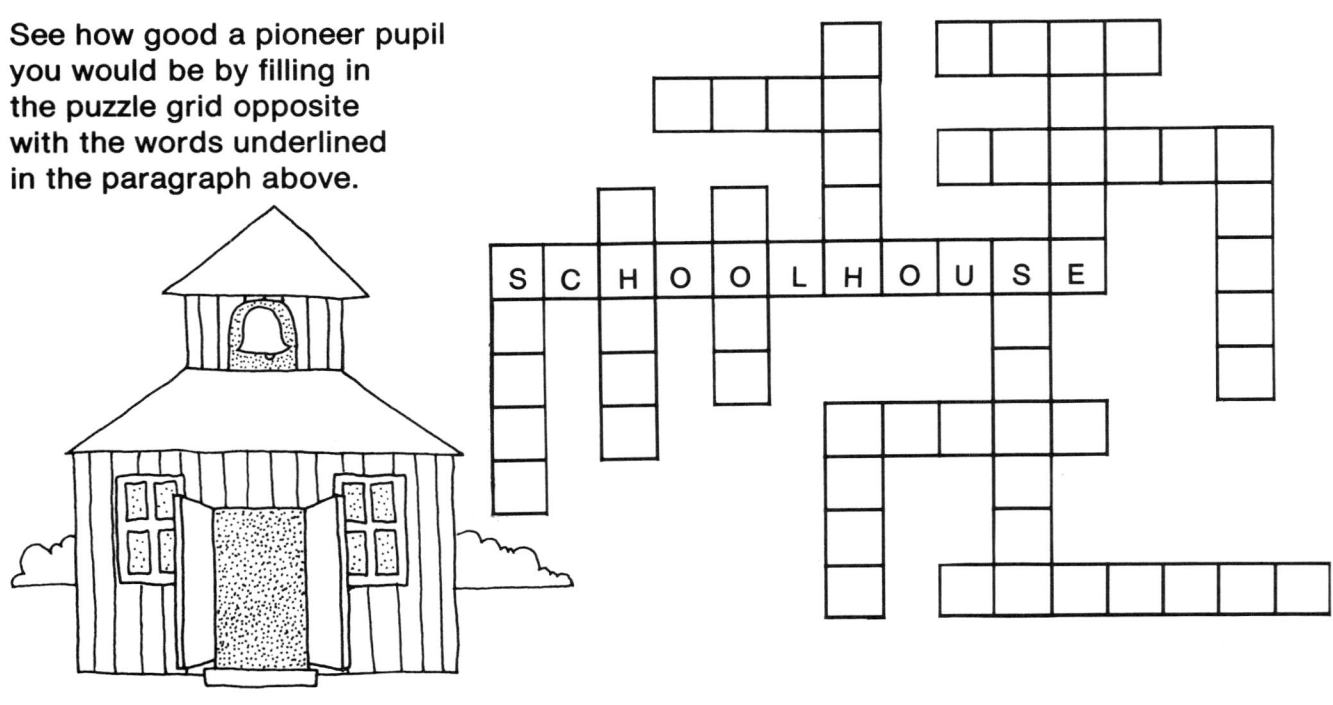

S C H O O L H O U S E

Teacher's Pet

See how much you can learn from the "teach."
Can you find at least ten different words of three letters or more in the word below?

T E A C H

1. _____   4. _____   8. _____

2. _____   5. _____   9. _____

3. _____   6. _____   10. _____

7. _____

FIRST DAY OF SCHOOL

Three Rs Plus

Today, students learn more than just the three Rs: "reading, 'riting and 'rithmetic." Unscramble the names below of all the subjects you'll be studying and then unscramble the circled letters to see what you'll get as a result of all your hard work!

REPOGHAGY   — — — — Ⓞ — — — —

CLAISO DETUSIS   — — — — —   — Ⓞ — — — —

HATSEMCITAM   — — — — — Ⓞ — — — —

GALNUGEA STAR   — Ⓞ — — — — —   — — — —

NESICEC   Ⓞ — — — — — — —

— — — — —!

A Trick Question

Can you pass the test?

What do you get when you cross a crab with a good student?

(Add and subtract the letters as shown to learn the answer.)

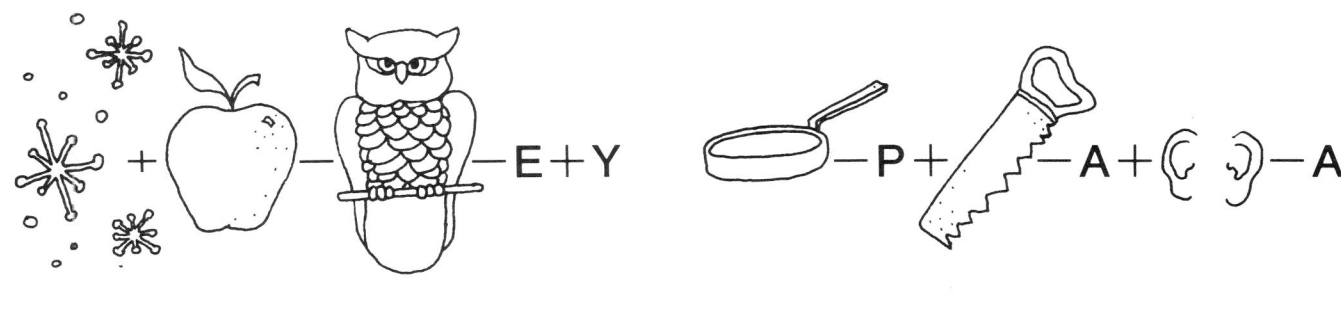

Name: _____

GRANDPARENTS' DAY

A Big Family

Some grandparents have many little grandchildren. The word GRANDPARENTS itself has many little words (of three letters or more) hidden in it. Can you find them? (There are at least 50.)

G R A N D P A R E N T S

1. _____	18. _____	34. _____
2. _____	19. _____	35. _____
3. _____	20. _____	36. _____
4. _____	21. _____	37. _____
5. _____	22. _____	38. _____
6. _____	23. _____	39. _____
7. _____	24. _____	40. _____
8. _____	25. _____	41. _____
9. _____	26. _____	42. _____
10. _____	27. _____	43. _____
11. _____	28. _____	44. _____
12. _____	29. _____	45. _____
13. _____	30. _____	46. _____
14. _____	31. _____	47. _____
15. _____	32. _____	48. _____
16. _____	33. _____	49. _____
17. _____		50. _____

GRANDPARENTS' DAY

Your Family Tree

Here's your chance to get the whole family together to honor your grandparents on their special day.

How many relatives can you find hidden in the tree opposite? For each relative you may use the letters given in any order, but only as often as they appear in the tree. One is done for you.

MOTHER
_____
_____
_____
_____
_____
_____

L M S H E I S
O B A A T N G
C U R R D X F

A Grand Riddle

You've got visitors for the holiday, but who *are* they?

Your brother-in-law's wife's great-aunt's only sister.

_____

Your niece's mother's father's mother's husband.

_____

Name: _____

MAYFLOWER DAY

Hoist Anchor!

On this day in 1620, 102 people set sail from England. They were headed for North America and the trip was expected to take months. They filled the hold (bottom) of their ship, the *Mayflower,* with barrels of things they would need for their life in the New World.

They brought <u>water</u> and <u>food</u>, <u>seeds</u> and <u>tools</u> for planting, plus <u>saws</u>, <u>axes</u>, and <u>hammers</u> for building <u>houses</u>. They also brought <u>cloth</u>, <u>beads</u>, <u>knives</u>, and little <u>mirrors</u> to trade with the <u>natives</u>.

Can you find all the underlined words in the puzzle opposite? They may be up, down, across, diagonal, or backwards. Circle each word as you find it.

```
H A M N E S A V S F
H W K C L O T H D B
A A P O D F S A E K
M T M I R R O R S X
S E K M I V F O S G
E R J B E A P A D M
V L P Z T R Q X E I
I S K S W A S E E R
N A L M H G T S S O
K V J S D A E B G Q
```

Land Ho!

Can you speed the passengers of the *Mayflower* on their journey by solving this riddle?

There are two English words of four letters each that are spelled the same, except for their first letters. One has to do with the ocean, the other with the land. What are they?

___ ___ ___ ___   ___ ___ ___ ___

Name: _____

CITIZENSHIP DAY

Sign Here

The signing of the Constitution of the United States took place on this day in 1787, at Independence Hall in Philadelphia. The Constitution was written to protect the rights of every U.S. *citizen,* and so the people are also honored on this day. (A citizen is a member of a nation either by birth or by choice. He or she has certain rights and owes loyalty to that nation.)

Can you unscramble the names of the two U.S. presidents who were also signers of the Constitution?

REGOGE SANGTWIHNO

___ ___ ___ ___ ___ ___   ___ ___ ___ ___ ___ ___ ___ ___ ___ ___

SEJMA DASONIM

___ ___ ___ ___ ___   ___ ___ ___ ___ ___ ___ ___

Extra Special

The Bill of Rights was added to the Constitution two years after the signing. These ten amendments promise U.S. citizens <u>freedom</u> of <u>speech</u>, <u>press</u>, <u>worship</u>, and <u>assembly</u> and the <u>right</u> to bear <u>arms</u>, to a <u>speedy</u> trial, and to a <u>trial</u> by <u>jury</u>.

Can you find each of the words underlined in the paragraph above in the puzzle? They may be up, down, across, diagonal, or backwards. Circle each word as you find it.

```
J  U  R  W  F  R  E  E  D  O
T  H  G  I  O  P  K  T  Z  N
R  Q  P  L  A  R  M  S  T  Y
I  K  S  H  N  E  S  X  H  D
E  F  R  P  G  S  Z  H  G  E
Y  L  B  M  E  S  S  A  I  E
R  I  Y  U  R  E  K  W  R  P
U  A  P  R  E  S  C  N  E  S
J  L  A  I  R  T  D  H  P  F
K  D  F  R  E  E  D  O  M  G
```

13

MICKEY MOUSE'S BIRTHDAY

Yea, Mickey!

Did you know that before Mickey Mouse made his official debut in the 1928 cartoon *Steamboat Willie,* he appeared in a silent cartoon called *Plane Crazy?* Only in that cartoon, he was called Mortimer Mouse, not Mickey! Invite some of Mickey's friends to his birthday party by completing the crossword puzzle below.

ACROSS:
2. A duck in a sailor suit.
5. The color of Bianca and Bernard mouse.
7. The birthday rodent himself.
9. Donald's girlfriend.
12. First initials of Eeyore and Piglet.
14. One of Donald Duck's nephews.
15. What the wicked stepmother said when Cinderella asked to go to the ball.
16. Us.
18. Donald's penny-pinching relative.
20. Kanga's baby.
21. Another one of Donald's nephews.
22. _____ and Dale.

DOWN:
1. Mickey's girlfriend.
2. A flying elephant.
3. Santa's nickname.
4. Sept. 19 is Mickey's birth_____.
5. Kooky canine who talks.
6. A notice to sell things. (plural)
8. A sad stuffed donkey.
9. A nephew of Donald Duck.
10. More than one yes vote.
11. Peter Pan could _____ over rooftops.
13. Mickey's canine pal.
17. A honey-loving bear.
19. What did Snow White do when she was lost in the woods?

Name: _____

AUTUMN

Ripe for the Picking

Autumn is a time for harvesting many different crops. Take a stroll into the apple orchard and see if you can solve this brain teaser.

If you took three apples from a basket that held ten apples, how many apples would you have?

_____

Bee Kind

Emily found a surprise in the apple she picked while working in the orchard with her friend, Abraham.

Can you figure out what they said to one another.

"M E, C D B?"

_____

"O S, A B, I C D B.

_____

S E Z 2 C D B!"

_____

AUTUMN

Name: _____

Autumn Harvest

Harvest your crop of knowledge by gathering all the answers you know and filling the crossword puzzle below. (One has already been done for you.)

WORD BANK

at	leaves
autumn	mine
bat	nil
D.C.	or
farmers	rake
faye	rd
five	re
football	right
geese	scarier
gnu	schools
grass	spot
harvest	term
he	top
hiker	TS
ll	UFO
it	yes

ACROSS:

1. A game whose object is to carry a ball across the opponent's goal line.
5. A lawn.
8. In the exact position of.
9. Opposite of left.
13. The gathering of a crop, often in early fall.
15. A tunnel in the earth that contains minerals.
16. The number of fingers you have on one hand.
17. Unidentified Flying Object.
18. To collect leaves with a large comblike tool.
19. September begins the fall ____ of school.
20. Abbrev. for road.
23. Opposite of no.
24. Nothing, zero.
26. More frightening. On Halloween, some children's masks are ____ than others.
27. A stain or mark.
28. Initials of Tom Sawyer.

DOWN:

1. People who plant and harvest crops.
2. A flying animal we think of on Halloween.
3. Same as #8 ACROSS.
4. The parts of trees that turn different colors in autumn.
5. Large Canadian birds that often fly south for the winter.
6. The season between summer and winter.
7. Buildings that students attend in order to learn.
10. Roman numeral for two.
11. A type of African antelope.
12. She and ____.
13. A person who likes to walk in the woods.
14. Abbrev. for regarding.
16. A girl's name.
19. Highest part.
21. Direct Current.
22. Neither, nor; either, ____.
25. Thing

AUTUMN

Name: _____

Lucky Leaves

Some people believe that it is very lucky to catch a leaf as it falls from a tree. How lucky are you? Try to find all the leaves listed below in the puzzle. The words may be up, down, diagonal, across, or backwards. Circle each word as you find it.

MAPLE OAK

ASH BIRCH

POPLAR ASPEN

WILLOW BEECH

ALDER ELM

```
O T W B E E C K R S
A N N I A Q Y A M A
L E E R L L I E S E
B L P C V L D U W L
I K S H S A O E R P
R R A L P O P W R A
B O A K B I E N T M
K A D Z J N L Y X G
T B E E C H M L A F
```

A Tricky TREE-t

Don't "leave" until you solve this riddle! Look at the pictures. Put the name of what you see in the spaces below each picture. The numbers under the spaces are a code that will help you get the joke.

How can you tell a dogwood tree from a maple tree?

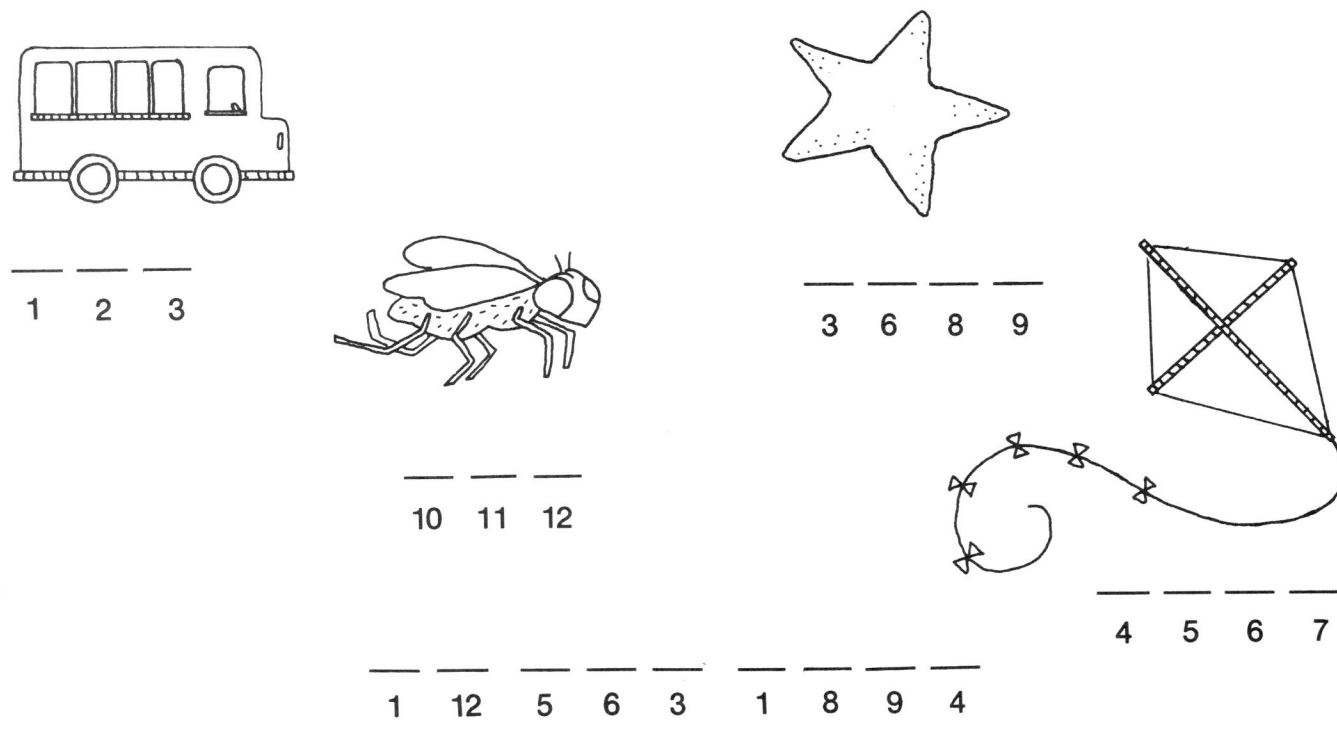

___ ___ ___
1   2   3

___ ___ ___
10 11 12

___ ___ ___ ___
3   6   8   9

___ ___ ___ ___
4   5   6   7

___ ___ ___ ___ ___ ___ ___ ___ ___
1   12 5   6   3   1   8   9   4

Name: _____

TẾT TRUNG-THU

Full Moon Festival

Tết Trung-thu, celebrated during the full moon in midautumn, is the most exciting holiday of the year for the children of Vietnam. On this day, the people make delicious sweets called "moon cakes." The list below shows some of the ingredients used. Can you find each word in the puzzle? The words may be up, down, across, diagonal, or backwards. Circle each word as you find it.

Moon Cakes

rice
lotus seeds
peanuts
duck egg
yolk
sugar
raisins
watermelon
seeds

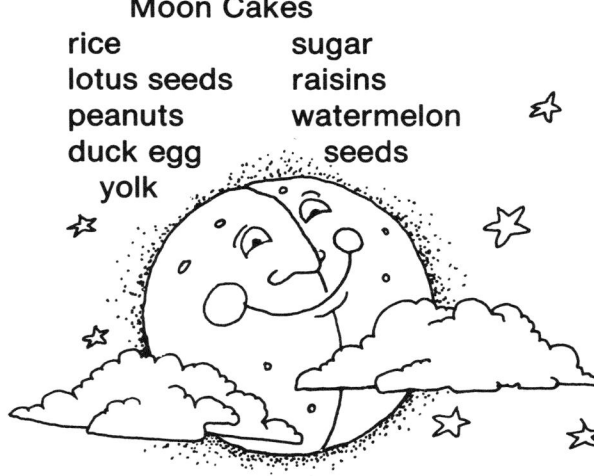

```
E C D R I C A K F S E E P M C
C U S U E G Q B P U W N R O A
I D P T C G K V T I Y O L O K
R K Q X B K G Y O L K S P N E
P A Z D C L O T U S S E E D S
A W I L O T I F Z S U G A R E
G A L S A E H J M R T Y N Q T
U T P E I N U Z X Q L A U B A
S D E E S N O L E M R E T A W
Q L R N T Z S U G O P L S M L
```

A Lantern Parade

On Tết Trung-thu, children make lanterns in the shapes of boats, dragons, cranes, and fish and parade through the streets with them.

Make a "lantern" of your own by completing the puzzle below.

Make a BOAT lantern that will GLOW.

Change one letter at a time keeping the letter order the same. Each change should result in a new word, until you have changed all four letters and solved the puzzle.

G L O W

_ _ _ _

_ _ _ _

_ _ _ _

B O A T

Name: _____

ROSH HASHANAH

Happy New Year!

The Jewish <u>New Year</u>, called Rosh Hashanah, begins on the first day of the Hebrew month of <u>Tishri</u> (Sept./Oct.). Legend has it that on this day the world was created. It is also a time of <u>judgment</u> when the Jewish people believe that a person's fate is inscribed (written down) and sealed in the <u>Book</u> of Life. The holiday begins at <u>sundown</u> when the <u>shofar</u>, or <u>ram</u>'s horn, is <u>blown</u> and the people are called together. Every family will have <u>honey</u> on its dinner table for a sweet year.

Can you find each of the underlined words in the puzzle opposite? They may be up, down, across, diagonal, or backwards. Circle each word as you find it.

```
J U D G B L R S U M
N U B L O V A H R C
E C D H O N E Y A R
W R J G K X Y K F E
Y E A S M L W Q O P
F A T M Z E E D H A
R T N W O D N U S G
A E I R H S I T Z H
N D B X B L O W N S
T I S H P D X K J L
```

Greetings

Starting with the letter "M", count off every third letter, going around the box three times. Print each letter as you come to it in the space below and circle it in the puzzle to learn the message. The first two letters are circled for you.

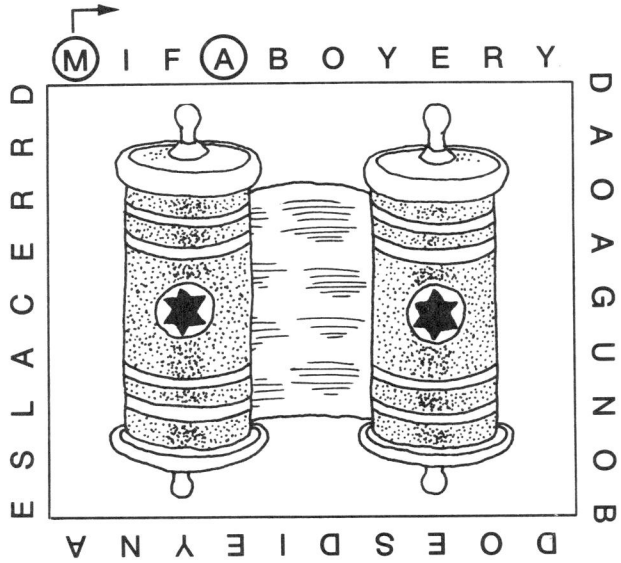

Name: _____

ROSH HASHANAH

Holiday Baking

When the ram's HORN is blown, it is time to BAKE the *challah* (pronounced hah-lah), a round egg bread, for the New Year.

Change one letter at a time, keeping the letter order the same. Each change should result in a new word, until you have changed all four letters and solved the puzzle.

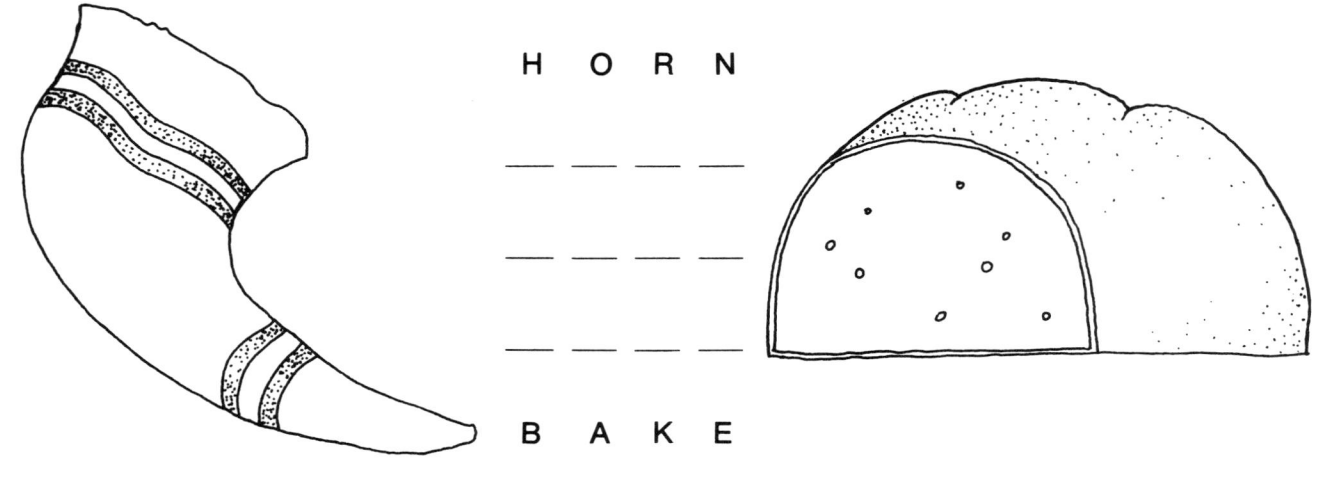

H   O   R   N

_ _ _ _

_ _ _ _

_ _ _ _

B   A   K   E

Harvest Foods

The fruits of the fall harvest are served with the <u>challah</u> on Rosh Hashanah. *Tzimmes* (pronounced tsim-mes) is made of sweet <u>potatoes</u>, <u>meat</u>, <u>prunes</u>, and <u>carrots</u>. There is <u>honey</u> cake and <u>apple</u> slices for dessert.

Can you fit each of the underlined words from the menu above in the puzzle grid? (One is already done for you.)

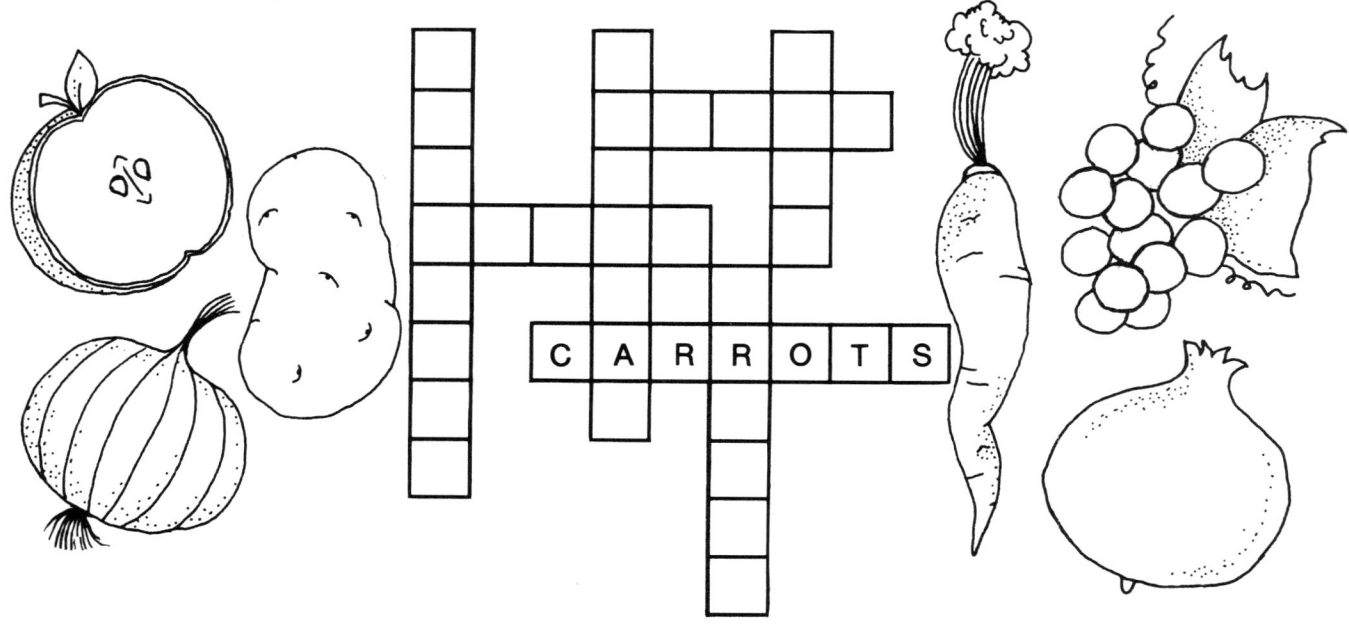

20

SUCCOT

Name: _____

Festival of Huts

In Israel, children build small <u>huts</u> during this holiday to represent those the Jews lived in during their forty years of wandering in the desert after the <u>Exodus</u> (when they all left Egypt). The <u>roof</u> of each hut is made of <u>branches</u> and <u>leaves</u> and decorated with <u>fruit</u>. Succot is an <u>autumn</u> <u>festival</u> of <u>thanksgiving</u> (for freedom and for a good harvest). It lasts for <u>eight</u> days.

Can you find each of the words underlined in the paragraph above in the puzzle? The words may be up, down, across, diagonal, or backwards. Circle each word as you find it.

```
T  K  B  R  A  L  E  A  U  F  G  J
H  H  R  Q  V  A  U  T  U  M  N  H
A  M  A  J  T  V  M  L  B  R  Z  G
N  P  N  N  W  I  B  X  N  D  V  S
R  G  C  L  K  T  P  F  E  S  T  E
S  D  H  U  D  S  T  U  H  X  P  V
Q  B  E  K  N  E  G  C  Z  M  Z  A
V  M  S  G  L  F  I  I  P  Y  I  E
E  X  O  D  U  S  R  Q  V  B  Q  L
I  H  J  Y  W  N  O  U  D  I  H  X
G  T  H  G  I  E  O  J  I  Z  N  S
N  F  O  O  N  X  F  L  Q  T  B  G
```

A Harvest Home

Help to build a "succah" or hut of your own by building words that have *hut* in them. How many can you do?

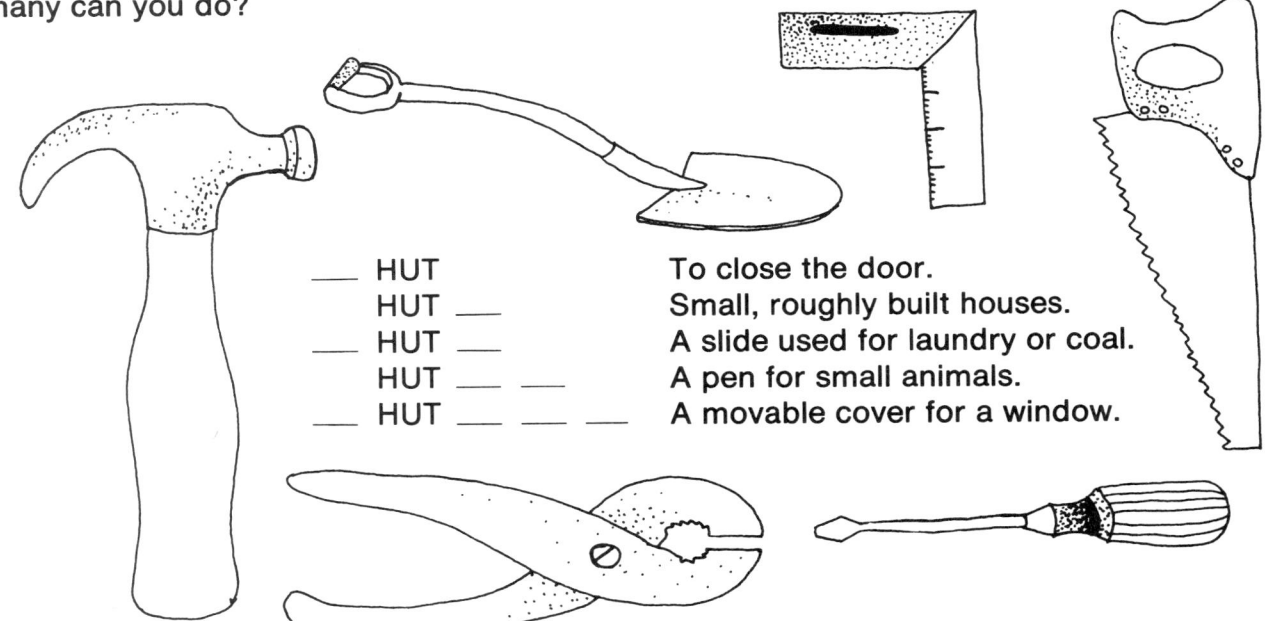

___ HUT	To close the door.
HUT ___	Small, roughly built houses.
___ HUT ___	A slide used for laundry or coal.
HUT ___ ___	A pen for small animals.
___ HUT ___ ___ ___	A movable cover for a window.

October 4   Name: _____

LAUNCH OF SPUTNIK I

Birth of the Space Age

On this day in 1957, the Soviet Union launched the first successful human-made *satellite*, Sputnik I. A satellite is a device that travels around the earth in order to send radio and television signals, observe weather conditions, or explore space.

  Take your own trip to the stars by solving these zany space riddles. Add and subtract the letters as shown.

What stars would be arrested if they could be caught?

[shoe] −E+ [pot] −P+ [ring] −R    −I

_____   _____.

Which weighs more—a full moon or a half moon?

A [hat] + [leaf] − [tea] [spoon]+1+AR− [pear]   A   F+ [bull] −B

__ _____ _____ , __ _____

[spoon]+1+AR− [pear]   [fist] −F−T   L+ [pig] + [hat] +N− [pan] +ER

_____ _____ _____.

What holds the sun up in the sky?

[submarine]+1− [bone] +N   [bear] −R+MS

_____   _____.

22

LAUNCH OF SPUTNIK 1

A Heavenly Message

The Soviet *Sputnik I*, the first satellite humans successfully launched into space, traveled around the earth for more than three weeks in 1957 sending back radio signals. Can you "receive" the signals coming from the crossword puzzle below?

WORD BANK

planet	eve	moon
man	Mars	suns
Earth	on	meteor
use	son	galaxy
astronaut	ans.	an
part	ear	space
sky	go	use
of	pa	name
st.	solar	S.E.
nods	top	star
hi	or	fa
	pt	

ACROSS:

1. The planet fourth in order from the sun.
5. Legend has it that there is a ____ in the moon.
7. The spaceship landed ____ the moon.
8. Rockets ____ fuel to work.
10. Earth is a ____.
12. Abbrev. for answer.
13. The evening or day before a holiday.
14. A piece of something.
15. Opposite of stop.
16. Abbrev. for street.
17. The planet third in order from the sun.
19. Homonym for sun.
22. Sally Ride was the first female ____.
24. Made with or from.
26. One of the parts of the body we use to hear.
27. The space above the earth.
28. Nickname for father.

DOWN:

1. The heavenly body that travels around the earth 13 times/year.
2. One.
3. The ____ system is made up of nine planets that revolve around the sun.
4. Stars are ____ very far away.
5. A shooting star.
6. Jupiter is the ____ of the largest planet in our solar system.
9. Abbrev. for southeast.
11. One of the insects sent aboard the space shuttle.
14. Abbrev. for part time.
15. A huge group of stars in space.
16. Outer ____.
18. Hello.
19. A heavenly body that can be seen on a clear night.
20. Neither, nor; either, ____.
21. Falls asleep, ____ off.
23. Highest part.
25. Musical note that comes after mi.

Name: _____

FIRE PREVENTION WEEK

Fire Drill

Do you know what to do in case of a fire in your home?
1. Know two ways to reach the ground safely from every room.
2. Arrange a place to meet outside for all who live in your home (in case of a fire).
3. Hold a home fire drill at least every six months.
4. Know your fire department's phone number.

```
W L P O U T S A K D T P
A Z J H G K V Z D O Q N
Y S W R O L U K F S N X
F G R O U N D E I Y C I
W N P O U G E M R B F W
O R L M E T K Q E M D A
N T J E C N S A F E L Y
K V B D A M X I S G T S
X L C G L L I R D Q P F
D N O H P X I B M E H G
```

Can you find each of the underlined words in the puzzle opposite? They may be up, down, across, diagonal, or backwards. Circle each word as you find it.

Your own fire department's phone number is:

_____

Help!

Can you break the code and figure out what three things you should do after you have gotten out of a burning building? (Hint: It's an 8-shift cipher.)

1. ___ ___ ___ ___   ___ ___ ___ ___   ___ ___ ___ ___ ___ ___ ___ ___ ___
U S D D   X A J W   V W H S J L E W F L

___ ___ ___ ___   ___ ___ ___ ___ ___ ___ ___   ___ ___ ___ ___ ___ ___ ___ ___ .
X J G E   G M L K A V W   T M A D V A F Y

2. ___ ___ ___ ___   ___ ___ ___ ___ ___ ___ ___   ___ ___ ___   ___ ___ ___ ___ .
Y A N W   S V V J W K K   S F V   F S E W

3. ___ ___ ___ ___ ___   ___ ___   ___ ___ ___ ___   ___ ___ ___ ___
F W N W J   Y G   T S U C   A F L G

___   ___ ___ ___ ___ ___ ___ ___   ___ ___ ___ ___ ___ ___ ___ ___ .
S   T M J F A F Y   T M A D V A F Y

Name: _____

FIRE PREVENTION WEEK

A Chain Reaction

Would you know how to cope if your house were burning?

Change the word BURN into COPE by changing only one letter at a time, keeping the letter order the same. Each time that you change a letter, form a new word for the next line.

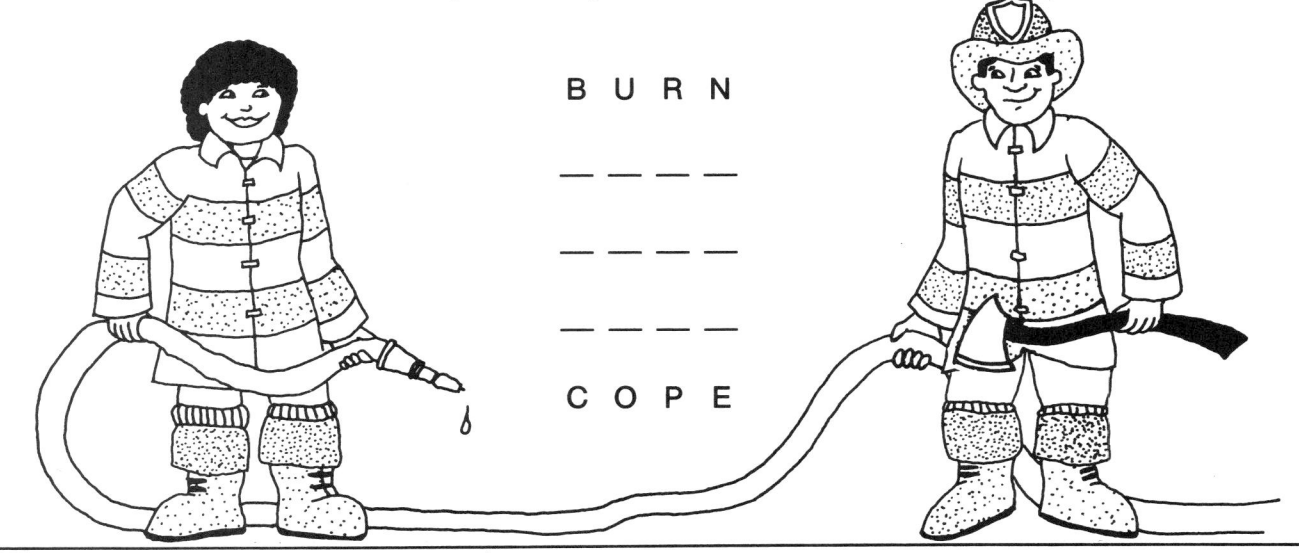

B U R N

_ _ _ _

_ _ _ _

_ _ _ _

C O P E

Fire!

Now read what you should do if your house or apartment *is* on fire.

1. <u>Feel</u> door if warm, <u>stay</u> in room and call for <u>help</u>.
2. Close <u>Windows</u> and <u>doors</u> as you leave.
3. Use <u>Stairs</u> never elevators.
4. <u>Pull</u> <u>Alarm</u>
5. Keep <u>Low</u> <u>crawl</u> to safety.

Complete the puzzle grid above by filling in the underlined words.

COLUMBUS DAY

Sailing

On August 3, 1492, Christopher Columbus set out from Spain with 120 men in three small ships, the *Niña*, *Pinta*, and *Santa Maria*. He was looking for a short route to India. What he discovered on October 12th, without knowing it, was the New World!

  Join Columbus on his voyage by solving the rebus riddles below. Add and subtract the letters as shown to get the answers.

What did the ocean say as the *Niña* sailed by?

N + 🚣 + G − 🛍 + H + 💍 − R   🧤 − M − 10

_____ ,   _____

🏺 + A + 📋 − 🪵   🪄 − ND + 🦺 + AR − ⭐ + D

_____   _____ .

What did Columbus have to watch when he was up in the crow's nest of the *Pinta*?

H + ✊ − F − T   S + 10 + 🌼 − 🕸 − AL

_____ _____ .

Why couldn't the sailors on the *Santa Maria* play cards?

🛋 + 👔 − 🪭 + 1   👗 − I − T

_____   _____

🪣 + 🪄 − 🧷 − D + 👁👁 − EE   S + 🧤 − 👔 + 💍 − R

_____   _____

1 − E   T + 🐔 − N   D + 👩 − N

_____   _____   _____

Name: _____

COLUMBUS DAY

Where Am I?

Christopher Columbus thought he had discovered a shorter route to India when he made his first voyage in 1492. Solve the puzzles below and find out where he really landed on his first, second, and third trips.

Look at each picture. Put the name of what you see in the spaces below each picture. The numbers under the spaces are a code that will help you find the answers.

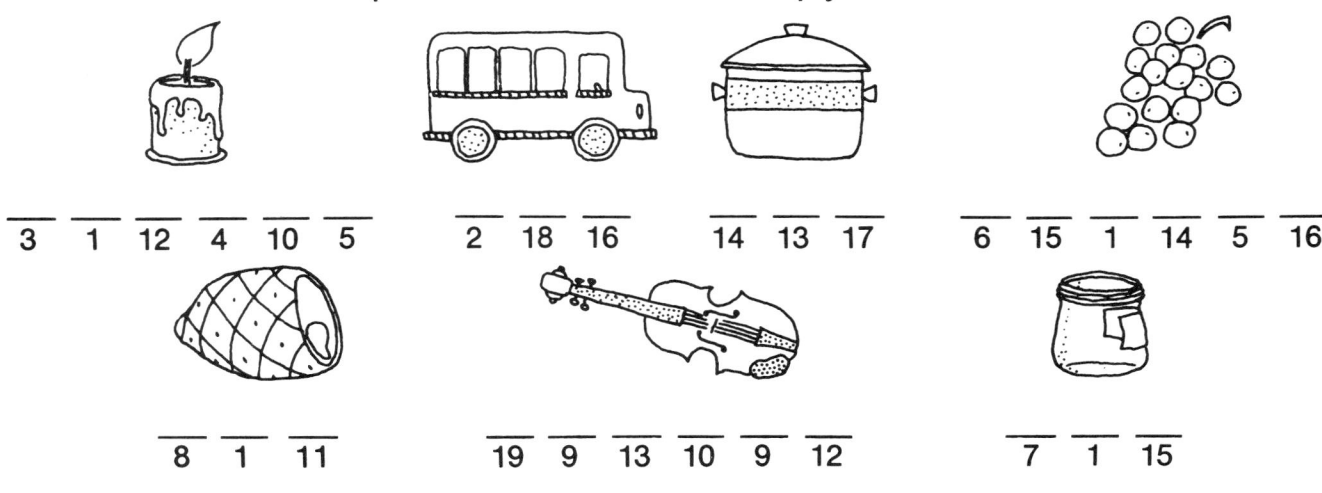

| 3 | 1 | 12 | 4 | 10 | 5 |

| 2 | 18 | 16 | | 14 | 13 | 17 | | 6 | 15 | 1 | 14 | 5 | 16 |

| 8 | 1 | 11 |

| 19 | 9 | 13 | 10 | 9 | 12 |

| 7 | 1 | 15 |

On his first trip (1492), Columbus discovered

___ ___ ___ ___ ___ ___ ___
2   1   8   1   11   1   16

On his second trip (1493), he found

___ ___ ___ ___ ___ ___   ___ ___ ___ ___
14 18 5   15 17 13   15   9   3   13

___ ___ ___ ___ ___ ___   ___ ___ ___ ___ ___ ___ ___
19   9 15   6   9   12   9 16 10   1 12   4 16

___ ___ ___ ___ ___ ___ ___
7   1 11   1   9   3   1

On his third trip (1498), he explored the coast of

___ ___ ___ ___ ___   ___ ___ ___ ___ ___ ___ ___
16 13 18 17   8   1 11   5 15   9   3   1

Name: _____

ALASKA DAY FESTIVAL

Up North

Do you know where <u>Alaxsxaq</u> is? Pronounced Al-ay-ek-sa, it is the name the Aleut people gave their homeland. In English, it is spelled, <u>Alaska</u>. To learn what the name means in English, solve the picture puzzle below. Add and subtract the letters as shown from the names of the objects pictured.

_____   _____

Cold Cash

On this day in 1867, U.S. Secretary of State William H. Seward paid the Russians $7,200,000 for the territory known as Alaska. At the time, many people in the United States could not understand why. Solve the puzzle below to learn what they called Alaska.

   Look at the pictures. Put the name of what you see in the spaces below each picture. The numbers under the spaces are a code that will help you discover the answer.

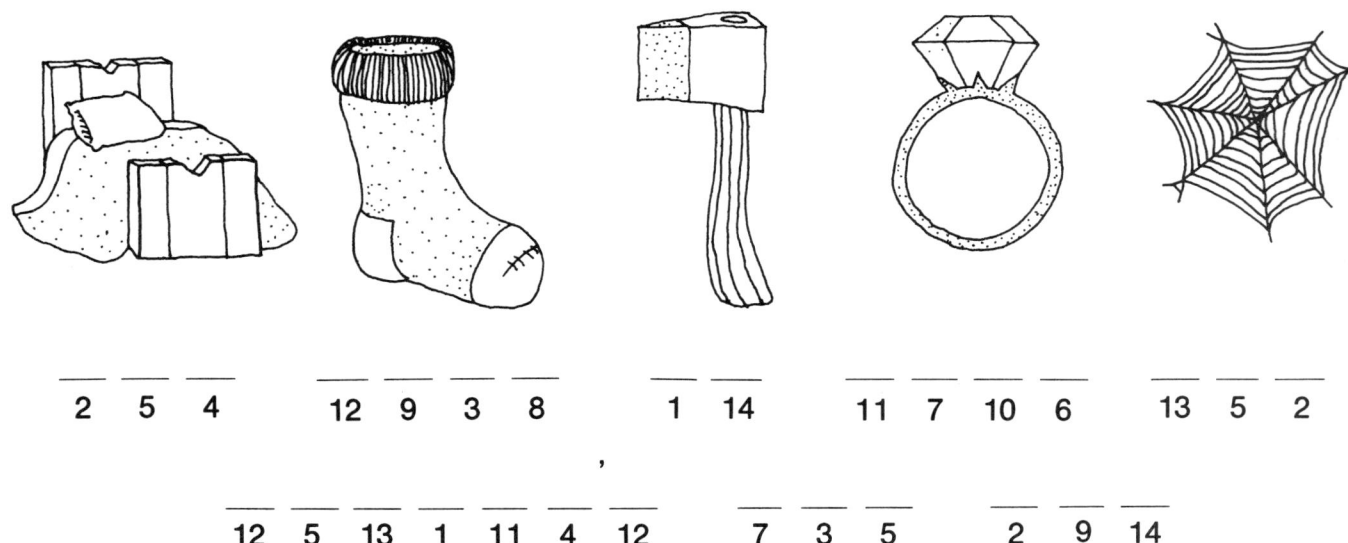

__ __ __   __ __ __ __   __ __   __ __ __ __   __ __ __
2 5 4   12 9 3 8   1 14   11 7 10 6   13 5 2

,

__ __ __ __ __ __ __   __ __ __   __ __ __
12 5 13 1 11 4 12   7 3 5   2 9 14

Brainteaser: Do you know an Eskimo word meaning "boat covered in sealskin" that is spelled the same forwards and backwards?

FIRST NATIONAL HORSE SHOW

Horse Sense

The first National Horse Show took place on this day in 1893 at Madison Square Garden in New York City. Many beautiful horses got to strut their stuff. Now you can strut yours by finding each of the parts of the horse listed below in the puzzle. The words may be up, down, across, diagonal or backwards. Circle each word as you find it.

MUZZLE	C	O	R	G	I	R	P	H	O	C
GIRTH	R	W	Q	I	K	M	U	M	I	O
WITHERS	E	J	I	R	C	E	T	U	L	F
HOCK	S	E	R	T	O	P	E	Z	X	O
CORONET	F	O	O	H	H	M	N	Z	K	M
CREST	W	L	Z	T	R	E	O	L	N	F
FLANK	I	J	A	S	N	C	R	E	S	T
DOCK	T	Q	Y	N	F	B	O	S	C	G
FETLOCK	H	D	O	C	K	R	C	P	T	V
HOOF	E	J	K	C	O	L	T	E	F	U

First Place

A horse named King jumped the gate perfectly and won a blue ribbon. Can you complete the magic word square below and take home the first place trophy too? (The answers should read the same across and down.)

1. Male monarch.
2. A thought.
3. The place in which a bird lays its eggs.
4. A door in a fence.

1	2	3	4
2			
3			
4			

Name: _____

UNITED NATIONS DAY

Good Neighbors

On this day in 1945, the United Nations was officially established. Celebrate the day by reading some of the words from the U.N. Charter. Then try to fit the underlined words in the puzzle grid below. (Two words have already been done for you.)

We the <u>peoples</u> of the <u>United</u>
<u>Nations</u> determine . . .
to live together in <u>peace</u> with
one another as good neighbors,
to work for the <u>equal</u> <u>rights</u> of
men and women and of nations
large and small, and
to promote <u>better</u> standards of
<u>life</u>.

A Special Goal

Can you unscramble the names of some of the U.N. Member Nations below? When you have done it, print the circled letters in order in the space below in order to learn what the United Nations is working toward.

DESWEN __ ◯ __ __ __ __   VOTISE __ __ __ __ __ __

ONINU __ __ __ ◯ __   GARTENANI __ ◯ __ __ __ __ __ __ __

SUITARALA __ __ __ __ __ __ ◯ __ __   DIANI __ __ ◯ __ __

GEPTY __ __ __ ◯ __   TRAGE __ __ ◯ __ __

TRABINI __ __ __ __ __ __ __   NADACA __ __ __ __ ◯ __ __

HACNI ◯ __ __ __ __ __

TENUDI __ __ __ __ __ __ __   TASSET __ __ __ __ ◯ __

__ __ __ __ __ __   __ __ __ __ __ __

Name: _____

DEDICATION OF STATUE OF LIBERTY

Liberty Trivia

Did you know that the Statue of Liberty was designed by Frederic Bartholdi and that it was modeled after his mother?

Did you know that the base of the statue is an 11-pointed star and that it rests on an 89-foot high granite pedestal?

Did you know that Grover Cleveland was president in 1886 when the Statue of Liberty was dedicated?

Did you know that the statue was sent to the United States from France in 214 pieces?

Did you know that the statue is 152 feet high from the base to the torch?

Did you know that the statue weighs 450,000 pounds?

Try to fit the underlined words from the facts listed above into the puzzle grid. One is already done for you.

DEDICATION OF STATUE OF LIBERTY

Lady Liberty

The poem below, by Emma Lazarus, appears on the pedestal of the Statue of Liberty. Read it and then try to find the underlined words in the puzzle. They may be up, down, across, diagonal, or backwards. Circle each word as you find it.

. . . Give me your <u>tired</u>, your <u>poor</u>,
Your huddled <u>masses</u> yearning to be <u>free</u>,
The wretched <u>refuse</u> of your teeming <u>shore</u>.
<u>Send</u> these, the <u>homeless</u>, tempest-tost to me,
I lift my <u>lamp</u> beside the golden <u>door</u>!

```
S N L A N P F J O P
H O M F L B M V B R
D O O R Q E A I D E
P W M E V S D N E S
R X L E Q U M G R W
E P M A L F A K I U
S H O R E E S D T E
F B L O C R S X M E
V C X L R F E S N R
G M K H T D S P Q E
```

Her First Name

The Statue of Liberty originally had a much longer name. To learn what it was, solve the puzzle below. Look at the pictures. Put the name of what you see in the spaces below each picture. The numbers under the spaces are a code that will help you solve the puzzle.

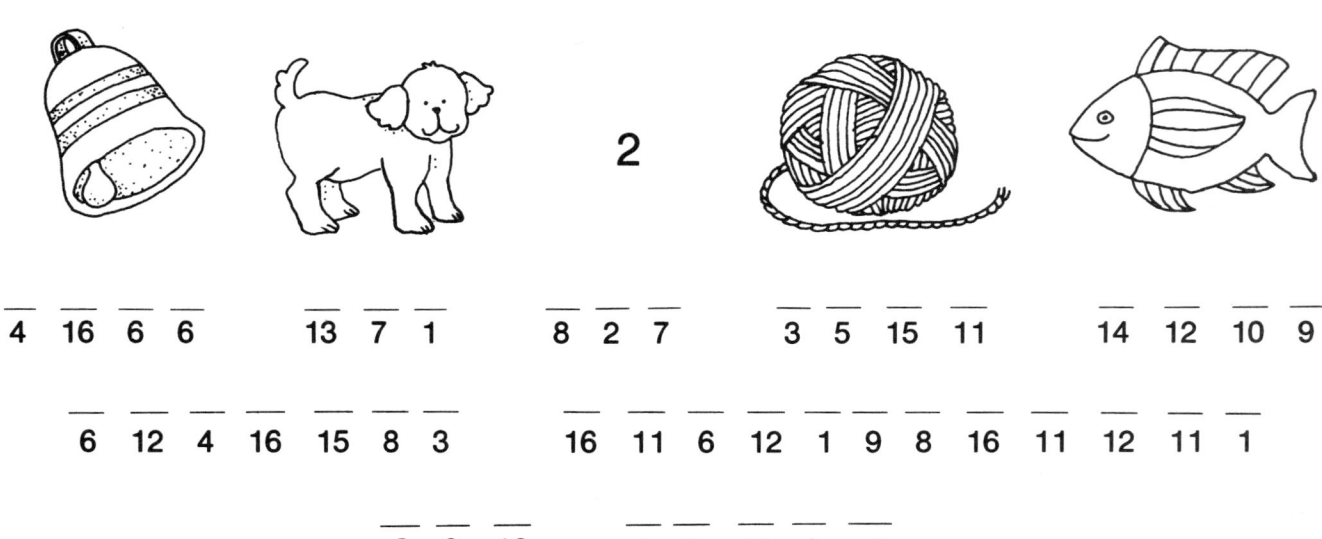

2

___ ___ ___ ___   ___ ___ ___   ___ ___ ___   ___ ___ ___ ___   ___ ___ ___ ___
4 16 6 6   13 7 1   8 2 7   3 5 15 11   14 12 10 9

___ ___ ___ ___ ___ ___ ___   ___ ___ ___ ___ ___ ___ ___ ___ ___ ___ ___ ___ ___
6 12 4 16 15 8 3   16 11 6 12 1 9 8 16 11 12 11 1

___ ___ ___   ___ ___ ___ ___ ___
8 9 16   2 7 15 6 13

HALLOWEEN

Name: _____

Pumpkin Patch Puzzle

On Halloween night, you may meet the ghost of a stingy, mean old man named Jack who is forced to wander the earth forever with his lantern. Don't be scared! Fill in the "jack-o'-lantern" puzzle below and old Jack will be your friend.

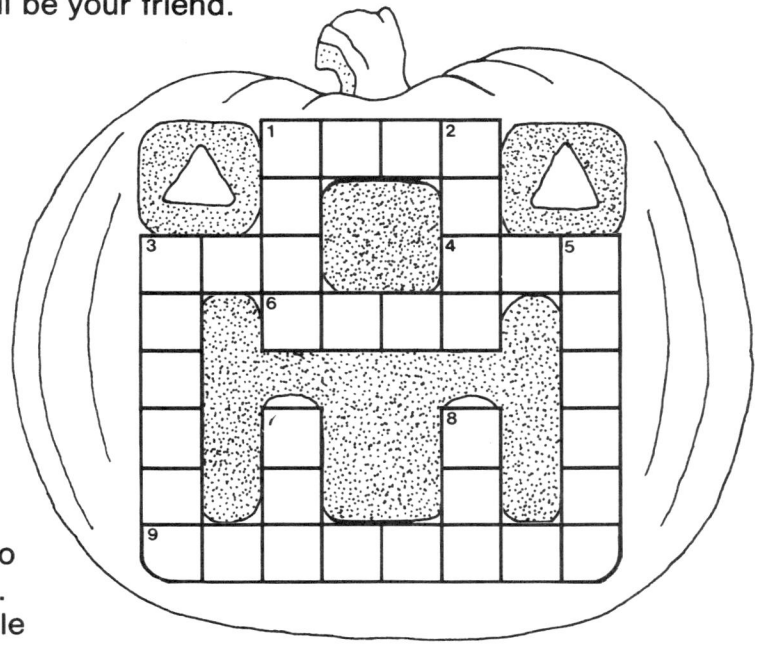

ACROSS:
1. The smile of your jack-o'-lantern.
3. The first letters of the words "trick or treat."
4. A cup with a handle that you use to drink hot cider.
6. The sharp, cutting side of a blade.
9. Large, round orange fruits that grow on a vine.

DOWN:
1. Opening in a fence.
2. Jack was the ____ of the stingy man forced to wander with his lantern.
3. Before pumpkins, people made jack-o'-lanterns from this vegetable.
5. Boo! The house is haunted by ____. (plural)

7. A hobo.
8. Something you do on snow, usually after Halloween.

Make Your Own Jack-O'-Lantern

By changing one letter at a time, can you make a new word?

CUT into the TOP of your pumpkin.	PICK out every SEED.	Carve a FACE and pop some CORN!
C U T	P I C K	F A C E
___ ___ ___ You drink from it.	___ ___ ___ ___ A light kiss.	___ ___ ___ ___ Money for a trip.
___ ___ ___ Nickname for police officer.	___ ___ ___ ___ To sneak a look.	___ ___ ___ ___ To be concerned.
	___ ___ ___ ___ To search.	___ ___ ___ ___ Center of an apple.
T O P	S E E D	C O R N

33

HALLOWEEN

Name: _____

Spooky Riddles

Can you decode the answers to the riddles below? You'll get the treat when you can figure out the trick! (Hint: the code used is known as a ten-shift cipher.)

What did the lovesick ghost say to his girlfriend?

O E K Q H U   R E E J Y V K B!

___ ___ ___ ___ ___ ___   ___ ___ ___ ___ ___ ___ ___ ___

What did the witch get when she went to the beauty parlor?

Q   D U M   I S Q H U - T   E.

___ ___ ___ ___ ___ ___ ___ ___ ___ - ___ ___

Why didn't the skeleton stay in the haunted house?

Y J   T Y T D' J   X Q L U   J X U   W K J I.

___ ___   ___ ___ ___ ___ ___   ___ ___ ___ ___   ___ ___ ___   ___ ___ ___ ___

What does a witch use to tell time?

Q   M Y J S X   M Q J S X.

___   ___ ___ ___ ___ ___   ___ ___ ___ ___ ___

Why is a person who never stops eating just like a ghost?

R U S Q K I U   J X U O' H U   R E J X

___ ___ ___ ___ ___ ___ ___   ___ ___ ___ ___ ___ ___   ___ ___ ___ ___

Q B M Q O I   Q - W E R R B Y D'.

___ ___ ___ ___ ___ ___   ___ - ___ ___ ___ ___ ___ ___ ___

HALLOWEEN

Witch's Brew

In Shakespeare's play *Macbeth*, three witches cook up a strange potion with these words:

"Double, double toil and trouble,
Fire burn and caldron bubble.
  Fillet of fenny snake,
  In the caldron boil and bake.
  Eye of newt and toe of frog,
  Wool of bat and tongue of dog.
. . .And now about the caldron sing
Like elves and fairies in a ring,
Enchanting all that you put in."

Cast your own spell by filling in the puzzle grid with the words
underlined in the chant above. (One has already been done for you.)

Black Cats

There is a superstition that says that black cats are the special friends of witches. Don't let one cross your path! Solve the puzzle below as fast as you can!

A cat is hidden
in each of the
words below!

CAT

CAT _ _   To get hold of.

CAT _ _ _   Cows.

CAT _ _ _ _   List of things.

CAT _ _ _ _ _   A group.

CAT _ _ _ _ _ _   A large church.

CAT _ _ _ _ _ _ _   Baby butterfly.

NATIONAL MAGIC WEEK

Hokus Pokus Harry

Harry Houdini, one of America's greatest magicians, died on this day in 1926. An amazing escape artist, he was famous for the sensational and dangerous tricks he performed. The week including Halloween has been dedicated to his memory and to the celebration of magic.

　Houdini never failed to escape from any of the devices designed to hold him. Here's your chance to be an escape artist too. Get out of each of the devices listed below by unscrambling them to see what they spell.

D A F F U N S H C　　　　　__ __ __ __ __ __ __ __ __

P E S O R　　　　　　　　__ __ __ __ __

S N A C I H　　　　　　　__ __ __ __ __ __

R I N S O P　 C L E L　　__ __ __ __ __ __　 __ __ __

Abracadabra!

By changing one letter at a time, can you make a new word?

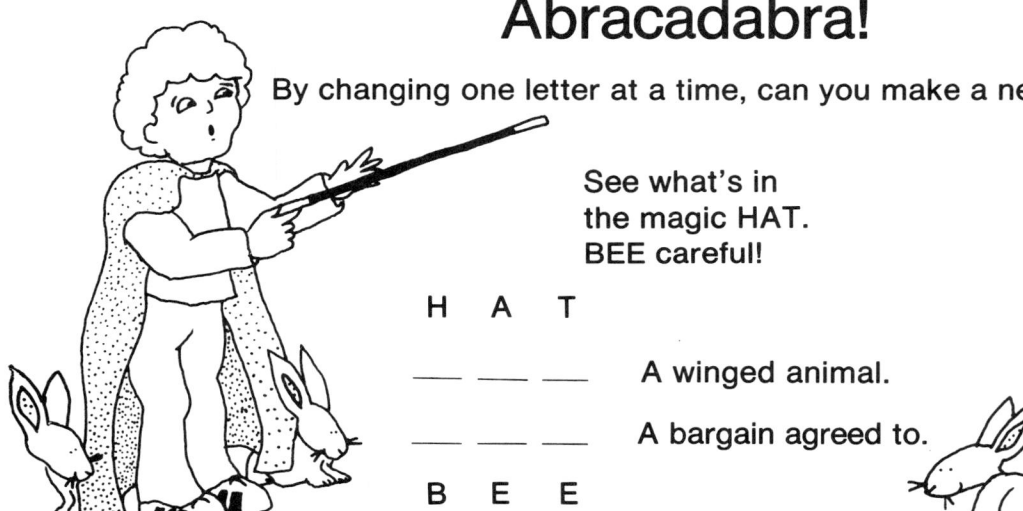

See what's in
the magic HAT.
BEE careful!

H A T

__ __ __　　A winged animal.

__ __ __　　A bargain agreed to.

B E E

Turn yourself into
a HERO with your
magic WAND.

This CARD trick
is for the dogs!

C A R D

__ __ __ __　　To nurse.

__ __ __ __　　Not covered.

__ __ __ __　　To make weary.

B O N E

W A N D

__ __ __ __　　It's quicker than the eye.

__ __ __ __　　Not easy.

__ __ __ __　　Group of animals.

H E R O

DIWALI

A Festival of Lights

All over India, Hindus celebrate one of their gayest festivals, *Diwali* (pronounced dee-wah-lee) at the end of the autumn harvest. Homes are cleaned and decorated with flowers. There are fireworks. Clay saucers are filled with mustard oil, and cotton wicks are floated in them. The wicks are lit and the lamps are placed on rooftops and windowsills. In northern India, it is believed that Lakshmi, the goddess of prosperity, will find and bless each lighted home.

Can you find the underlined words in the puzzle opposite? They may be up, down, across, diagonal, or backwards. Circle each word as you find it.

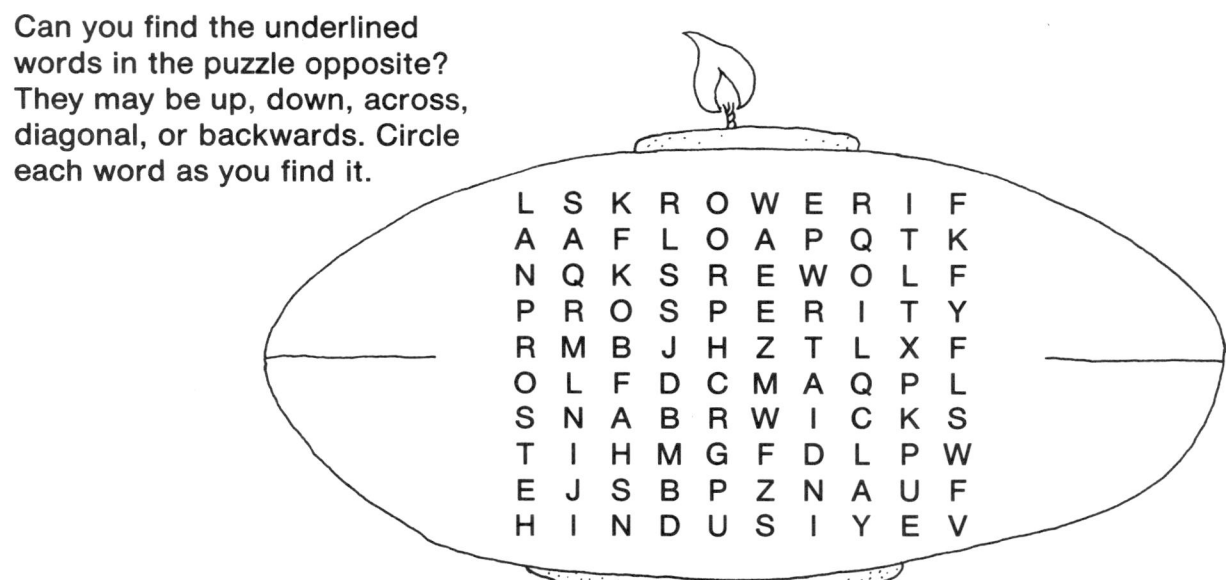

```
L  S  K  R  O  W  E  R  I  F
A  A  F  L  O  A  P  Q  T  K
N  Q  K  S  R  E  W  O  L  F
P  R  O  S  P  E  R  I  T  Y
R  M  B  J  H  Z  T  L  X  F
O  L  F  D  C  M  A  Q  P  L
S  N  A  B  R  W  I  C  K  S
T  I  H  M  G  F  D  L  P  W
E  J  S  B  P  Z  N  A  U  F
H  I  N  D  U  S  I  Y  E  V
```

Lucky Lamps

In the city of Banares, women and girls float their lighted clay lamps across the Ganges River. They believe it is a sign of good luck if the light still shines when it reaches the other shore.

Help the girls *float* their lamps across the river by subtracting one letter at a time. (Each step should form a new word.)

F L O A T

Name: _____

DANIEL BOONE'S BIRTHDAY

Frontier Fun

Born in 1734, Daniel Boone was probably America's most famous pioneer. Solve the cryptograms below and learn some important facts about his exciting life on the frontier.

Each number under the blanks below stands for a letter. The numbers that stand for the letters in Daniel Boone's name are given to you. Fill in the letters you know, then try to figure out what the others might be.

D A N I E L   B O O N E
11 7 17 18 9 10   12 14 14 17 9   12 10 7 25 9 11   7

19 21 7 18 10   16 21 14 2   23 18 21 1 18 17 18 7

18 17 19 14   5 9 17 19 8 3 5 22

_____

6 9   15 7 4   7 11 14 20 19 9 11   7 4   7

2 9 2 12 9 21   14 16   19 6 9   4 6 7 15 17 9 9

18 17 11 18 7 17   19 21 18 12 9

_____

6 9   16 14 8 17 11 9 11   12 14 14 17 9 4 12 14 21 14

14 17   19 6 9   5 9 17 19 8 3 5 22   21 18 23 9 21

Name: _____

ELECTION DAY

Vote!

On General Election Day, which falls on the first Tuesday after the first Monday in November, U.S. citizens who meet certain requirements can vote for the persons of their choice to govern their country, state, and county, city, or town.

Read the list below. Now, cast your vote by filling in the puzzle grid with the underlined words. (One is already done for you.)

Elected Offices:

(local)   County <u>Executive</u>
             Town <u>Supervisor</u>
             City <u>Mayor</u>

(state)   State <u>Governor</u>
             Member of <u>State</u> <u>Legislature</u>

(country)   U.S. <u>President</u>
             U.S. <u>Senator</u> (U.S. Congress)
             U.S. <u>Member</u> of <u>House</u> of <u>Representatives</u>

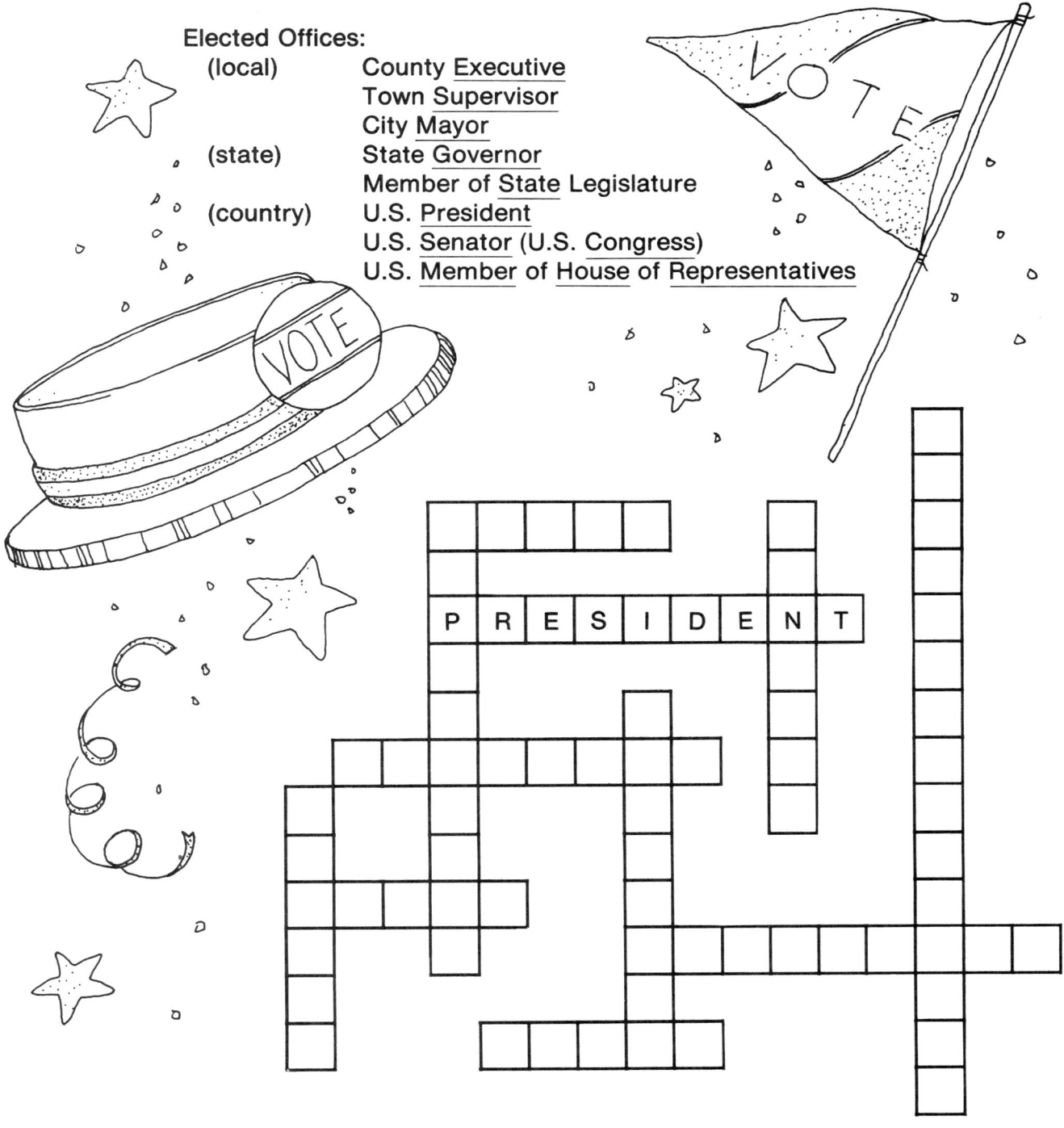

Name: _____

ELECTION DAY

A Pebble for Your Thoughts

The tradition of voting by secret ballot was begun in ancient Greece. To vote for a public official, a person would drop a round stone into a box. A white stone meant one voted "for" the candidate; black meant "against."

Here's your chance to vote. Be sure to pick the BEST candidate by completing the magic word square below. (The answers will be the same across and down.)

1. Good, better, _____.
2. To give back or repeat sound.
3. To display.
4. Larger than a village but smaller than a city.

And the Winner Is. . .

The ancient Greek method of voting with stones left someone a lot of counting to do! Help out by completing the puzzle below. Subtract one letter at a time so that each step forms a new word.

S   T   O   N   E   S

___ ___ ___ ___ ___

___ ___ ___ ___

___ ___ ___

___ ___

Name: _____

VETERANS DAY/REMEMBRANCE DAY

Never Forget

Ever since 1918, when the fighting in World War I ended, we have honored anyone who has fought for his or her country. Study the puzzle below and learn part of the inscription on the tomb of the American Unknown Soldier.

```
  (H) R  R (E) E  K  R  D  N  E
E ┌─────────────────────────┐ G
O │                         │ O
D │                         │ R
N │                         │ L
D │                         │ W
O │                         │ E
G │                         │ O
L │                         │ N
  │                         │ S
  │                         │ R
  │                         │ B
H └─────────────────────────┘ T
  O  O  N  T  S  I  T  A  S  U  Y
```

Starting with the letter "H", count off every third letter, going around the box three times. Print each letter as you come to it and circle it in the puzzle to learn the inscription. (The first two letters are circled for you.)

_____

_____

_____

_____

Many Were Called

Many men and women gave their lives in order to defend their countries. These people are known as veterans. Find at least fifty smaller words of three letters or more in the word:

V E T E R A N S

____	____	____	____	____
____	____	____	____	____
____	____	____	____	____
____	____	____	____	____
____	____	____	____	____
____	____	____	____	____
____	____	____	____	____
____	____	____	____	____
____	____	____	____	____

Name: _____

FREDERICK BANTING'S BIRTHDAY

An Important Discovery

Sir Frederick Banting, a Canadian doctor, discovered something in 1923 that would help millions of people suffering from diabetes. That something was insulin. For this achievement, Banting, along with J.J.R. MacLeod, won the Nobel Prize in Medicine. He shared the honor with a coworker, C.H. Best. In 1941, Banting was killed in a plane crash while on a medical war mission.

Can you fit the underlined words from the paragraph above into the puzzle grid? (One has already been done for you.)

Medical Miracle

One discovery in medical research often leads to another. In the puzzle below, one word will lead to another. Can you find at least 10 smaller words of two letters or more in the word:

M E D I C I N E

1. _____   6. _____

2. _____   7. _____

3. _____   8. _____

4. _____   9. _____

5. _____   10. _____

NATIONAL CHILDREN'S BOOK WEEK

Read On!

Books and reading have been celebrated during this week since 1919. Discover the slogan for the first Book Week poster by adding and subtracting the letters as shown from the picture puzzle below.

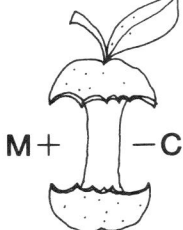 M+ −C   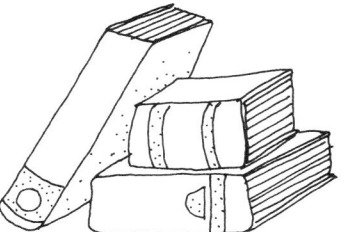   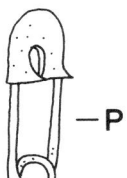 −P   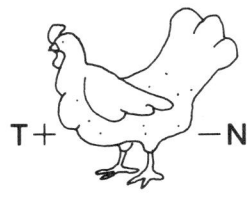 T+ −N

_____   _____   _____   _____

C+ 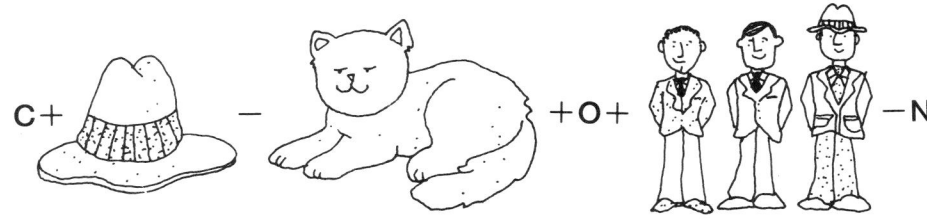 − +O+ −N

_____

Book Fun

Build a bookcase of words that contain the word book in them. Try to guess the answers first without looking at the clues opposite.

BOOK __   (A library has many.)

BOOK __ __   (Registered.)

BOOK __ __ __   (A little one.)

BOOK __ __ __ __   (A pair to hold them up.)

BOOK __ __ __ __ __   (A place where you can buy them.)

BOOK __ __ __ __ __ __   (A person who handles accounts.)

NATIONAL FAMILY WEEK

The Gang's All Here

Help celebrate Family Week with a family portrait. Find the names of all family members listed below in the puzzle. The names may be up, down, across, diagonal, or backwards. Circle each name as you find it.

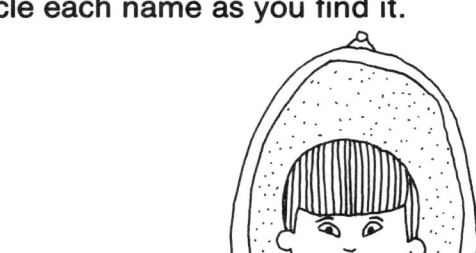

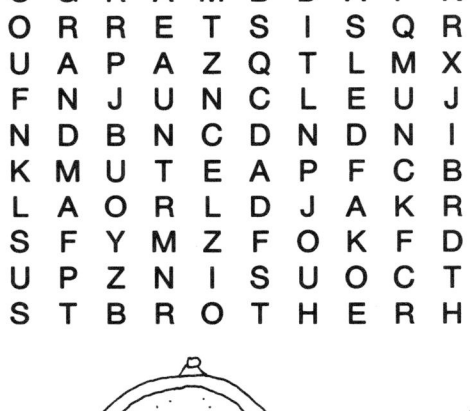

MOM	C G R A M B D A P K
DAD	O R R E T S I S Q R
SISTER	U A P A Z Q T L M X
BROTHER	F N J U N C L E U J
YOU	N D B N C D N D N I
GRANDMA	K M U T E A P F C B
GRANDPA	L A O R L D J A K R
AUNT	S F Y M Z F O K F D
UNCLE	U P Z N I S U O C T
COUSIN	S T B R O T H E R H

The Family Joke

Solve the riddle below by unscrambling the answer.
What is everyone in the family doing at the same time?

T E G I N G T   D E R O L

_____   _____

THANKSGIVING

Name: _____

A Fabulous Feast

Ninety Native American braves joined 55 Pilgrims for the first Thanksgiving dinner in 1621. There were only four women at the party and they did all the cooking! Give them a hand by finding each of the foods listed below in the puzzle. The words may be up, down, diagonal, across, or backwards. Circle each word as you find it.

VENISON   OYSTERS   (WILD) GRAPES   DUCK   STUFFING
TURKEY   BERRIES   CORNBREAD   GRAVY   GOOSE

```
G O O S G R A P E S
S V T U R K C U D G
T O E M A T X J G N
U Y D N P K L R T I
F S U Q I J G H U F
F T C I Z S O Z R F
K E R L O P O U K U
G R A V Y N S N E T
P S E I R R E B Y S
C O R N B R E A D R
```

Words-A-Plenty

The Pilgrims were grateful for a bountiful harvest. How many smaller words of three letters or more can you produce from your own HARVEST? (There are at least 35.)

1 _____	10 _____	19 _____	28 _____
2 _____	11 _____	20 _____	29 _____
3 _____	12 _____	21 _____	30 _____
4 _____	13 _____	22 _____	31 _____
5 _____	14 _____	23 _____	32 _____
6 _____	15 _____	24 _____	33 _____
7 _____	16 _____	25 _____	34 _____
8 _____	17 _____	26 _____	35 _____
9 _____	18 _____	27 _____	

Name: _____

THANKSGIVING

Pilgrim Children

There were about thirty children among the Pilgrims who landed at Plymouth, Massachusetts, in 1620. Two boys were even born on the *Mayflower*—Oceanus Hopkins (who died before he turned two) and Peregrine White (who lived to be 83!).

The children had to work as hard as their parents. Read the list of their chores. Then try to fit the underlined words into the puzzle grid below. (One is already done for you.)

<u>Pull</u> weeds.
<u>Gather</u> nuts
   and berries.
<u>Rock</u> baby's
   cradle
<u>Fell</u> trees.
<u>Spin</u>.
<u>Weave</u>.
<u>Knit</u> stockings.
<u>Sow</u> and <u>reap</u>
   crops.
<u>Bake</u>.
Fish and <u>hunt</u>.

It wasn't all hard work, though. For fun, the children would:

Make <u>dolls</u> from
   <u>cornhusks</u> and <u>rags</u>.
<u>Whittle</u> <u>toys</u> from
   <u>wood</u>.
<u>Swim</u>.
<u>Fish</u>.
Invent <u>games</u>.

THANKSGIVING

Give Thanks

Every culture has celebrated its harvests with ceremonies that include parades, music, games, and special foods—much like our own Thanksgiving. Here's your chance to do what even ancient cultures have done and say "thanks."

Look at the letters in the circles below. Can you make a one-letter word, a two-letter word, a three-letter word, a four-letter word, a five-letter word, and a six-letter word from them? (Be sure to use each letter only once in every word.)

(A) (N) (S) (H) (T) (K)

—

— —

— — —

— — — —

— — — — —

— — — — — —

Harvest the Crops

Can you find the names of four different crops hidden in the sentences below? (Hint: three are grains and one is a fruit.) Underline the word when you find it.

Wow, he ate all the cookies!

The nurse, Ms. Maco, R.N., bandaged my arm.

The doctor who will be operating, R.A. Pesci, is an excellent surgeon.

Snow or ice can make roads slippery.

MARK TWAIN'S BIRTHDAY

What's in a Name?

Mark Twain, the famous American author, was born on this day in 1835. He worked as a printer and a Mississippi River pilot before becoming a writer. In fact, Mark Twain was not his real name at all. "Mark twain" was actually a river call that told the boat pilots that the water in a certain spot was two fathoms deep.

   To learn Twain's real name, solve the puzzle below. (Hint: The code is a 4-shift cipher. A=E, B=F, C=G, and so on.)

O W I Q A H   Y H A I A J O

___ ___ ___ ___ ___ ___   ___ ___ ___ ___ ___ ___ ___

Storybook Heroes

Twain spent his childhood in Hannibal, Missouri. Two of the most famous characters in his books were based on experiences he had in Hannibal. To learn the names of these characters, do the math shown in the blanks and then use the answers as a code to fill in the letters.

A=3	E=1	K=6
C=11	L=10	R=12
I=15	S=18	W=17
B=5	F=13	O=9
H=7	Y=4	N=2
T=8	M=16	U=14

___ ___ ___   ___ ___ ___ ___ ___ ___
4+4 5+4 8+8 9+9 4-1 9+8 6-2 3-2 6+6

___ ___ ___ ___ ___ ___ ___ ___ ___ ___
4+3 8+6 6+5 9-3 6+4 3-2 6-1 3-2 6+6 6+6 6-2

___ ___ ___ ___
7+6 9+6 3-1 3-1

48

ADVENT

Name: _____

A Sweet Treat

Advent is the four week period before Christmas. It is a time of great preparation. Many people begin to bake special foods now so they will have them for Christmas.

You can help with the baking by unscrambling the names of the ingredients of (or directions for) a popular holiday dessert. When you have unscrambled them, print the circled letters in order in the space below to learn what you have made.

S N A R I S I   _ Ⓞ _ _ _ _ _

R O L U F   Ⓞ _ _ _ _

T U R B E T   _ _ _ _ _ Ⓞ

G A R U S   _ Ⓞ _ _ _

C E P S I S   _ _ Ⓞ _ _ _

N A T W U L S   _ _ _ _ _ Ⓞ _

R E C H S I E R   Ⓞ _ _ _ _ _ _ _

R E G O A N   D R I N   _ _ Ⓞ _ _ _   _ _ _ _

K E A B   _ _ Ⓞ _

S G E G   Ⓞ _ _ _

_ _ _ _ _ _ _ _ _ _ _ _

Light the Way

An Advent wreath is a circle of evergreens with four candles—three purple and one pink. A different candle is lit each of the four Sundays of Advent.

Complete the four steps of the puzzle below in order to light all the candles of the Advent wreath. (Each step should make a new word.)

W R E A T H

Drop a letter and unscramble to make a grain.   _ _ _ _ _

Drop a letter to keep things hot.   _ _ _ _

Drop a letter and unscramble to make a drink.   _ _ _

Drop a letter and you'll be ____ the end of the puzzle!   _ _

Name: _____

ST. NICHOLAS DAY

A Shoe-ful of Goodies

In many European countries, it is St. Nicholas, not Santa Claus, who brings holiday gifts to good children. Arriving on a white horse or donkey, St. Nicholas places small toys in the shoes left out by children on this special day. He has a helper, often dressed in black, who warns bad children to behave by leaving a bunch of birch twigs in their shoes.

 Can you unscramble the names of some small gifts St. Nicholas has left in your shoes?

N A D C Y _____   R I N A T _____

L O D L _____   R E G N O A _____

Z U L P E Z _____   L A L B _____

T R S O Y K O B O _____

Holiday Magic

St. Nicholas wears a long white robe with a scarlet cape. He has a white beard, carries a staff, and has a red *mitre* (pronounced: my-tur), a bishop's hat, on his head. According to legend, St. Nicholas performed many miracles. Try your hand at some holiday magic by solving the word squares. (The answers will be the same down and across.)

1. St. Nicholas's mitre is his _____.
2. Past tense of eat.
3. A drink.

1. Nickname for Nicholas.
2. A thought.
3. One penny.
4. Nickname for Katherine.

1. St. Nicholas wore a scarlet _____.
2. A space. (Length x Width = _____.)
3. A fruit.
4. You hear with these.

Name: _____

HUMAN RIGHTS DAY

The Right to Be Free

Today, we celebrate the freedoms that people have fought for throughout the ages and the rights they still hope to gain.

Can you decode the names of three events that marked peoples' search for equal rights? (Hint: They are written as ten-shift ciphers. A=K, B=L, C=M, and so on.)

● A document signed in 1215 by King John of England. In it, people demanded the right to a fair trial and the right to keep the things they owned.

C Q W D Q   S Q H J Q

_ _ _ _ _   _ _ _ _ _

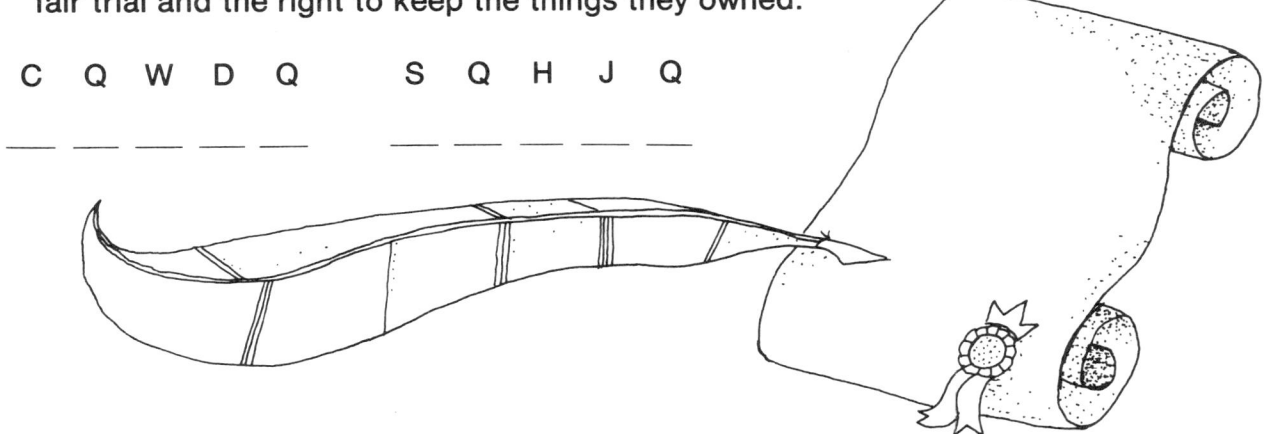

● In 1773, American colonists threw certain goods off ships to protest the fact that they were taxed by England, yet they were not represented in that government.

R E I J E D   J U Q   F Q H J 0

_ _ _ _ _ _   _ _ _   _ _ _ _ _

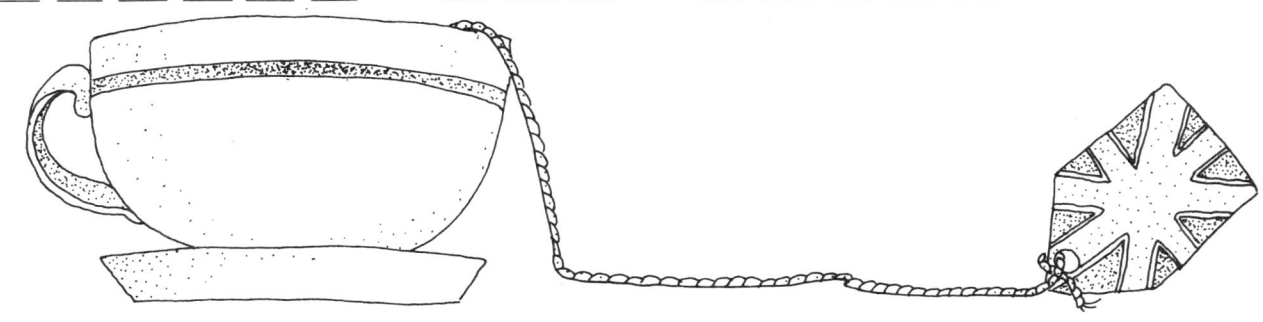

● A revolt in France in 1789 in which people demanded the same rights for the poor as for the rich.

V H U D S X   H U L E B K J Y E D

_ _ _ _ _ _   _ _ _ _ _ _ _ _ _ _

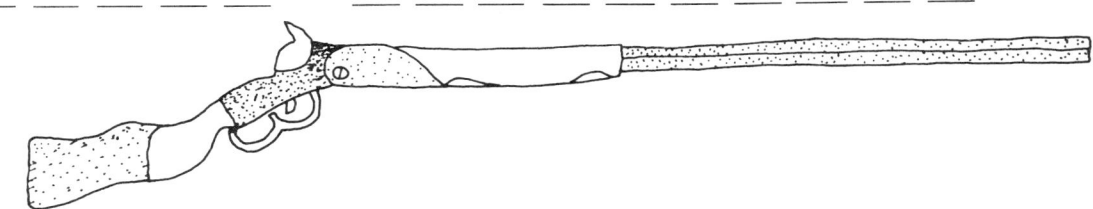

SANTA LUCIA DAY

Lighting the Way

In Sweden, boys and girls honor the Italian saint, Lucia, whose name means <u>light</u>, on one of the shortest days of the year. The oldest daughter in the family wears a long, white <u>dress</u> tied with a crimson <u>sash</u>. On her head is placed a <u>crown</u> of <u>greens</u> topped with lighted <u>candles</u>. Her brother might wear a tall, pointed <u>hat</u> covered with <u>stars</u>. Together, they serve coffee and special <u>buns</u> to their parents and <u>sing</u> the song, "Santa Lucia."

Can you fit the underlined words into the puzzle grid below? (One has already been done for you.)

Lucia Buns

The buns served on *Luciadagen* (pronounced loo-see-ah-dah-gen by the Swedes), or Lucia Day, are made of yeast dough flavored with saffron. They are twisted into different shapes that have special meanings. Read the clue for each different bun and see if you can figure out what they are supposed to represent.

Rhymes with filly; a flower. _____

Rhymes with hat; an animal. _____

Rhymes with joy; a person. _____

Rhymes with gown; a headpiece. _____

WRIGHT BROTHERS DAY

Taking Flight

Ever since people observed animals that could fly, they have wanted to be able to take off too. How many living creatures that fly can you find in the puzzle below? (There are at least five.) For each answer, you may use the letters given in any order, but only as often as they appear in the puzzle.

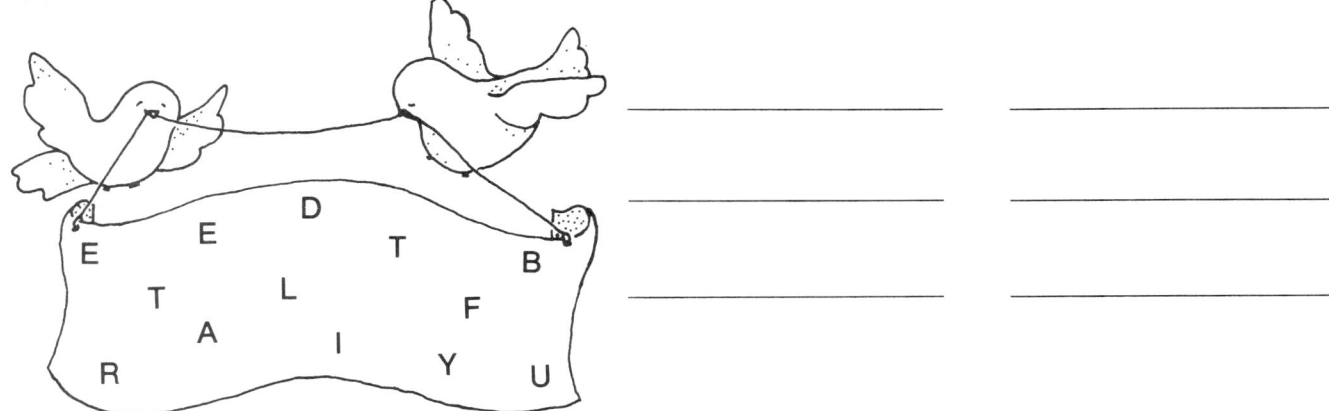

On December 17, 1903, Wilbur and Orville Wright built a flying machine that really worked. On its first flight, Orville flew their plane 120 feet in 12 seconds.

People have since invented many different devices and machines that fly. The names of five of them appear below. Can you unscramble the letters and head for the wild blue yonder?

T E K I   _ _ _ _

D L E G I R   _ _ _ _ _ _

R A I L P E N A   _ _ _ _ _ _ _ _

T J E   _ _ _

K O R T E C   _ _ _ _ _ _

Winter Wonderland

Watch Jack Frost give everything his icy touch
in this winter wonderland of a crossword puzzle.

WORD BANK

snowflakes	white	hat
bobsleds	that	rub
ski	fire	raw
socks	ole	chill
la	so	snap
more	lip	roof
dad	or	lend
D.C.	winter	of
ET	the	cold
S.A.	me	IDs
hit	be	ha
at	iceskates	er
		of

ACROSS:

1. To move your hands together briskly to warm them.
3. Greater in number.
6. To move over snow on a pair of long, narrow strips of plastic strapped to the boots.
8. A Spanish sporting exclamation.
10. Neither, nor; either, ____.
11. To exist.
12. Direct Current.
13. Tiny, white snow crystals.
16. The air temperature is ____ in the winter.
17. Several forms of identification (abbrev.).
18. When the weather suddenly turns chilly, it is sometimes called a cold ____.
19. A laugh.
20. In the exact position of.
21. This and ____.
23. A homonym for sew.
25. The color of newly fallen snow.
26. The musical note that comes after so.
27. Build a bon____ to keep the skaters warm.
28. A favorite alien.

DOWN:

1. A damp, cold January day.
2. Long sleds each made of two short sleds joined by a plank.
3. I.
4. The part of one's house that can be covered with snow.
5. A person that skis is a ski____.
6. Wear two pairs of ____ to keep your feet warm.
7. Shoes fitted with blades for moving on ice.
9. To allow someone to use a thing.
12. Father.
14. The season that comes between autumn and spring.
15. A part of your mouth that can become chapped by the cold.
16. A sudden cold feeling in the body.
18. Abbrev. for South America.
19. Wear one to keep your head warm.
21. Used to refer to a particular person or thing.
22. Don't ____ me with that snowball!
24. Words ____ wisdom.

WINTER

Name: _____

Winter Sports

Can you help your favorite department store restock its sporting goods for the winter season? Hidden in each of the sentences below is something you play with in the snow. Can you find each item? (Take a look at the sample sentence to see how it's done.)

SAMPLE: Charles <u>led</u> Diane to the campsite.

Dan's horse came in last, but Bob's led the pack.

A cask is used to hold wine.

Use two different kinds of rices, Kate, so the recipe will be correct.

Snow Kidding!

Subtract one letter at a time in order to "melt" the snow!

S   N   O   W   Y

___ ___ ___ ___

___ ___ ___

___ <u>N</u>

A Frosty Riddle

Add and subtract the letters as shown to solve the riddle.

How do kids kill time in the winter?

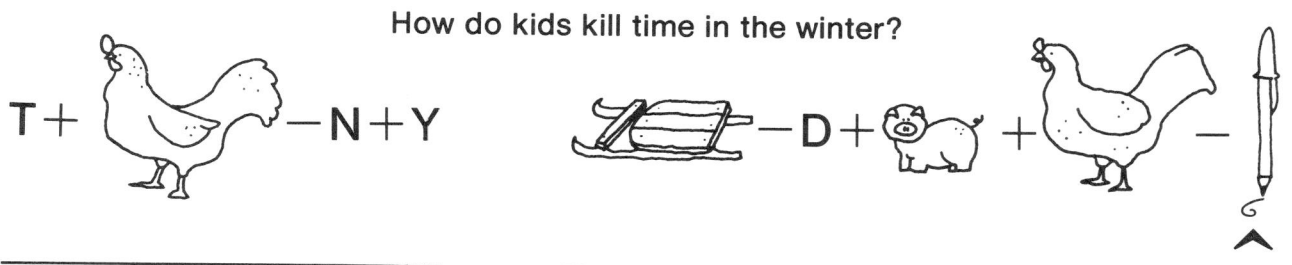

_____

WINTER

Name: _____

A Word Storm

Like the many tiny snowflakes you see falling during a storm, no two exactly alike, you should be able to find many different smaller words of three letters or more in the word below. (There are at least 50.)

SNOWFLAKES

1. _____
2. _____
3. _____
4. _____
5. _____
6. _____
7. _____
8. _____
9. _____
10. _____
11. _____
12. _____
13. _____
14. _____
15. _____
16. _____
17. _____

18. _____
19. _____
20. _____
21. _____
22. _____
23. _____
24. _____
25. _____
26. _____
27. _____
28. _____
29. _____
30. _____
31. _____
32. _____
33. _____

34. _____
35. _____
36. _____
37. _____
38. _____
39. _____
40. _____
41. _____
42. _____
43. _____
44. _____
45. _____
46. _____
47. _____
48. _____
49. _____
50. _____

PILGRIMS' DAY

Name: _____

Pilgrims Land

No one is exactly sure what the Pilgrims' ship, the <u>Mayflower</u>, looked like. It was probably about <u>ninety</u> feet long and 25 feet wide. After a voyage of more than <u>two</u> months, Captain Christopher <u>Jones</u> landed the ship and its 102 passengers at <u>Plymouth</u>, Massachusetts.

Can you fill in the puzzle grid with the words underlined in the paragraph above? One has already been done for you.

Plymouth Rock

Help the Pilgrims LAND on Plymouth ROCK.

Change one letter at a time, keeping the letter order the same. Each change should result in a new word, until you have changed all four letters and solved the puzzle.

L A N D

___ ___ ___ ___

___ ___ ___ ___

___ ___ ___ ___

R O C K

HANUKKAH

Name: _____

Freedom to Worship

Hanukkah, the Jewish "Festival of Lights," honors an event that took place more than 2,000 years ago. Judas Maccabeus and a small band of men drove out the Syrians, under King Antiochus and won a battle for religious freedom. When they went to relight the menorah (holy candelabra) in their temple, they found only a tiny bit of oil. Even so, the menorah is said to have burned for eight days.

Can you find each of the underlined words in the puzzle opposite? They may be up, down, across, diagonal, or backwards. Circle each word as you find it.

```
T E M S O F R E D L I G
I K L U Q I P T Z A J K
G S T H G I L R L V P F
M A C C A B E U S I X R
E M N O L E I G H T N E
N I P I D E D I C S Y E
O Q C T E M P L E E B D
R I D N H R U B C F W O
A G E A S V B R O N T M
H N A I Z P Q F R E E R
```

Light the Candles

Can you light each of the eight candles in the menorah? Find eight different words of three letters or more in the word . . .

C A N D L E

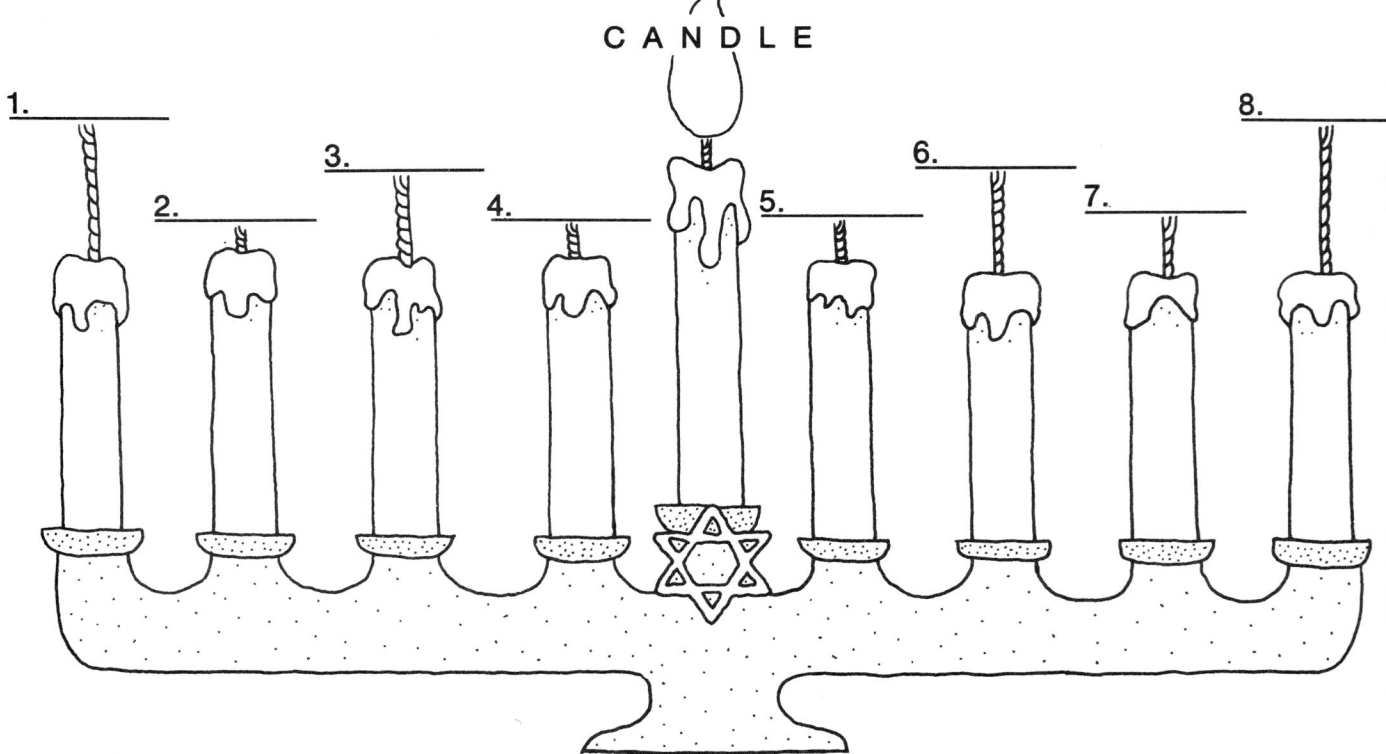

1. _____
2. _____
3. _____
4. _____
5. _____
6. _____
7. _____
8. _____

HANUKKAH

Spin the Dreidel

The *dreidel* (pronounced: dray-duhl) is a spinning top used to play games of chance. Each of the four sides of the dreidel has a Hebrew letter on it.

(Nun)
N

(Gimmel)
G

(Hay)
H

(Shin)
S

The four letters stand for the words "a great miracle happened here."
  Can you fill in the missing letters in the words below with letters from the dreidel? (Use the English versions, of course, not the Hebrew.)

__ A __ U K K A __   L I __ __ T __

E I __ __ T   __ I __ __ T __

Holiday Pancakes

Special pancakes called *latkes* (pronounced:laht-kehz) are a favorite Hanukkah meal.
Fill in the crossword puzzle below and learn the ingredients for latkes.

ACROSS:
2. White substance found in sea water.
3. Fine meal of ground wheat or crackers.
4. These are laid by chickens.
5. The rootlike bulb of a certain plant used as a vegetable.

DOWN:
1. Red fruits that grow on trees.
2. Butter or lard.
5. A spice made of ground, hot-tasting berries.
6. The bulbs of a plant with a strong odor.

CHRISTMAS

Name: _____

"A Right Jolly Old Elf"

In 1822, Clement Moore wrote a poem that described, for the first time, a very popular character. Can you read the picture puzzle below and guess who it is?

His 👁 👁 —how they twinkled! his dimples how merry!

His cheeks were like 🌹 🌹, his 👃 like a 🍒 !

His droll little 👄 was drawn up like a 🎀 ,

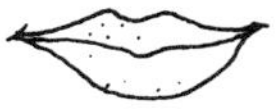

And the 🧔 on his chin was as white as the ❄ ;

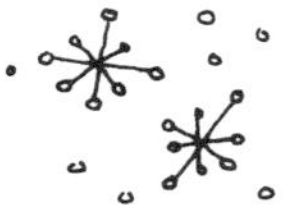

The stump of a 🪈 he held tight in his 😁 ,

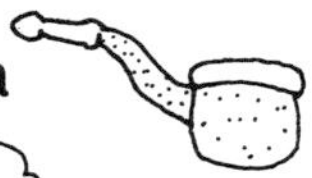

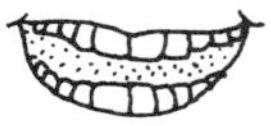

And the 💨 it encircled his head like a 🎄 ;

He had a broad face and a little round belly,

That shook when he laughed like a 🥣 full of JELLY .

He is _____ .

Ho! Ho! Ho!

Here's a holiday chuckle just for you.
If an athlete gets athlete's foot, what does an astronaut get?

Name: _____

CHRISTMAS

Away in a Manger

Today most Christians celebrate the birth of Christ. Because there was no room in any of the inns of Bethlehem, Mary and Joseph took shelter in a stable. Legend tells us that several animals saw the birth of Jesus and huddled close to keep him warm. How many farm animals can you find in the puzzle? (There are at least five.) For each animal, you may use the letters given in any order, but only as often as they appear in the puzzle.

R
C   S
O   X   E
D   K
E   H   P
N   W
Y

_____
_____
_____
_____
_____

Star Bright

On the night of Christ's birth, the "Star of Bethlehem" was said to have shone more brightly than any other star in the sky. Complete the puzzle below and see the star shine. Follow the directions and create a new word for each step.

__ __ __ __ __ __   Add a letter.

__ __ __ __ __   Add a letter.

S   T   A   R

__ __ __   Subtract a letter.

__ __ __   Reverse the letters.

__ __   Subtract a letter.

__   Subtract a letter.

CHRISTMAS

Trim the Tree

Help decorate the Christmas tree with all the different "ornaments." How many hidden smaller words of three letters or more can you find? (There are at least fifty.)

O R N A M E N T S

1. _____
2. _____
3. _____
4. _____
5. _____
6. _____
7. _____
8. _____
9. _____
10. _____
11. _____
12. _____
13. _____
14. _____
15. _____
16. _____
17. _____

18. _____
19. _____
20. _____
21. _____
22. _____
23. _____
24. _____
25. _____
26. _____
27. _____
28. _____
29. _____
30. _____
31. _____
32. _____
33. _____

34. _____
35. _____
36. _____
37. _____
38. _____
39. _____
40. _____
41. _____
42. _____
43. _____
44. _____
45. _____
46. _____
47. _____
48. _____
49. _____
50. _____

Name: _____

CLARA BARTON'S BIRTHDAY

Lady of the Red Cross

Clara Barton was a very special woman. She served as a nurse in three wars and formed a bureau to search for soldiers missing during the Civil War. She founded the American Red Cross which gave help to thousands of victims of disasters.

Can you find each of the words underlined in the paragraph above in the puzzle? They may be up, down, across, diagonal, or backwards. Circle each word as you find it.

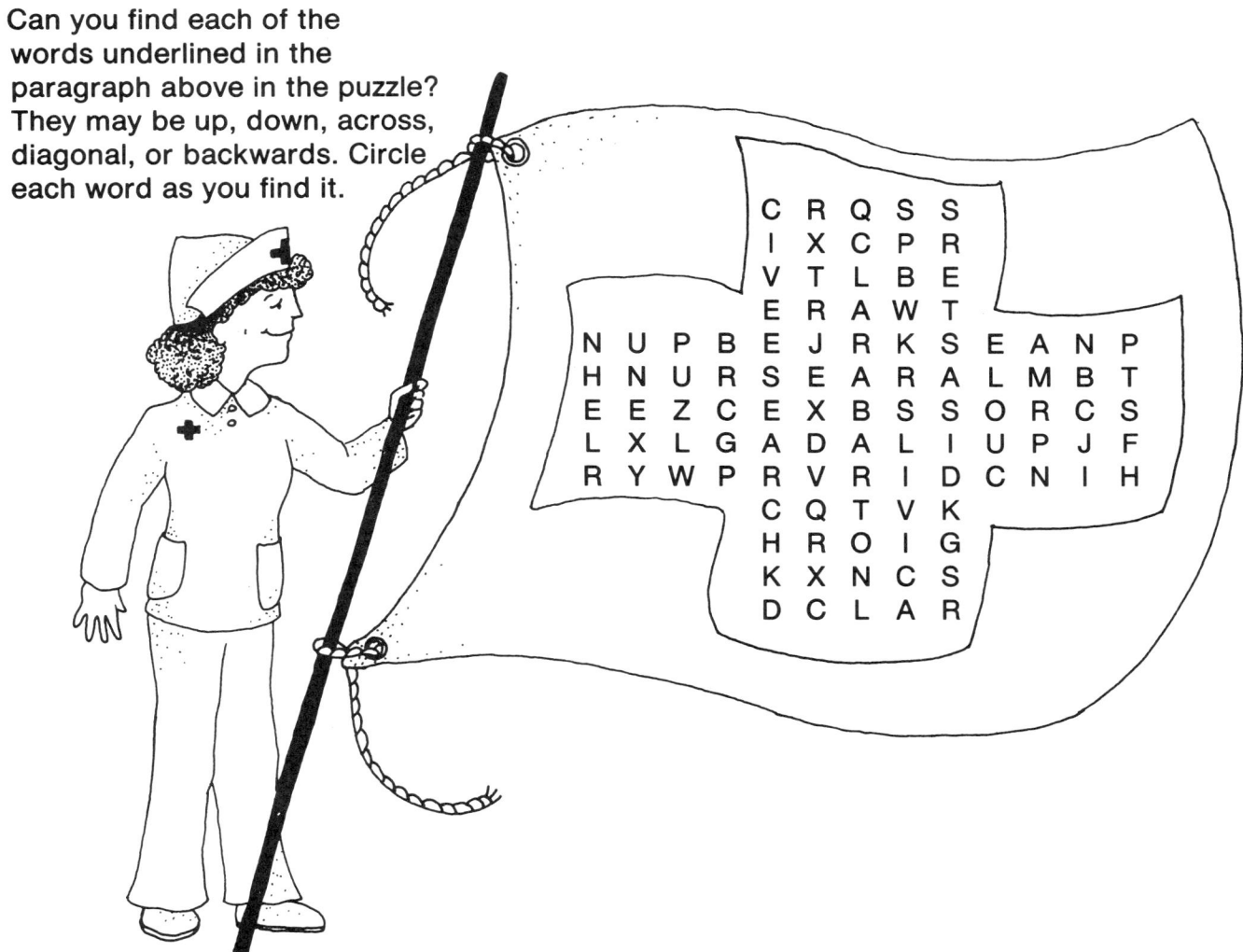

```
              C R Q S S
              I X C P R
              V T L B E
              E R A W T
  N U P B E J R K S E A N P
  H N U R S E A R A L M B T
  E E Z C E X B S S O R C S
  L X L G A D A L I U P J F
  R Y W P R V R I D C N I H
              C Q T V K
              H R O I G
              K X N C S
              D C L A R
```

Civil War Nurse

Clara Barton was famous for her care of wounded soldiers and was given a special nickname by the press. Can you unscramble the letters to learn what the name was?

GELNA   FO   HET   LABTETDELIF

_____   _____   _____

BOXING DAY

Name: _____

Gift Boxes

In Canada and Great Britain, today is the first weekday after Christmas and the day when people said thank you to those who worked for them, with gift boxes or money.

Finish wrapping the boxes below by solving the three magic word squares. The answers in each puzzle will be the same across and down.

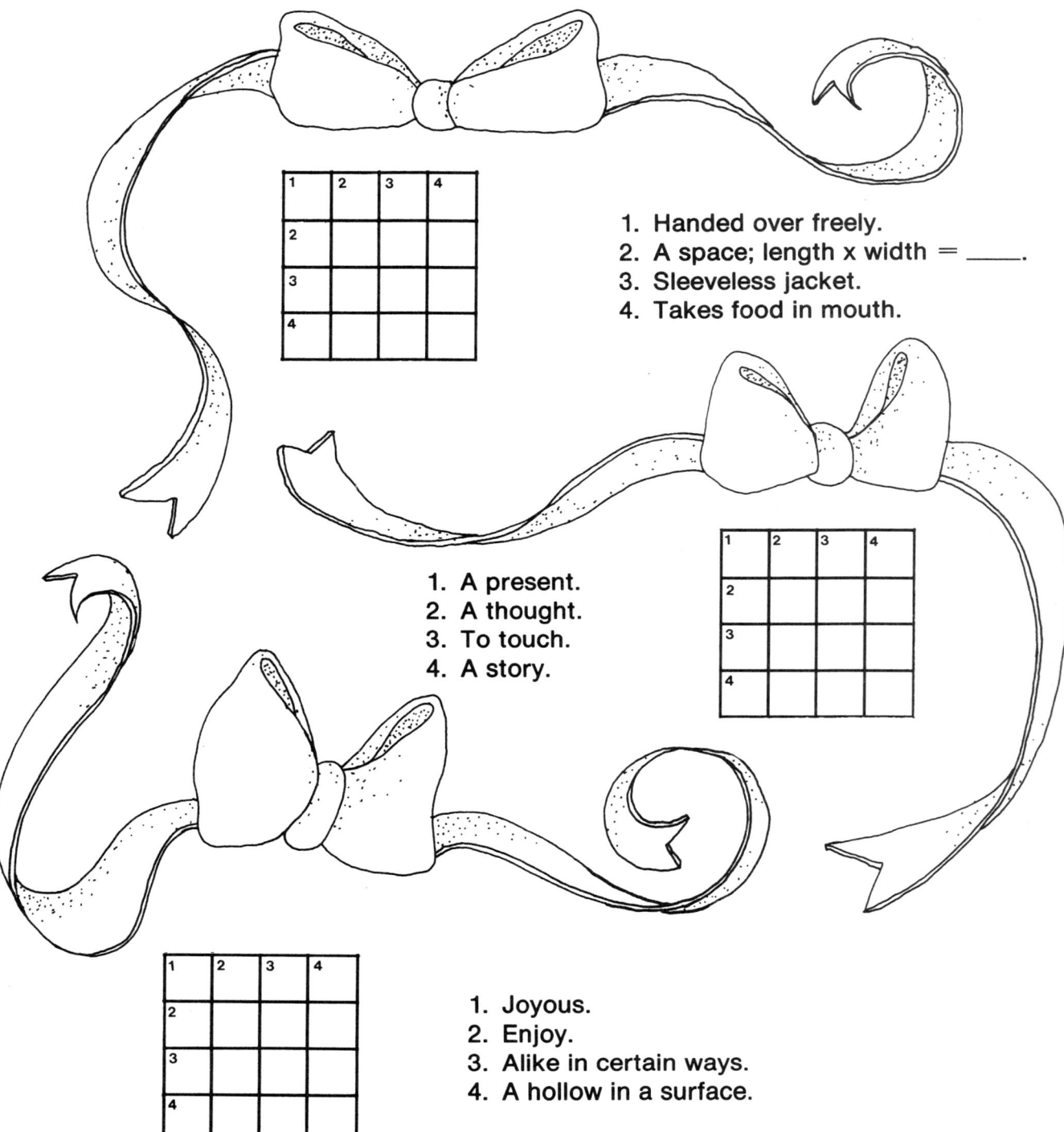

1. Handed over freely.
2. A space; length x width = _____.
3. Sleeveless jacket.
4. Takes food in mouth.

1. A present.
2. A thought.
3. To touch.
4. A story.

1. Joyous.
2. Enjoy.
3. Alike in certain ways.
4. A hollow in a surface.

Name: _____

NEW YEAR'S EVE

Ringing in the New

In many cultures, it is the custom to "ring in" the new year by making a lot of noise. Some primitive people believed that the noise would chase away evil spirits. Here's your chance to greet the new year with a lot of noise by doing the crossword puzzle below.

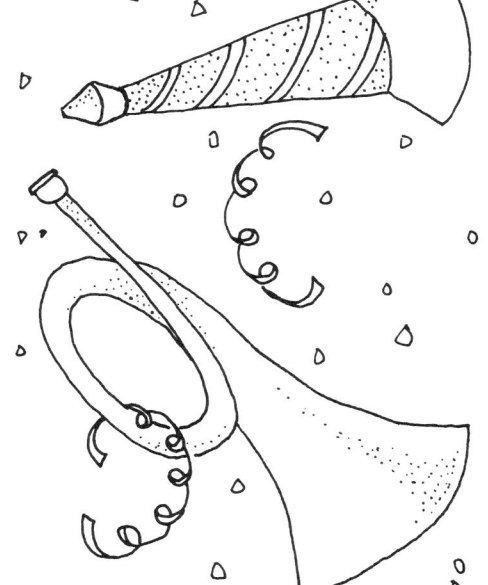

DOWN:
1. Paper sacks you can blow up and burst to make a noise.
2. Using the voice to make musical sounds.
3. Abbrev. for regarding.
4. Pleasant sounds made by a voice or instrument.
5. Painting, drawing, or sculpture.
6. The evening before Jan. 1 is New Year's _____.
7. Initials of For Information.
10. Brass musical instruments.
11. An untruth.
12. It makes a ringing sound.
14. Yes.
15. To tear.
16. Citizen's Band radio.

WORD BANK

bell	horns	firecracker
siren	whistle	guns
make	bags	fur
re	Eve	music
NY	lose	pop
big	CB	singing
lie	art	FI
rip		aye

ACROSS:
2. A device for making a loud sound; a police car has one.
4. It's fun to _____ a lot of noise on New Year's Eve.
7. Hair on certain animals.
8. Muskets were colonial _____ used to make noise at the new year.
9. Device that is blown into to make a shrill sound.
13. A small roll of paper containing gunpowder and a fuse.
17. Initials of New Year.
18. #13 ACROSS can make a _____ noise.
19. Opposite of find.
20. A short, sharp noise; also a nickname for Dad.

Name: _____

NEW YEAR'S DAY

Look on the Bright Side

Janus is the ancient Roman god for whom the month of January is named. He was said to have two faces and could look both forward and backward at the same time. On January 1st, we look back on the old year and ahead to the new.

Turn your FACE and LOOK ahead to a wonderful new year. Change one letter at a time keeping the letter order the same. Each change should result in a new word, until you have changed all four letters and solved the puzzle.

```
F   A   C   E
__  __  __  __

__  __  __  __

__  __  __  __
L   O   O   K
```

First Footer

In Scotland, it was considered good luck if a dark-haired man was the first person to set foot in the door of one's house on New Year's Day.

Black-haired cousin Fred is the first person to set FOOT in your house today and you're GLAD.

Change the word FOOT to GLAD by changing one letter at a time.

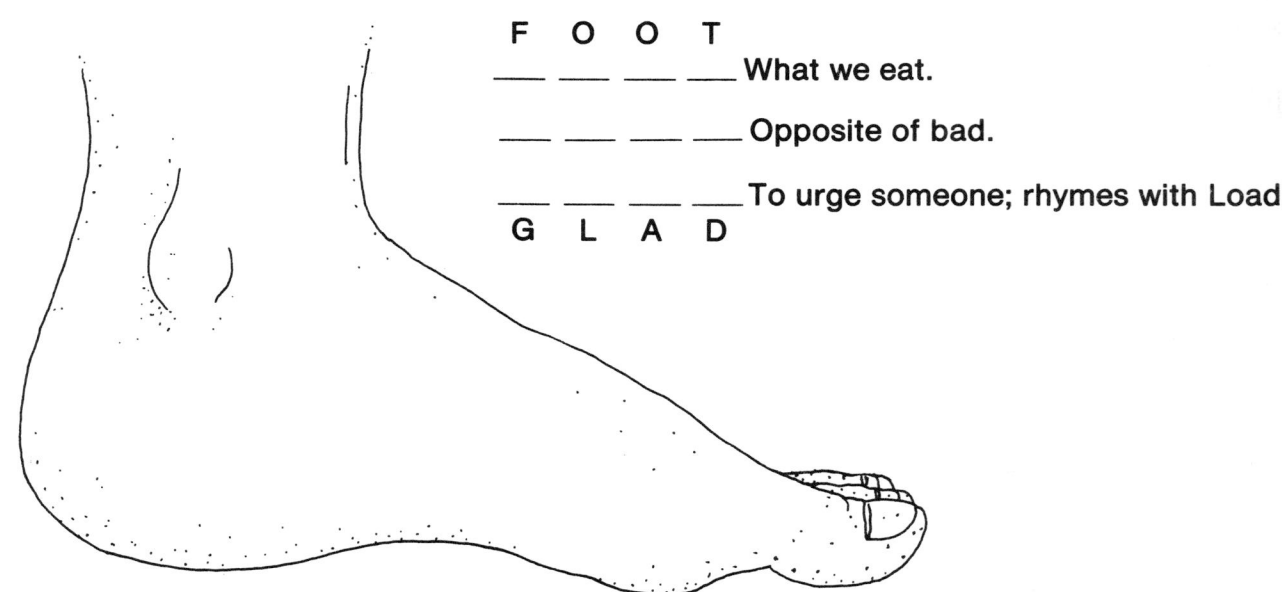

```
F   O   O   T
__  __  __  __  What we eat.

__  __  __  __  Opposite of bad.

__  __  __  __  To urge someone; rhymes with Load.
G   L   A   D
```

A Parade of Flowers

Every year, on New Year's Day, in Pasadena, California, a very special parade is seen by millions of people. It is the Tournament of Roses Parade. Magnificent floats are made entirely of real flowers just for today.

Help to decorate a float of your own for the parade by solving the flower riddles below. Look at the pictures. Put the name of what you see in the spaces below each picture. The numbers under the spaces are a code that will help you get the joke.

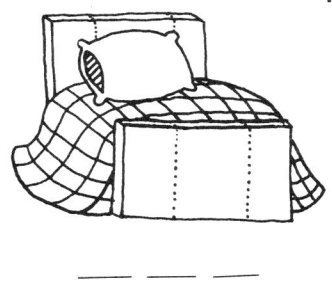   

___ ___ ___   ___ ___ ___ ___   ___ ___ ___ ___   ___ ___ ___
 8   7   2   15 10   3 11   13   5 16 11   17 12 18

___ ___ ___ ___ ___   ___ ___ ___ ___ ___
 6   1   5 15   7   9   4   3 14   7

What did the big flower say to the little flower?

___ ___ , ___ ___ ___ .
 1 10   8 12   2

Why are flowers so lazy?

___ ___ ___ ___   ___ ___ ___   ___ ___ ___ ___ ___   ___ ___   ___ ___ ___ .
 4   1   7 13   5 16   7   5 15   6   5 13 9   10 11   8   7   2

Why is a spring garden like your mouth?

___ ___ ___ ___   ___ ___ ___ ___   ___ ___ ___ ___ ___ ___ ___ .
 8   3   4   1   1   5 14   7   4 12 15 10 18   9

NATIONAL HOBBY MONTH

The More the Merrier

This month we celebrate all the things people enjoy doing just for fun. Dancing, playing sports, reading, gardening, and painting are all hobbies. So is collecting things. Take a look at the puzzle below and try to find all the different collectibles listed. The words may be up, down, across, diagonal, or backwards. Circle each word as you find it.

```
M A B J B U T F O N N D P B P
B A U T O G P E D N A T S J O
D S T I C K E R S H Z P D C S
F P T C S T I Q K F R S R Q T
G O O Y H G P S M L X K A I G
I R N Z R B C N S M D B C M X
J T S F X J O I S T E N T A Y
K S H P A R G O T U A O S Y B
S C K J P Z Q C K N Q M O T P
Q A S B C M N F P C K F P C X
X R J C X F R T Y D O L L S I
Y D R N S Z F H K J L V D B D
W S H F L L B J P F H X E F O
P Q R Z U E G Z S N U Y G R L
T Y P F C D M A Q S L L E H S
```

BUTTONS
STICKERS
MATCHBOOK COVERS
AUTOGRAPHS
COINS
STAMPS
POSTCARDS
SHELLS
DOLLS
SPORTS CARDS

Hobby Ha-Ha

Solve the riddle by unscrambling the answer.

What is Santa Claus's favorite hobby?

R A N G D E G I N.   E H   S O G E   O E H,   O E H,   O E H.

_____. _____, _____, _____.

JAKOB GRIMM'S BIRTHDAY

Famous Folktales

Jakob Grimm was born on this day in 1785. He and his brother, Wilhelm, preserved for all time some German folktales that had been handed down by word of mouth for generations.

Can you figure out the titles of some of these famous tales? Just unscramble the letters to learn them.

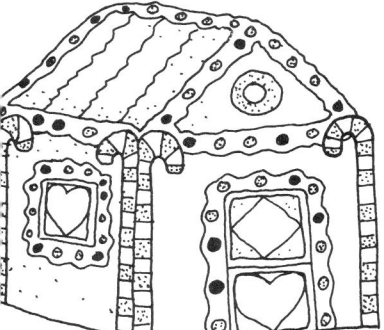

Two children who want to eat a witch out of house and home.

N E S H A L   D A N   T E R G L E

____ ____ ____ ____ ____   ____ ____ ____   ____ ____ ____ ____ ____ ____

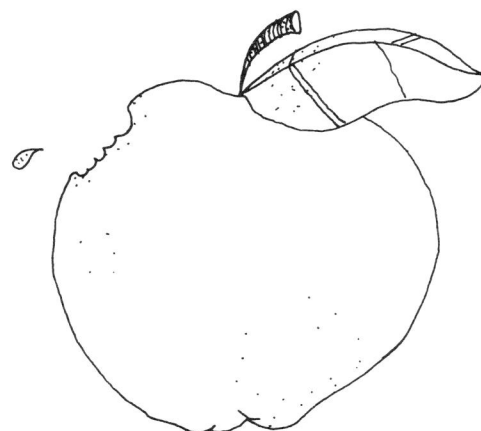

A princess who bites a bad apple.

W O N S   H E T I W

____ ____ ____ ____   ____ ____ ____ ____

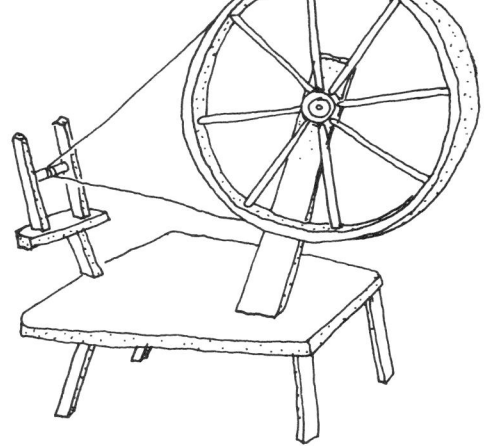

A little man who spins straw into gold.

M U P R E L L I S T T N I K S

____ ____ ____ ____ ____ ____ ____ ____ ____ ____ ____ ____ ____ ____

A girl who takes on a wolf.

T E L T I L   D E R   D R I G I N   D O H O

____ ____ ____ ____ ____ ____   ____ ____ ____   ____ ____ ____ ____ ____ ____   ____ ____ ____ ____

69

Name: _____

LOUIS BRAILLE'S BIRTHDAY

Tiny Dots

Louis Braille, born on this day in 1809, invented a type of printing with raised dots that allows the blind to read and to write.

Study the braille alphabet and then try to read the answers to the riddles below.

A B C D E F G H I J K L M N O P

Q R S T U V W X Y Z

What can you have in your pocket when your pocket is empty?

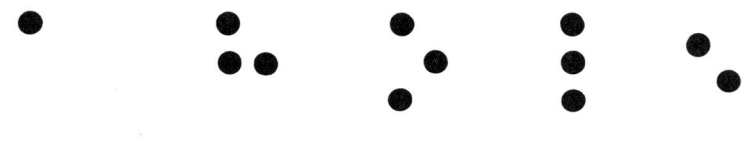

_____

What do you lose every time you stand up?

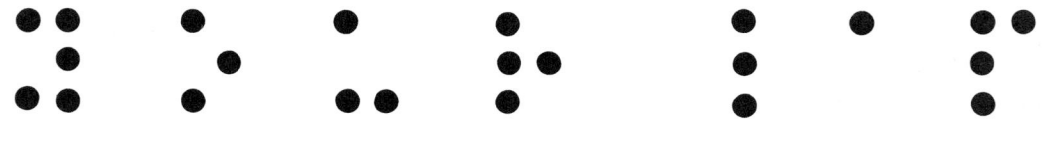

_____

What can you keep even if you give it away?

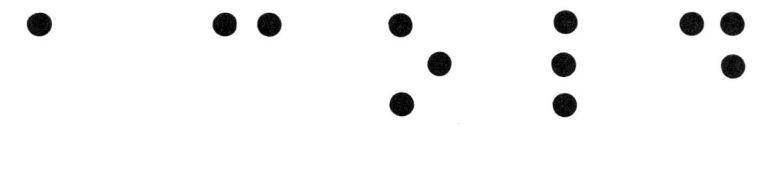

_____

GEORGE WASHINGTON CARVER

Not Just Peanuts

George Washington Carver, the famous black American scientist, died on this day in 1943. Because of his research in agriculture, he discovered hundreds of uses for the peanut, the sweet potato, and the soybean. He figured out ways to get many products from cotton waste and he made red, blue, and purple pigments from a certain kind of clay found in the South.

How many of the words underlined in the paragraph above can you find in the puzzle? They may be up, down, across, diagonal, or backwards. Circle each word as you find it.

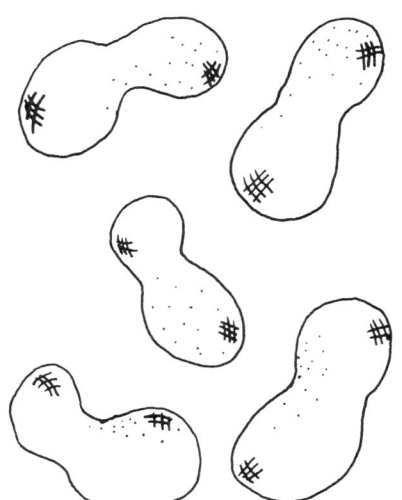

```
E  S  T  N  E  M  G  I  P  B  D
T  H  U  N  D  R  E  D  S  F  D
S  K  N  G  L  F  W  B  O  M  C
A  W  A  C  R  S  E  S  U  B  A
W  J  E  M  C  Q  M  W  T  P  R
B  X  P  E  B  L  U  E  H  U  V
R  D  C  O  T  T  O  N  J  R  E
K  E  V  G  T  U  S  Z  G  P  R
Z  H  D  N  Y  A  L  C  Q  L  S
P  R  O  D  U  C  T  S  T  E  U
B  C  N  A  E  B  Y  O  S  M  Z
```

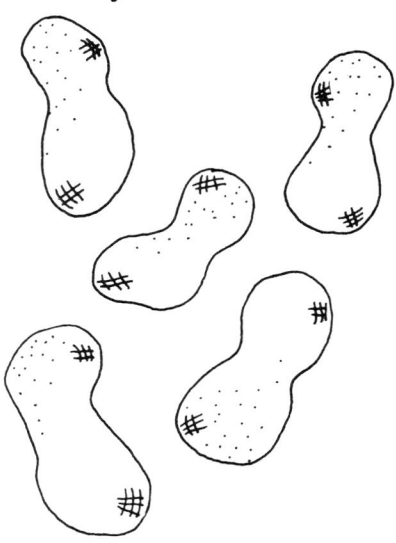

Nutty Puzzles

Here's your chance to assist G. W. Carver in his research on peanuts.

Can you change the word PEA to NUT? Change one letter at a time keeping the letter order the same. Each change should result in a new word, until you have changed all three letters and solved the puzzle.

P   E   A

___   ___   ___

___   ___   ___

N   U   T

Complete the two magic word squares below. The answers for each puzzle will be the same across and down.

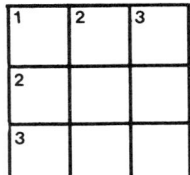

1. A vegetable that grows in a pod.
2. One of the things you hear with.
3. Painting and sculpture.
4. Almond or pecan.
5. To put into service.
6. A hot drink.

Name: _____

TWELFTH NIGHT

Twelve Gifts

Your "true love" has been very generous this Christmas! Take a look at the list of gifts that were sent to you. Now, try to fit each of the underlined words into the puzzle grid below. (Two have already been done for you.)

1 <u>partridge</u> in <u>pear</u> tree
2 <u>turtle</u> <u>doves</u>
3 <u>french</u> <u>hens</u>
4 calling <u>birds</u>
5 golden <u>rings</u>
6 <u>geese</u> a-laying
7 <u>swans</u> a-swimming
8 <u>maids</u> a-milking
9 <u>ladies</u> dancing
10 <u>lords</u> a-leaping
11 <u>pipers</u> piping
12 <u>drummers</u> drumming

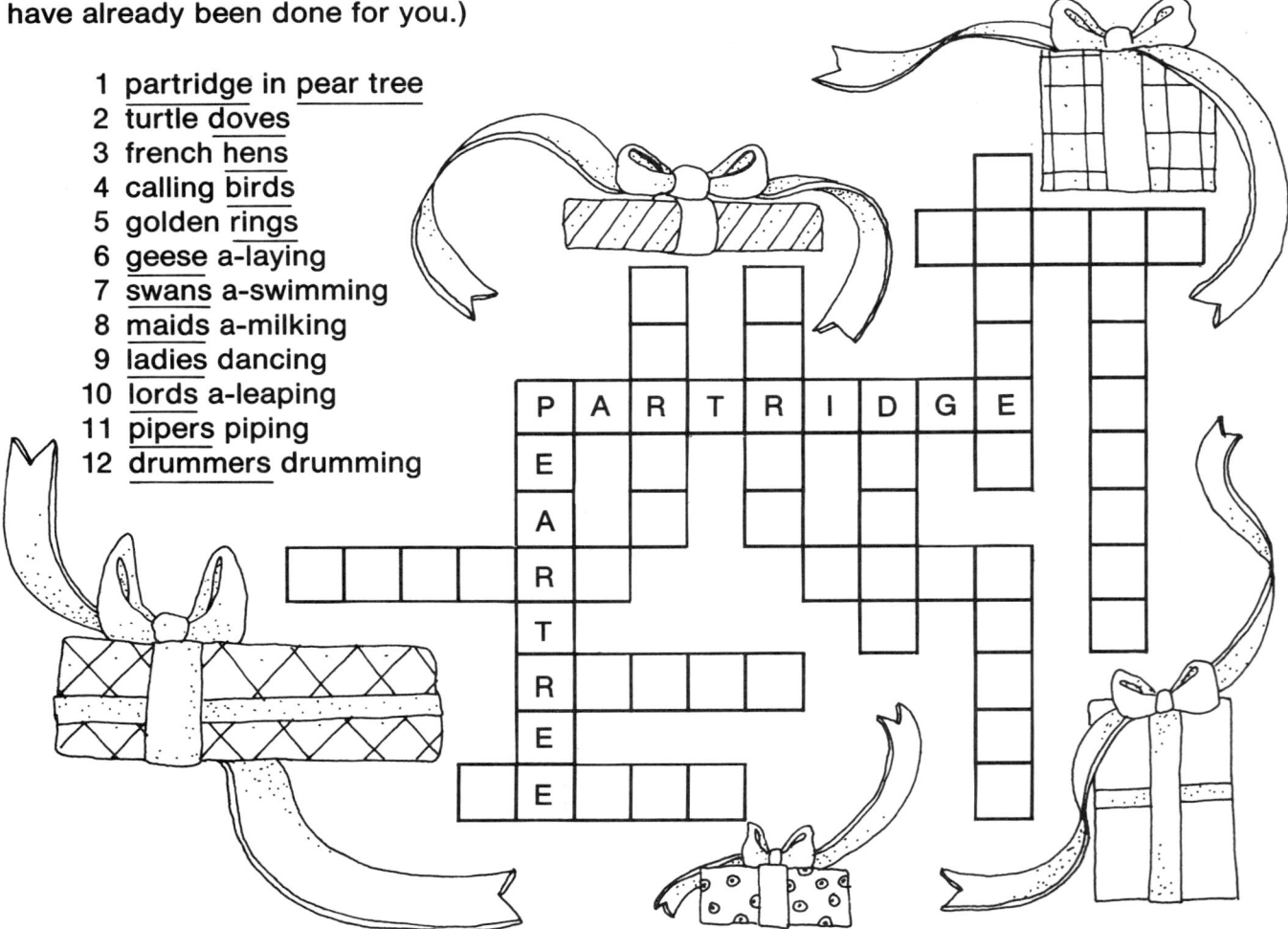

Find the Bean

In France, it is a tradition to bake a "King's Cake" on this day and to hide a bean in it. The person who finds the bean becomes "King or Queen of the Bean" and wears a paper crown. Other countries have similar customs and it is always considered lucky to be the person to find the bean.

Are you lucky? Try to find three different kinds of beans in the sentences below. (Hint: two are vegetable beans and one makes a drink.) Underline the words when you find them.

My friend, Ali, made lunch for me.

The ogre entered the room with a roar.

The zookeeper accused Mac of feeding the bears.

EPIPHANY

Name: _____

Three Wise Men

Today Christians celebrate the coming of the three Magi. The Magi, or wise men, were said to have followed a very bright star to the place in which Jesus Christ was born. Each of the wise men carried a special gift for the infant. Can you break the code and figure out the names of each of the three wise men and the gifts they brought? (Hint: The code is a 3-shift cipher. Skip the first three letters of the alphabet and A becomes D; B=E, C=F, and so on.)

___ ___ ___ ___ ___ ___ ___ ___ ___
Y X I Q E X P X O

___ ___ ___ ___ ___ ___ ___ ___ ___ ___ ___
C O X K H F K Z B K P B

___ ___ ___ ___ ___ ___ ___ ___ ___ ___ ___
J B I Z E F L O   D L I A

___ ___ ___ ___ ___ ___ ___ ___ ___ ___ ___
D X P M X O   J V O O E

Be Wise, Too

Can you solve the two magic word squares below? The answers for each puzzle will be the same across and down.

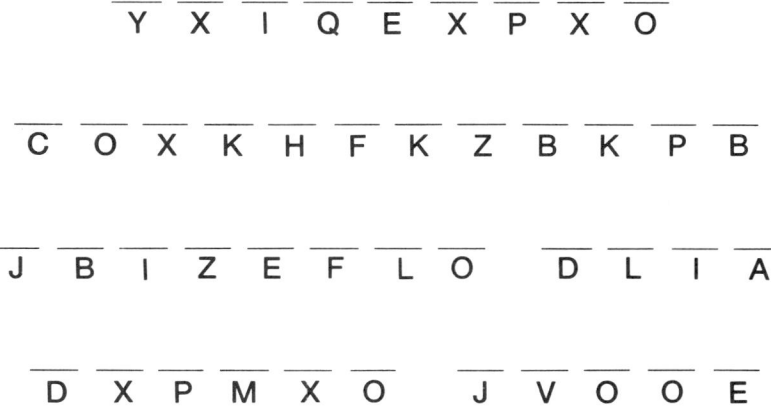

1. Smart.
2. Used to press wrinkles.
3. Given in return for money.
4. The last parts of anything.

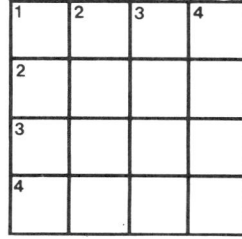

1. Male people.
2. A period of history.
3. A short sleep.

JOHN A. MACDONALD'S BIRTHDAY

Canada's Finest

Today is the birthday of Canada's first prime minister, John A. MacDonald, who took office in 1867, when the Dominion of Canada was formed.

Can you solve the picture puzzles below and discover the names of four Canadian provinces? Add and subtract the letters as shown from the names of the pictures.

H + [queen] − [hen] + [cookie jar] + C − D

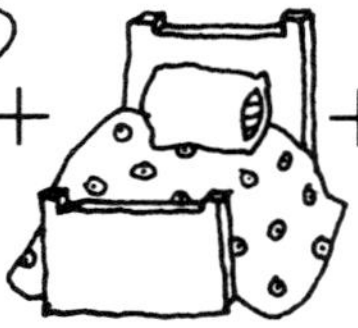

_____

[bone] + E − [bee] + [pail] − G + R + [pie] + AR − [pear] + O

_____

[man] + I + [toe] − E + [bag] − G

_____

[ball] − B + [bear] + MP − [lamp] + [pail] − G

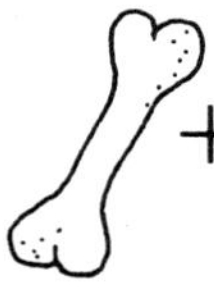

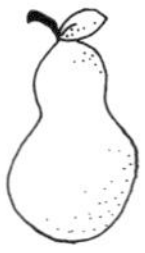

_____

CHARLES PERRAULT'S BIRTHDAY

Favorite Fairy Tales

Charles Perrault (pronounced: peh-roh) was a French poet who was born on this day in 1628. He is famous for the eight stories he collected for a book he called <u>Tales</u> of <u>Olden</u> <u>Times</u>. The titles of three of the stories appear below. Add and subtract the letters as shown from the names of the objects pictured.

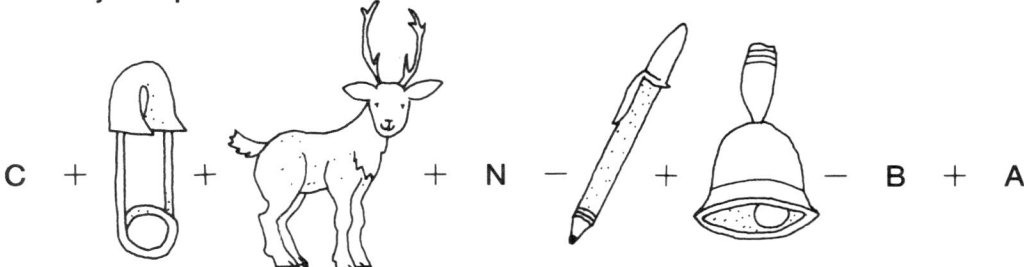

C + [pin] + [deer] + N − [pen] + [bell] − B + A

_____

[bag] − R + S − E 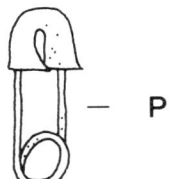 [pin] − P 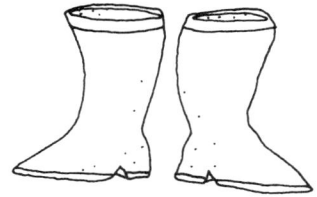 [boots]

_____

S + [blocks] − [socks] + U + [bee] + D − [bed] + [teddy bear] + D

_____

Name: _____

MARTIN LUTHER KING'S BIRTHDAY

A Drum Major for Peace

Dr. Martin Luther King, Jr., born on this day in 1929, was a great American civil rights leader. He devoted his life to the fight for equality for all people and, in 1964, he won the Nobel Peace Prize for his work. He was shot and killed in 1968, but his inspiration lives on. When asked how he wanted to be remembered, he said, "Say that I was a drum major for peace."

Can you fit each of the underlined words in the paragraph above into the puzzle grid? One has already been done for you.

Equality for All

In 1963, Dr. King led the "March on Washington." More than 200,000 people marched from the Washington Monument to the Lincoln Memorial to dramatize the fight for equality.

Translate the words below to learn the name of a song that was played during the March. (Hint: It is written as a 3-shift cipher. A=D, B=E, C=F, and so on.)

"I B Q   C O B B A L J   O F K D"

___ ___ ___   ___ ___ ___ ___ ___ ___ ___   ___ ___ ___ ___

BENJAMIN FRANKLIN'S BIRTHDAY

Colonial Inventor

Benjamin Franklin was born on this day in 1706. A <u>scientist</u> as well as a <u>statesman</u>, <u>printer</u>, and <u>writer</u>, he invented <u>bifocal</u> <u>spectacles</u>, the <u>lightning</u> <u>rod</u>, a <u>harmonica</u>, and the <u>Franklin</u> <u>stove</u>.

    How many of the words underlined in the sentence above can you find in the puzzle? They may be up, down, across, diagonal, or backwards. Circle each word as you find it.

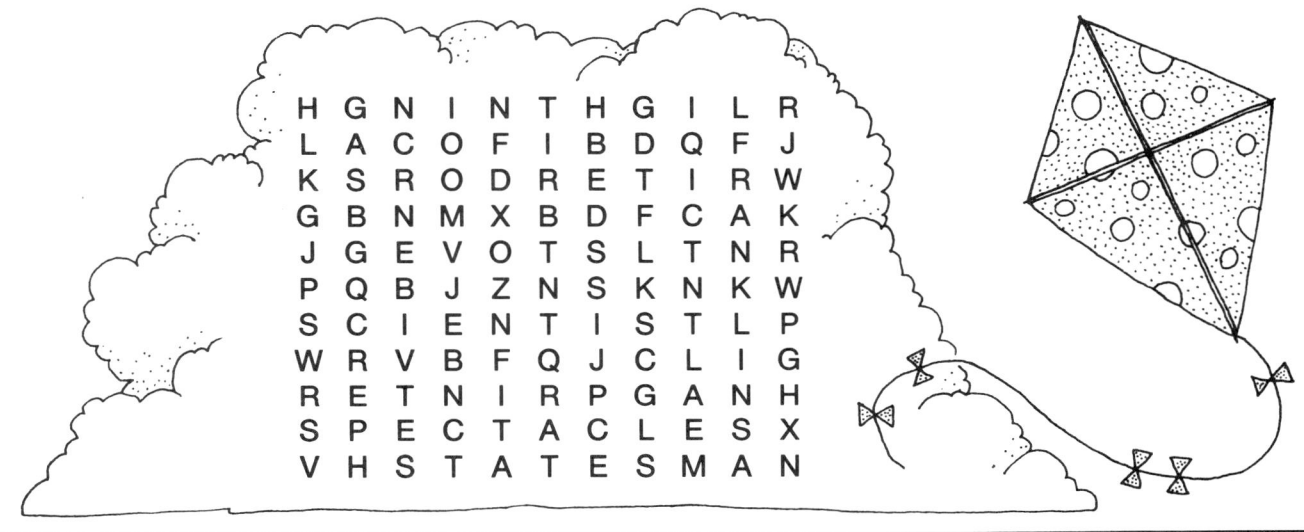

```
H  G  N  I  N  T  H  G  I  L  R
L  A  C  O  F  I  B  D  Q  F  J
K  S  R  O  D  R  E  T  I  R  W
G  B  N  M  X  B  D  F  C  A  K
J  G  E  V  O  T  S  L  T  N  R
P  Q  B  J  Z  N  S  K  N  K  W
S  C  I  E  N  T  I  S  T  L  P
W  R  V  B  F  Q  J  C  L  I  G
R  E  T  N  I  R  P  G  A  N  H
S  P  E  C  T  A  C  L  E  S  X
V  H  S  T  A  T  E  S  M  A  N
```

An Electric Experience

You'll get a kick out of this riddle!

Look at the pictures. Put the name of what you see in the spaces below each picture. The numbers under the spaces are a code that will help you get the joke.

What did Benjamin Franklin do the moment he discovered electricity?

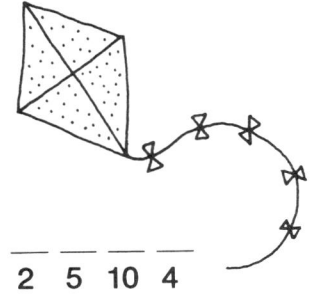

___ ___ ___ ___
2 5 10 4

___ ___ ___ ___
3 6 8 7

___ ___ ___
9 1 11

___ ___ ___ ___
7 1 12 13

___ ___ ___ ___ ___ ___ ___ .
8 1 10 3 5 8 12

___ ___
3 4

___ ___ ___
11 6 13

___ ___ ___
10 1 1

___ ___ ___ ___ ___ ___ ___ .
13 3 1 9 2 4 7

Name: _____

INAUGURATION DAY

Taking the Oath

Today a newly elected President of the United States takes the oath of office. Read the oath below and then try to fit the underlined words into the puzzle grid. (Two have already been done for you.)

| | P | R | E | S | I | D | E | N | T | |

I do solemnly swear that I will faithfully execute the office of President of the United States, and will, to the best of my ability, preserve, protect and defend the Constitution of the United States.

U N I T E D S T A T E S

Presidential Privilege

A new President is able to appoint many people to different government jobs. See how many "appointments" you can make by finding as many smaller words of three letters or more as you can in the word below. (There are at least 50. Continue on the back of this page.)

P R E S I D E N T

1._____   8._____   15._____

2._____   9._____   16._____

3._____   10._____   17._____

4._____   11._____   18._____

5._____   12._____   19._____

6._____   13._____   20._____

7._____   14._____   21._____

Name: _____

January 20

INAUGURATION DAY

First Facts

Can you figure out the names of the U.S. presidents named in the puzzles below? The first letter of the name of each picture is a letter in the name of the president. (The first puzzle is done for you).

(1) He was called the "Father of the Constitution."

 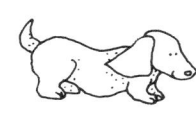   

M   A   D   I   S   O   N

(2) He was the first four-star general in the United States.

___   ___   ___   ___   ___

(3) He was the only person to be both president *and* chief justice.

  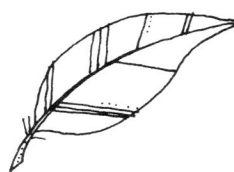 

___   ___   ___   ___

(4) He was the first president to have earned a Ph.D.

 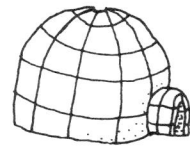    

___   ___   ___   ___   ___   ___

(5) He made the decision to drop the first atom bomb during World War II.

___   ___   ___   ___   ___   ___

Name: _____

FIRST BASKETBALL GAME

The Main Man

The first basketball game was played on this day in 1892. Basketball was invented by a physical education teacher at the YMCA college in Springfield, Massachusetts. To learn his name, look at the pictures below. Put the name of what you see in the spaces below each picture. The numbers under the spaces are a code that will help you find out the answer.

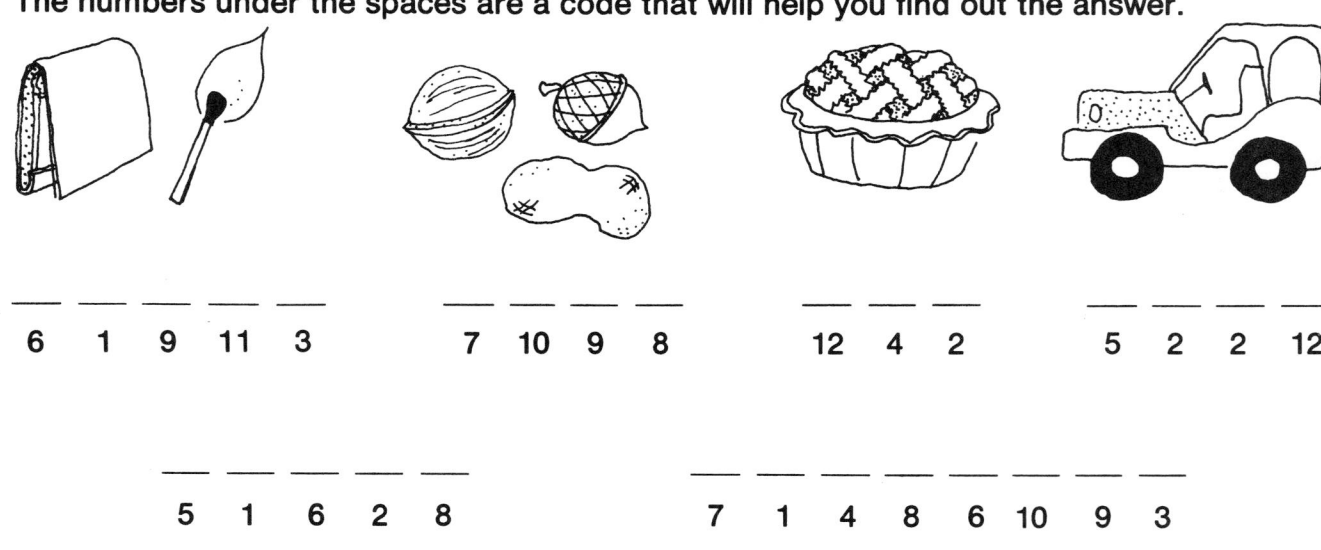

___ ___ ___ ___ ___
6   1   9   11   3

___ ___ ___ ___
7   10   9   8

___ ___ ___
12   4   2

___ ___ ___ ___
5   2   2   12

___ ___ ___ ___ ___
5   1   6   2   8

___ ___ ___ ___ ___ ___ ___ ___
7   1   4   8   6   10   9   3

Way to Go!

See how many points you can score by finding as many smaller words of three letters or more as you can in the word below. (There are at least 30.)

B A S K E T B A L L

1. _____	11. _____	21. _____
2. _____	12. _____	22. _____
3. _____	13. _____	23. _____
4. _____	14. _____	24. _____
5. _____	15. _____	25. _____
6. _____	16. _____	26. _____
7. _____	17. _____	27. _____
8. _____	18. _____	28. _____
9. _____	19. _____	29. _____
10. _____	20. _____	30. _____

Name: _____

AUSTRALIA DAY

Animals of the Outback

On this day in 1788, the first English settlement was started in Australia. The colonists discovered some very unusual animals in their new home.

Can you fit the names of each of the animals listed into the puzzle grid? (One has already been done.)

KANGAROO (carries its young in a pouch)

KOALA (eats only eucalyptus leaves)

EMU (flightless bird, similar to an ostrich)

WALLABY (looks like a small kangaroo)

PLATYPUS (a mammal that has a bill and lays eggs)

KOOKABURRA (called a laughing jackass because of its loud braying)

K
A
N
G
A
R
O
O

Word-Go-Round

The English settlers learned many new words from the native people living in Australia. One was *boomerang*—a curved piece of wood that can be thrown so that it returns to the thrower.

Try to find as many smaller words of three letters or more as you can in the word

BOOMERANG   (There are at least 35.)

1. _____
2. _____
3. _____
4. _____
5. _____
6. _____
7. _____
8. _____
9. _____
10. _____
11. _____
12. _____

13. _____
14. _____
15. _____
16. _____
17. _____
18. _____
19. _____
20. _____
21. _____
22. _____
23. _____
24. _____

25. _____
26. _____
27. _____
28. _____
29. _____
30. _____
31. _____
32. _____
33. _____
34. _____
35. _____

Name: _____

WAYNE GRETSKY'S BIRTHDAY

Hockey Superstar

Wayne Gretsky, born on this day in 1961, is considered by many to be the world's best ice hockey player.

The game of ice hockey was first played in Canada in the 1870s. Each team in a hockey game has six players: the goalie, the center, two defense players, and two forwards.

Can you fill in the blanks in the four words below? Each word can be found in the paragraph above.

```
__ E __ T __ R

__ __ A  L __ E

__ __ F __ N __ E

__ O __ W __ __ D
```

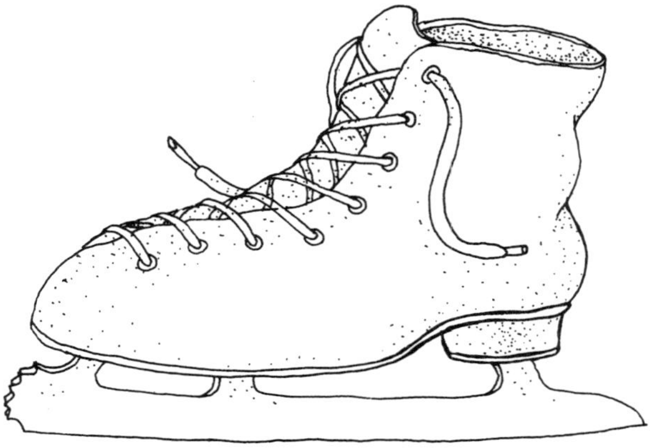

Matching Game

Below is a list of the teams in the National Hockey League. Can you fill in the blanks in the sentences below with the names of the correct teams. (Team names can be used only once.)

Islanders	Flames	Flyers	Whalers
Maple Leafs	Jets	Bruins	Devils
Rangers	Penguins	North Stars	Sabres
Blues	Red Wings	Nordiques	Black Hawks
Kings	Canadiens	Oilers	Capitals
			Canucks

1. The _____ grow on trees.

2. The _____ can make things really hot!

3. The _____ live with water all around them.

4. The _____ and _____ take off into the wild blue yonder.

5. The _____ and _____ are both names for people who live

   in Canada.

6. The _____ shine brightly in the night sky.

7. The _____, the _____ _____ and the

   _____ _____ are birds of a feather!

The Prima Ballerina

Anna Pavlova, the greatest ballerina of her time, was born in Russia in 1882. Her most famous performance was in the ballet, "A Dying Swan."

Can you complete the magic word square below? The answers will be the same across and down.

1. A large, white swimming bird with a long, curved neck.

2. Contraction for we are.

3. Dance, painting, and music are all parts of the _____.

4. The place in which a bird lays its eggs.

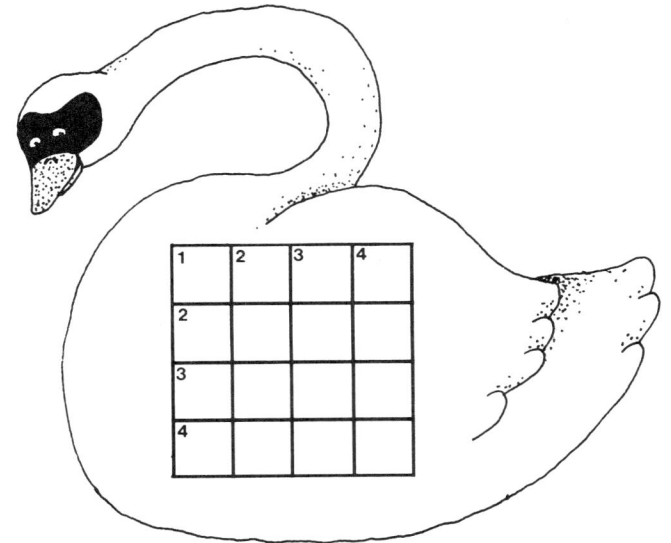

Fancy Footwork

Pavlova was also famous for her dancing in another ballet. This ballet was based on a story about a girl and ghosts. To learn the name of the ballet, look at the pictures below. They show a ballerina's feet in the five positions used in ballet. The number under each picture becomes a code. Do the math and then use the answers to fill in the letters in the spaces provided.

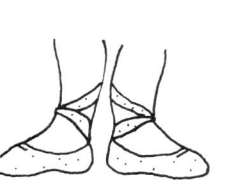

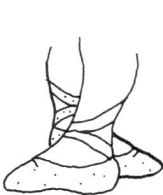
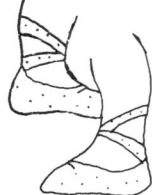

1	2	3	4	5
(I)	(S)	(G)	(L)	(E)

___   ___   ___   ___   ___   ___   ___
9-6   1+0   5-3   4+1   8-4   3+1   11-6

CHINESE NEW YEAR

Parade of the Dragon

The Chinese New Year is celebrated with a special parade. The most important marcher is a dragon—a symbol of strength and goodness. Its huge, red head is made of wood or papier-mâché, with silver horns and a green beard. It is carried by as many as 50 people, who walk and dance under its cloth and bamboo body.

Help carry the dragon by solving the puzzles below.

The HEAD of the dragon is also decorated in GOLD paint. Can you change the word HEAD into the word GOLD by changing one letter at a time, making a new word at each step?

H E A D

___ ___ ___ ___

___ ___ ___ ___

G O L D

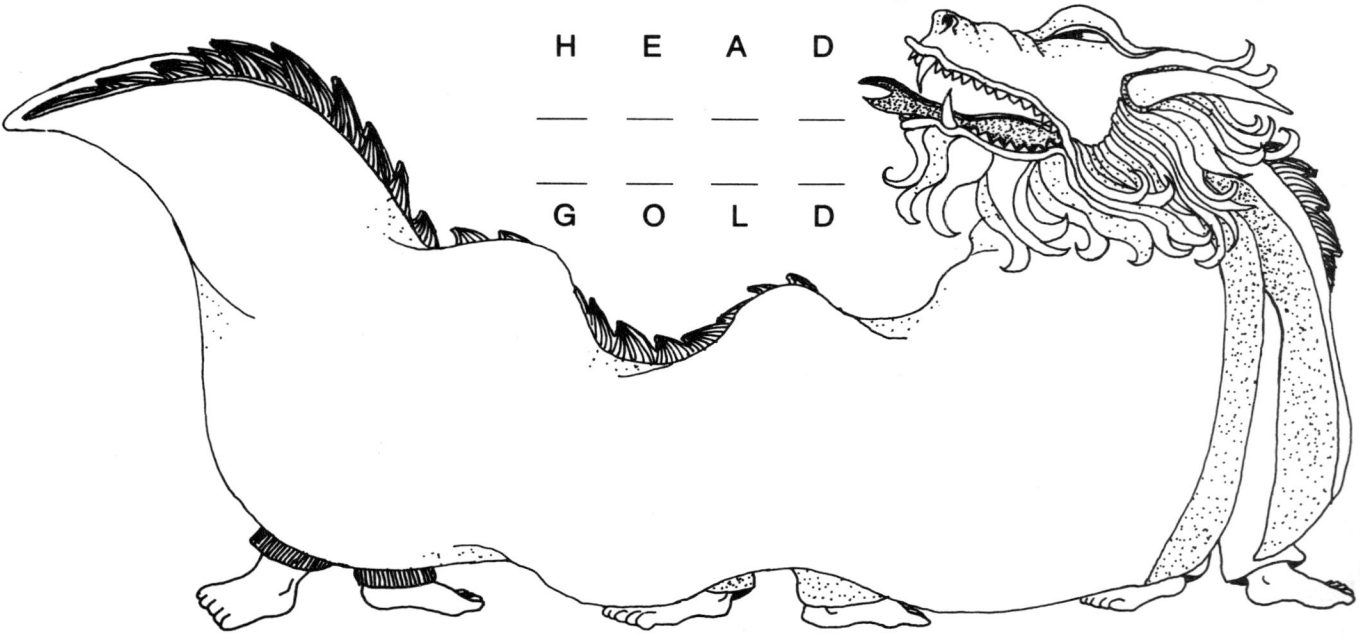

Join the parade and see how many smaller words of three letters or more you can find in the word below. (There are at least 12.)

P A R A D E

1. _____   4. _____   7. _____   10. _____

2. _____   5. _____   8. _____   11. _____

3. _____   6. _____   9. _____   12. _____

Firecrackers are lit during the parade to scare away evil spirits and to bring good luck in the New Year. Complete the word pyramid below by subtracting one letter at a time so that each step is a new word.

B A N G

___ ___ ___

___ ___

___

CHINESE NEW YEAR

A Day Circled in Red

In China, people hang red paper decorations for the New Year and burn red candles. Red is considered to be a very lucky color.

Get some good luck for yourself by completing the magic word square below. (Hint: the answers will be the same across and down.)

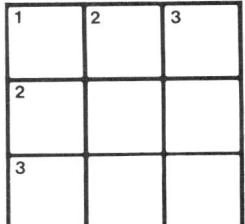

1. A lucky color.
2. One of the things you hear with.
3. Opposite of wet.

Here's another puzzle to try. If you complete it, you'll have helped to make the special candy, made of a nut mixture rolled in rice flour, that is a popular New Year's treat.

1. A walnut is one.
2. To put into service.
3. A hot drink.

A Very Happy Day

In addition to wishing one another Happy New Year on this day, what else do many people in China and Japan say to each other?

Add and subtract the letters as shown from the names of the pictures to learn the answer.

[picture] + [picture] − [picture] +B+ [picture] − [picture] +Y

[picture] −D+B+ [picture] − [picture] +B+ [picture] +K− [picture] +A +Y

(In the Orient, it is the custom to consider January 1st as everyone's birthday!)

Name: _____

BLACK HISTORY MONTH

Two Special Teachers

Mary McLeod Bethune, born in 1875, was an educator who worked to improve educational opportunities for blacks. She was the first black woman to head a U.S. federal agency.

Try to fit each of the underlined words from the paragraph above into the puzzle grid. (One has already been done for you.)

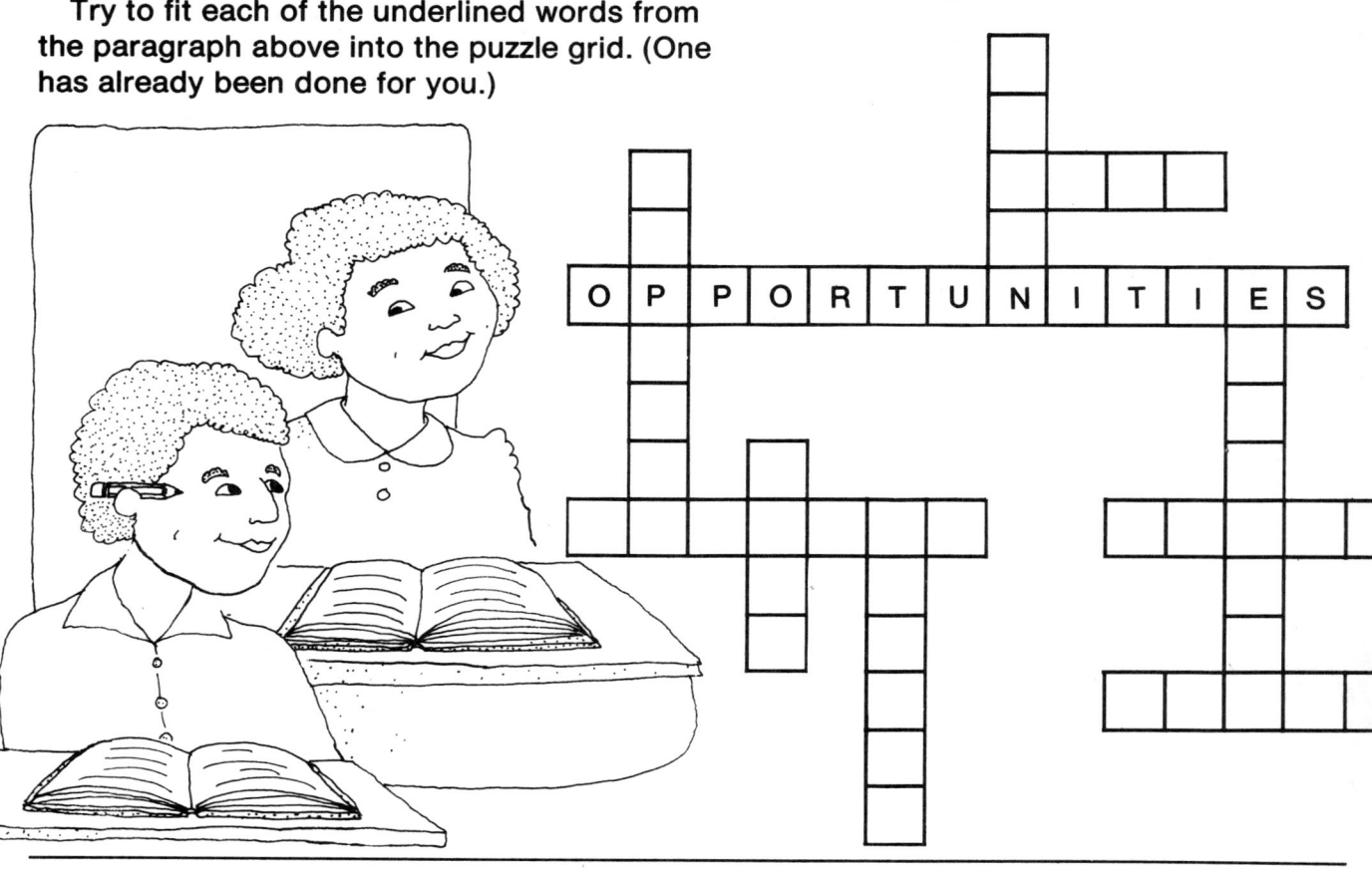

Booker T. Washington was born a slave in 1856. He grew up to become an important leader and teacher of black people. He founded Tuskegee Institute, a school that has produced many teachers, nurses, engineers, and scientists.

Can you find each of the underlined words from the paragraph above in the puzzle below? The words may be up, down, across, diagonal, or backwards. Circle each word as you find it.

```
B  O  Q  K  F  R  L  E  B  D  F  G  B
S  G  R  S  C  I  E  N  T  I  S  T  S
L  B  O  O  K  E  R  R  I  V  J  F  X
V  K  R  W  A  S  H  I  N  G  T  O  N
B  M  D  T  M  L  N  P  S  B  U  U  T
Q  L  R  E  D  A  E  L  T  C  S  N  S
K  V  A  A  X  V  B  K  I  W  K  D  K
S  L  J  C  P  E  G  C  T  J  E  E  G
E  C  K  H  K  J  L  R  U  F  G  D  M
S  B  R  E  G  Q  R  E  T  D  E  X  R
R  D  X  R  M  B  C  J  E  K  E  V  P
U  F  Q  W  P  F  B  C  X  C  M  Q  D
N  G  E  N  G  I  N  E  E  R  S  B  L
```

BLACK HISTORY MONTH

Freedom Workers

Frederick Douglass was born around 1817. His own escape from slavery enabled him to work to stop slavery completely. He organized two regiments of blacks during the Civil War and was minister to Haiti.

Try to fit each of the underlined words from the paragraph above into the puzzle grid. (One has already been done for you.)

Harriet Tubman, born around 1820, also escaped from slavery and went on to lead over 300 more slaves to freedom. During the Civil War, she served as a nurse, did laundry for the soldiers, and was a spy for the North.

Can you find each of the underlined words from the paragraph above in the puzzle below? The words may be up, down, across, diagonal, or backwards. Circle each word as you find it.

```
L   E   A   B   N   S   L   A   W   F   R   V   B
H   E   K   J   O   G   H   D   K   M   L   R   V
A   H   A   R   R   I   E   T   T   J   B   D   C
R   J   G   D   T   L   A   U   N   D   R   Y   I
R   P   W   K   H   F   R   B   E   D   Q   N   W
J   M   X   G   Q   C   D   M   B   G   H   M   I
F   B   K   M   E   S   C   A   P   E   D   K   L
R   C   J   P   W   L   P   N   U   R   S   E   X
E   D   L   V   Z   A   F   Y   W   A   D   G   Y
F   R   P   C   I   V   I   L   K   A   W   B   J
P   G   R   F   R   E   E   D   O   M   R   K   M
Q   H   Z   X   Y   R   J   K   Q   Y   G   N   L
M   V   J   K   Q   Y   V   C   F   H   P   R   S
```

February 2 Name: ____________________

GROUNDHOG DAY

Furry Forecaster

Did "Punxutawney (punk-suh-taw-nee) Phil," the famous Pennsylvania groundhog, see his shadow today? If he did, legend tells us that we're in for six more weeks of winter!

Here's a riddle that old Phil would enjoy. Can you solve it? Add and subtract the letters from the names of the pictures as shown.

W+ 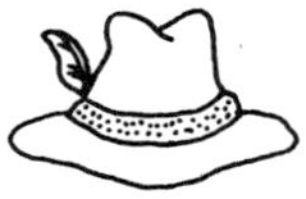 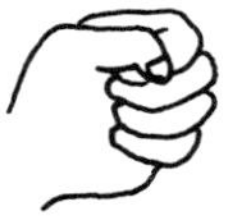 −F−T 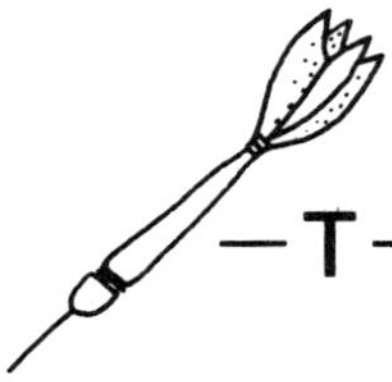 −T+K 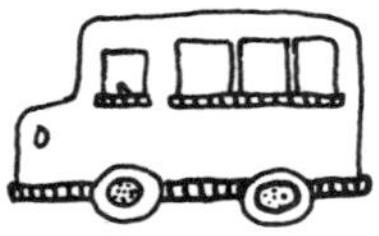 −S+T

__________ __________ __________ __________

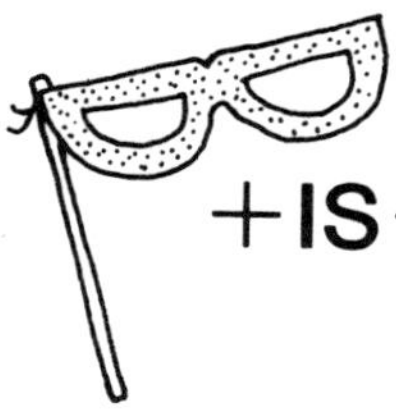 +IS− 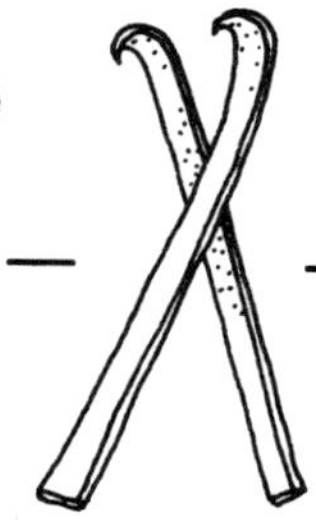 + 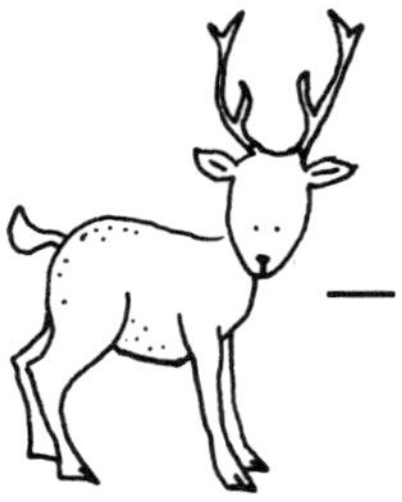 −ER C+ 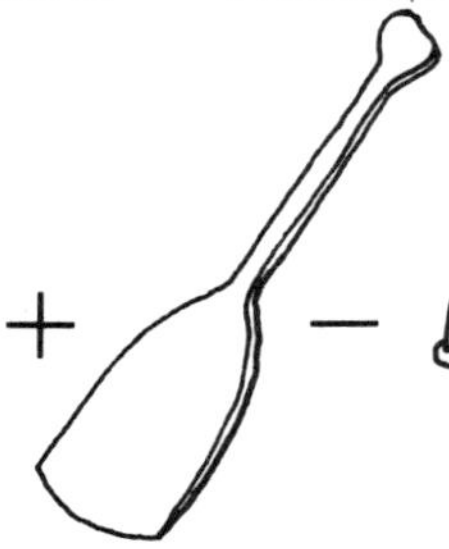 − 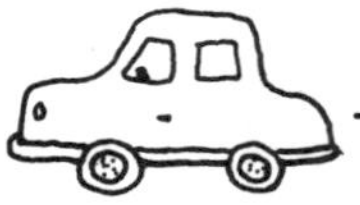 +F

______________________________ ____________________

L+ 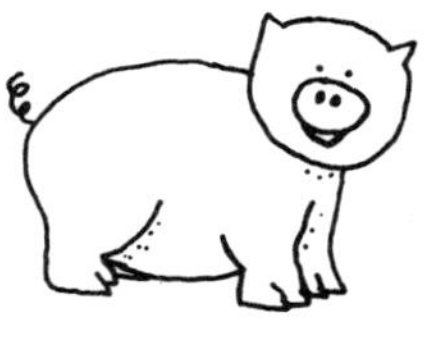 + 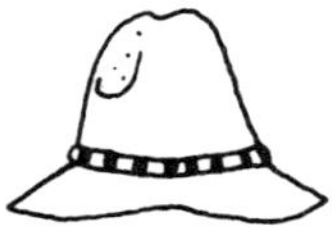 +N− 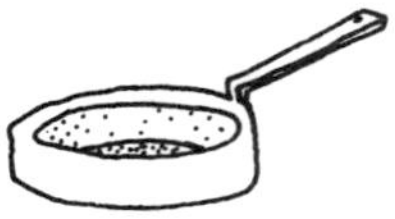

____?

A T+ 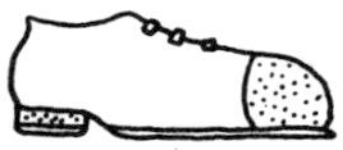 − 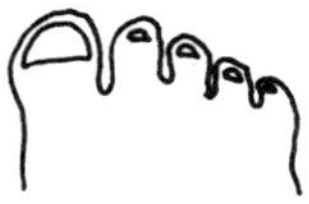 +A+ 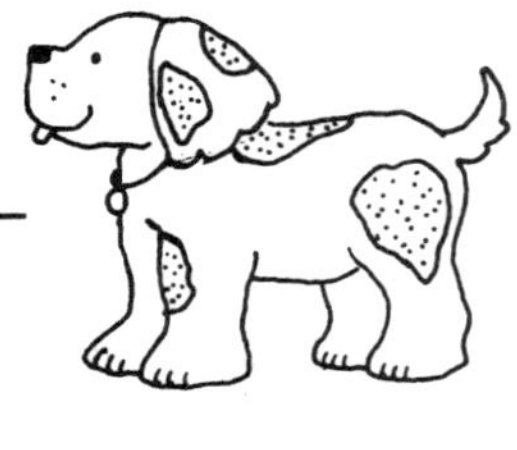 −G+W

_____ ____.

CANDLEMAS

Name: _____

Festive Fire

Candles are blessed in many churches on this day. In Luxembourg, boys and girls carry their lighted candles to the doors of elderly people and shut-ins and sing a special song about light.

Can you get the FIRE ready to light the holiday candles by completing the magic word square below? (The answers will be the same down and across.)

¹F	²I	³R	⁴E
²I			
³R			
⁴E			

2. A thought.
3. The back part.
4. What you hear with.

Holiday Candles

Now, light your candle for Candlemas by completing the puzzle below. Follow the directions and form a new word for each step.

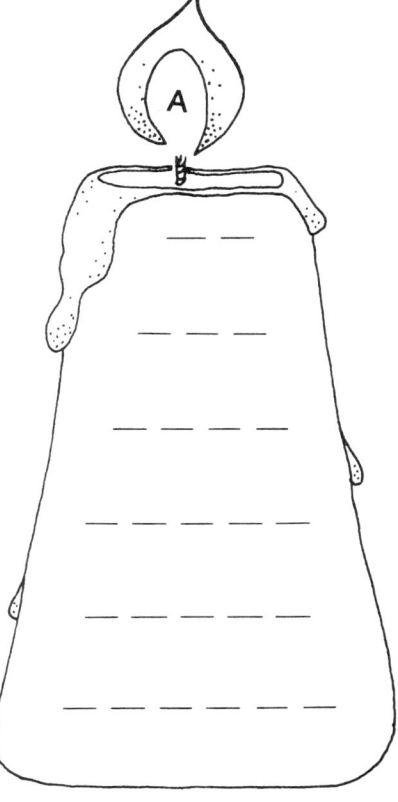

A

___ ___

___ ___ ___

___ ___ ___ ___

___ ___ ___ ___ ___

___ ___ ___ ___ ___ ___

___ ___ ___ ___ ___ ___

Add a letter; _____ apple.

Add a letter; pencil _____ paper.

Add a letter; part of your arm below the wrist.

Add a letter; to be skillful.

Substitute a letter; a sweet treat.

Subtract a letter and then add two new letters; something you'll light on this holiday.

ELIZABETH BLACKWELL'S BIRTHDAY

First Woman Doctor

Elizabeth Blackwell was born on this day in 1821. She was the <u>first</u> <u>American</u> <u>woman</u> to receive a <u>medical</u> <u>degree</u>. Doctor Blackwell founded a <u>hospital</u> and a <u>school</u> for training more women to be doctors.

   Can you fit each of the underlined words in the paragraph above into the puzzle grid? (Two have already been done for you.)

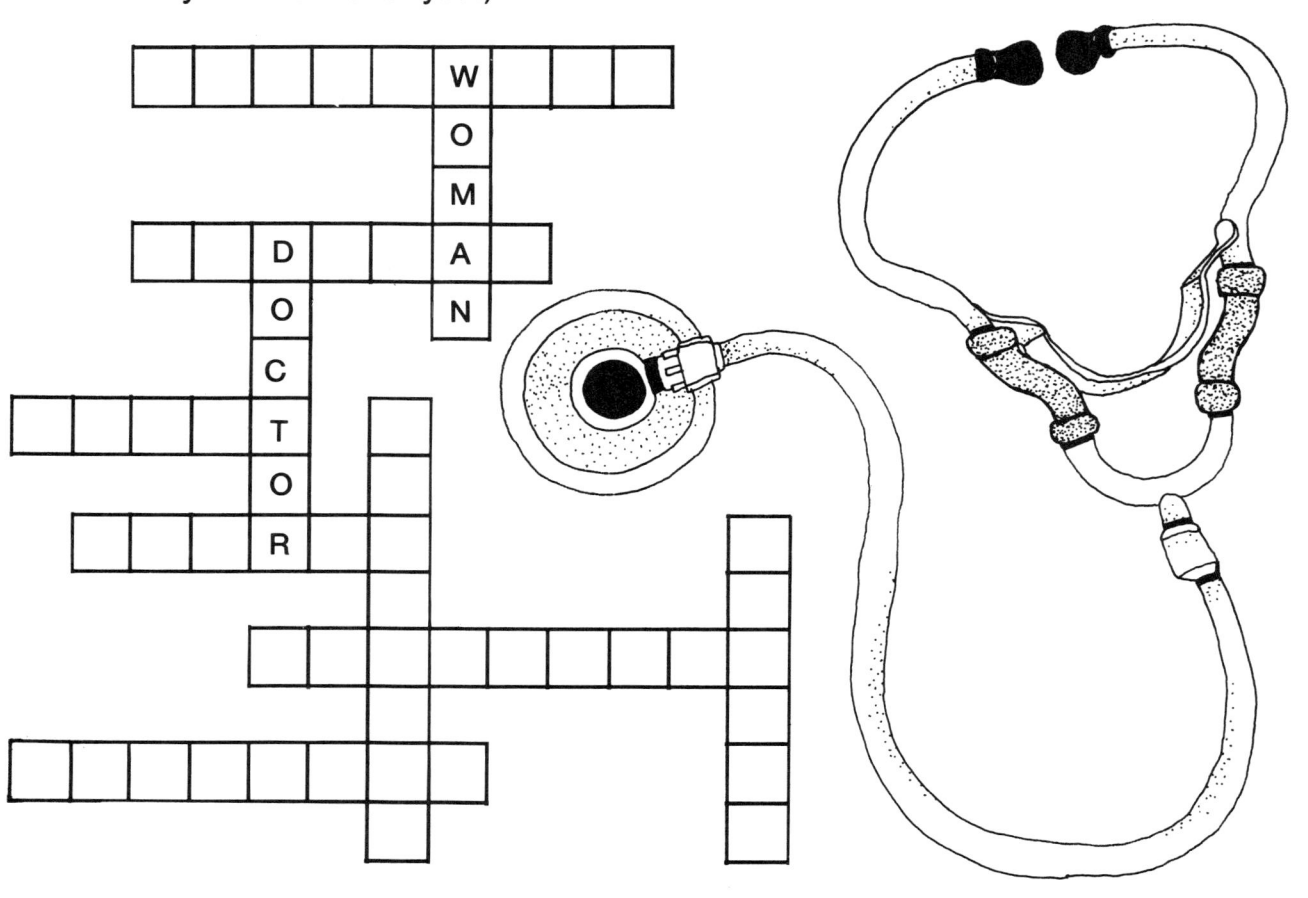

First Degree

How many smaller words of three letters or more can you find hidden in the word DOCTOR? (There are at least ten.)

D O C T O R

1. _____   4. _____   8. _____

2. _____   5. _____   9. _____

3. _____   6. _____   10. _____

                          7. _____

BABE RUTH'S BIRTHDAY

The Bambino

George Herman Ruth, known as Babe or "The Bambino," was born on this day in 1895. One of the greatest baseball players of all time, he was a world series-winning pitcher and an all-time great home run hitter.

Hit some home runs yourself by completing the three magic word squares below. (Hint: the answers in each puzzle will be the same across and down.)

1. Round object used in a game.

2. A space (length x width = ___).

3. When it rains, the roof has a ___.

4. Large body of water. (Rhymes with bake.)

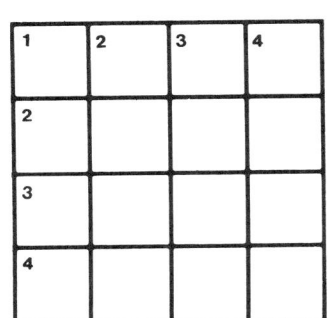

1. The bottom part of a thing, on which it rests.

2. A space (length x width = ___).

3. A chair. (Rhymes with feet.)

4. Takes food into mouth.

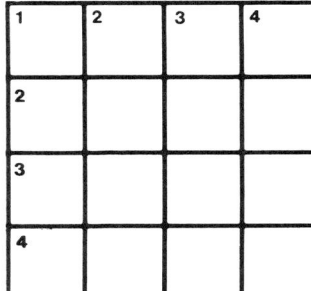

1. Wooden stick used in a game.

2. A long, long time ___.

3. Opposite of bottom.

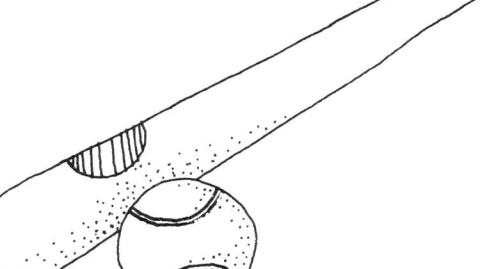

From House to Hall

Babe Ruth helped to make the game of baseball very popular. He was the second player to be elected to the Baseball Hall of Fame. (Ty Cobb was the first.) His popularity gave the original Yankee Stadium in New York City a special name. To find out what it was, unscramble the letters in the words below.

H E T   S O E H U   H T A T

___ ___ ___   ___ ___ ___ ___ ___   ___ ___ ___ ___

T H U R   L I B U T.

___ ___ ___ ___   ___ ___ ___ ___

Name: _____

BOY SCOUTS FOUNDED

Scout Motto

The Boy Scouts of America were founded on this day in 1910 by William Boyce. Do you know the motto of both the Boy Scouts and Girl Scouts? The first letter of the name of each picture is a letter in the motto.

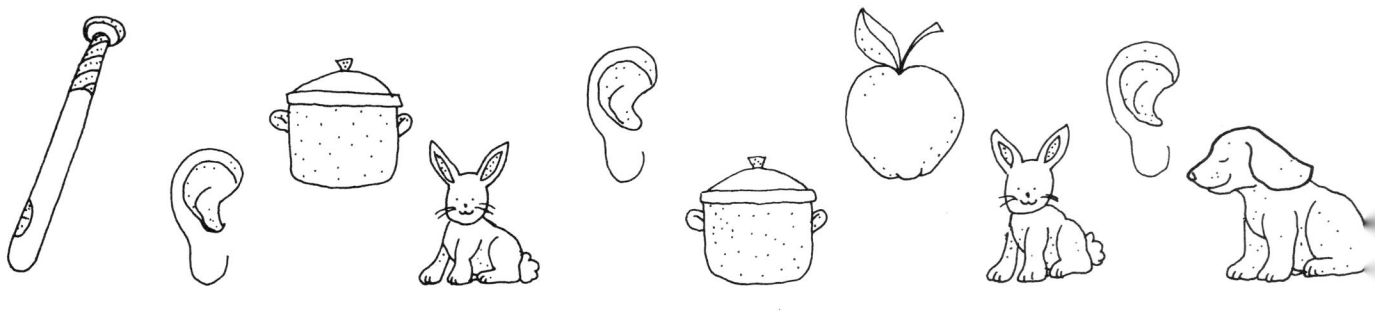

___ ___ ___ ___ ___ ___ ___ ___ ___ ___

The Boy Scout Law

A scout is trustworthy, loyal, helpful, friendly, courteous, kind, obedient, cheerful, thrifty, brave, clean, and reverent.

Can you find each of the words underlined in the Boy Scout Law in the puzzle below? They may be up, down, across, diagonal, or backwards. Circle each word as you find it.

```
T R R E V E R E N T K J
C L E A N F R I F N P R
F M V J K G M S Q L B D
R D A H N S F L K Q C R
I T R U S T W O R T H Y
E H B G J S P Y Q X E T
N F F G D R L A Y C E F
D K B L U F P L E H R I
L B I V R S B K J C F R
Y C X N D Z U G B H U H
P O B E D I E N T X L T
R Z C O U R T E O U S Z
```

Did you know that there are Boy Scouts in more than 100 different countries?

Name: _____

THOMAS EDISON'S BIRTHDAY

Turn On the Light

Thomas Edison was born on this day in 1847. One of the greatest inventors of his time, Edison created the first practical electric light, the phonograph, and the first central electric power plant in the world. His laboratories in New Jersey are now museums.

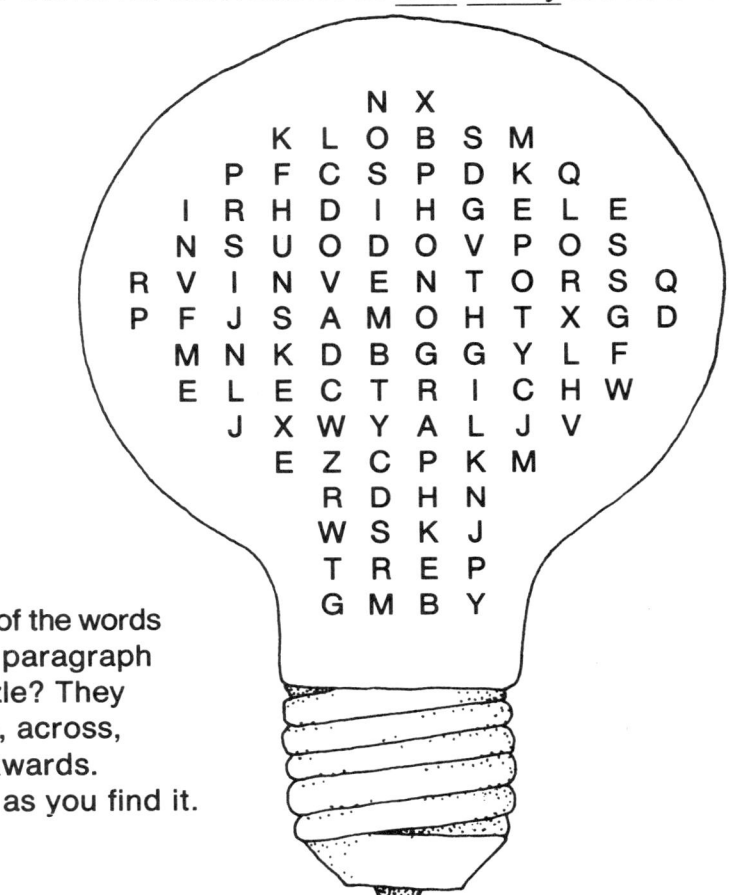

Can you find each of the words underlined in the paragraph above in the puzzle? They may be up, down, across, diagonal, or backwards. Circle each word as you find it.

A Busy Genius

Thomas Edison held more than 1,000 patents for his inventions. He was a very busy inventor. Can you find at least 25 smaller words of two letters or more in the word below?

INVENTOR

1 _____	6 _____	11 _____	16 _____	21 _____
2 _____	7 _____	12 _____	17 _____	22 _____
3 _____	8 _____	13 _____	18 _____	23 _____
4 _____	9 _____	14 _____	19 _____	24 _____
5 _____	10 _____	15 _____	20 _____	25 _____

Name: _____

ABRAHAM LINCOLN'S BIRTHDAY

Happy Birthday, Mr. Lincoln

Read this list of important events in the life of our 16th president. Then try to fit the under-lined words into the puzzle grid below. (One is already done for you.)

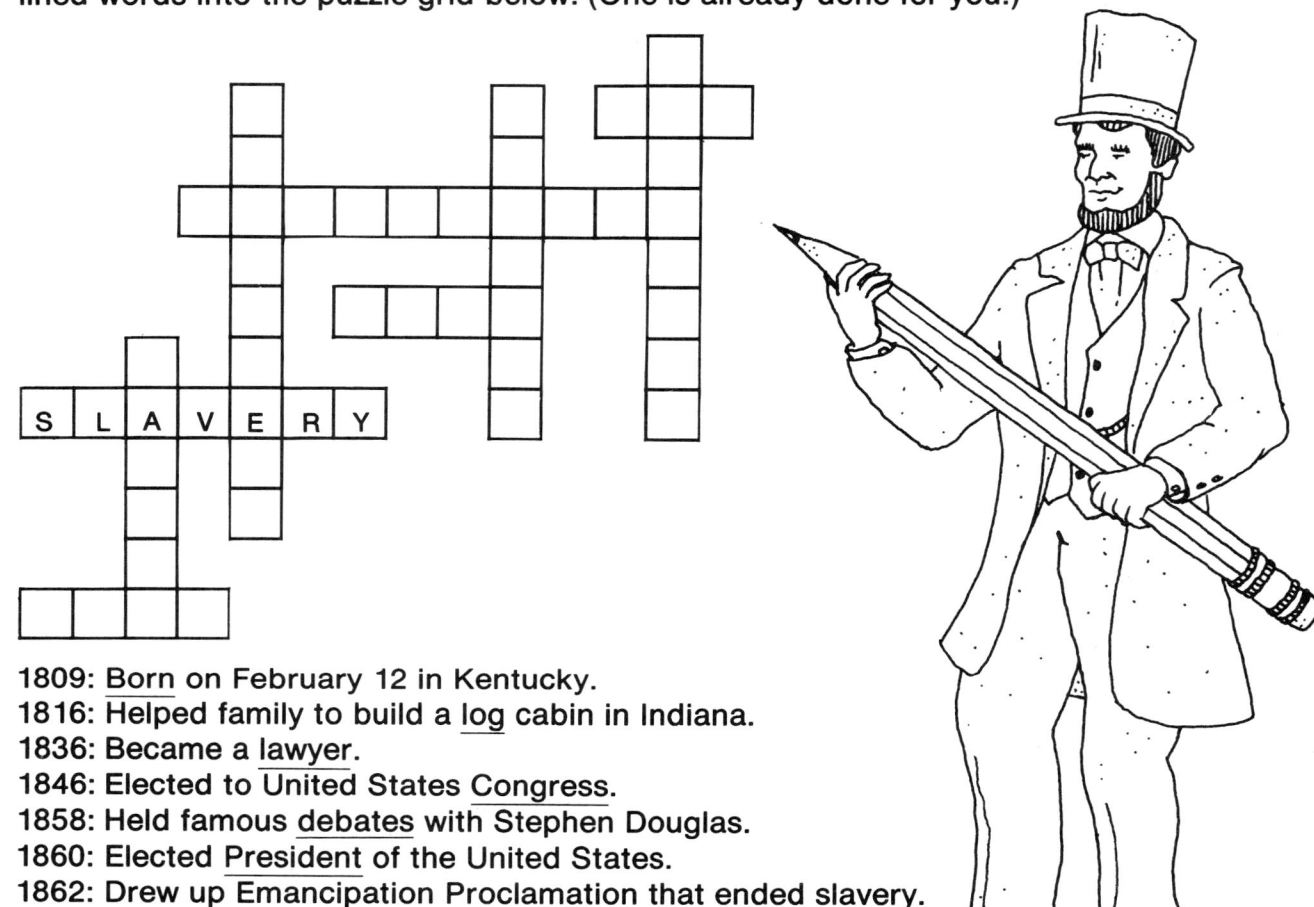

1809: Born on February 12 in Kentucky.
1816: Helped family to build a log cabin in Indiana.
1836: Became a lawyer.
1846: Elected to United States Congress.
1858: Held famous debates with Stephen Douglas.
1860: Elected President of the United States.
1862: Drew up Emancipation Proclamation that ended slavery.
1863: Delivered the Gettysburg Address.
1865: Shot by John Wilkes Booth in Ford's Theatre.

Lincoln Logs

Help young Abe build his log cabin. Follow the clues and fill in each square with five different words that have a "log" in them.

☐ LOG   To stop up.
LOG ☐ ☐   Clear thinking.
☐ ☐ ☐ LOG ☐   Study of living things.
LOG ☐ ☐ ☐   A tangle of logs in a river.
☐ LOG   To beat with a stick.

ABRAHAM LINCOLN'S BIRTHDAY

A Presidential Fact

Solve the cryptogram below and you will get President Lincoln's number!

Each number under the blanks below stands for a letter. The numbers that stand for the letters in President Lincoln's name are given to you. Fill in the letters you know, then try to figure out what the others might be.

```
P  R  E  S  I  D  E  N  T     L  I  N  C  O  L  N
6  3  2  4  5  1  2  8  9     7  5  8 10 12  7  8
```

```
__ __ __     __ __ __     __ __ __ __ __ __ __ __ __
11 13  4      9 14  2      4  5 15  9  2  2  8  9 14
```

```
__ __ __ __ __ __ __ __ __     __ __     __ __ __
 6  3  2  4  5  1  2  8  9     12 16      9 14  2
```

```
__ __ __ __ __ __     __ __ __ __ __ __
17  8  5  9  2  1      4  9 13  9  2  4
```

Lincoln Monuments

There are many buildings, roads, and places in the United States that have been named in honor of Abraham Lincoln. Can you unscramble the words below in order to learn the names of many of those places?

LINCOLN   N   E   T   R   E   C   A place to see the opera, ballet,
__ __ __ __ __ __   etc. in New York City.

LINCOLN   G   I   H   W   A   Y   H   A road that stretches across
__ __ __ __ __ __ __   the United States.

LINCOLN   N   U   T   L   E   N   A path under the Hudson River
__ __ __ __ __ __   connecting New Jersey to New
       York City.

LINCOLN   N   U   V   I   R   I   E   S   T   Y   A school in Tennessee founded
__ __ __ __ __ __ __ __ __ __   in 1863.

LINCOLN   M   O   L   E   M   I   R   A   A monument in Washington, D.C.
__ __ __ __ __ __ __ __

February 12 Name: ______________________

JUDY BLUME'S BIRTHDAY

Happy Birthday, Judy!

Judy Blume, a very popular author of children's books, was born on this day in 1938. To learn the titles of some of her books, solve the puzzles below. The first letter of the name of each picture is a letter in the title of a book. (The first one is already done for you.)

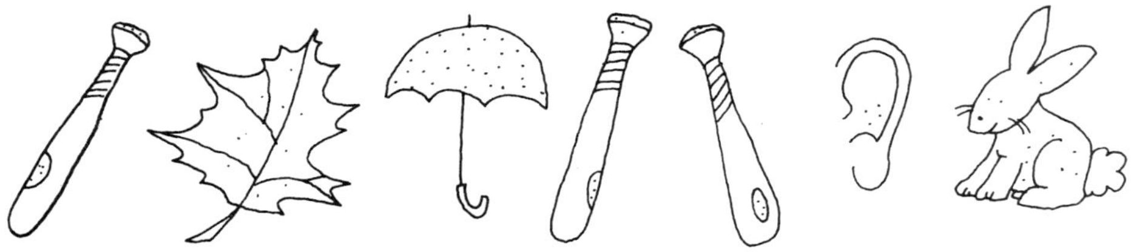

B L U B B E R

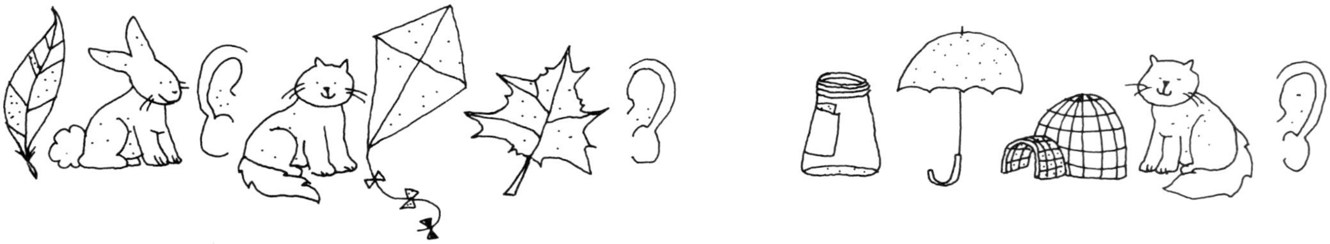

___ ___ ___ ___ ___ ___ ___   ___ ___ ___ ___ ___

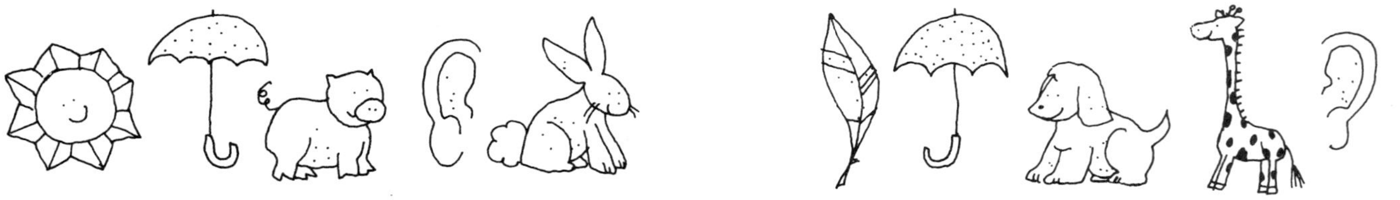

___ ___ ___ ___ ___   ___ ___ ___ ___ ___

___ ___ ___ ___ ___' ___   ___ ___ ___ ___ ___

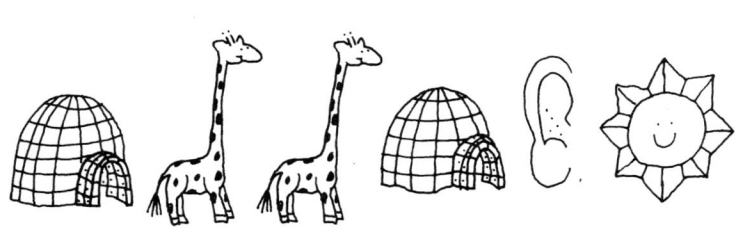

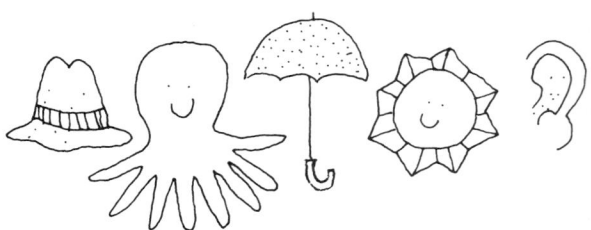

Name: _____

VALENTINE'S DAY

Cupid's Arrows

Cupid is a favorite subject of Valentine cards. Cupid comes from Greek mythology. The dimpled baby son of the goddess Venus, Cupid loved to eat ambrosia and nectar, the food and drink of the gods, but he never seemed to grow. Though he remained a baby, he could fly and he had a tiny bow and many little golden arrows that the god of fire, Vulcan, had made for him. His mother, Venus, the goddess of love, gave the arrows a special power. If Cupid shot you with his arrow, you fell in love with the first person you saw.

```
C  U  P  D  I  P  U  C  E  N
N  A  R  R  O  N  B  M  A  E
V  B  M  K  V  E  N  U  S  C
U  O  G  B  Q  D  N  X  P  T
L  E  D  O  R  L  E  R  N  B
C  L  U  V  L  O  V  E  E  P
A  Q  Z  H  I  G  S  F  C  L
N  F  J  R  V  W  J  I  T  O
P  C  L  S  W  O  R  R  A  V
Q  Z  E  Y  S  B  L  K  R  F
```

Can you find all of the underlined words in the puzzle opposite? They may be up, down, across, diagonal, or backwards. Circle each word as you find it.

Love at First Sight

Cupid shot a LAD with an arrow from his BOW,
and the boy FELL madly in love with the first GIRL he saw.

Help Cupid do the deed by completing the two magic word chains below. Make a new word by changing only one letter at a time, keeping the letter order the same. Each change should result in a new word, until you have solved the puzzle.

B   O   W   F   E   L   L

__ __ __   __ __ __ __

__ __ __   __ __ __ __

L   A   D   G   I   R   L

Name: _____

VALENTINE'S DAY

Love Letters

See how many words of three letters or more you can find hidden in the word below.

V A L E N T I N E

1. _____	11. _____	21. _____	31. _____
2. _____	12. _____	22. _____	32. _____
3. _____	13. _____	23. _____	33. _____
4. _____	14. _____	24. _____	34. _____
5. _____	15. _____	25. _____	35. _____
6. _____	16. _____	26. _____	36. _____
7. _____	17. _____	27. _____	37. _____
8. _____	18. _____	28. _____	38. _____
9. _____	19. _____	29. _____	39. _____
10. _____	20. _____	30. _____	40. _____

Love Birds

Many years ago, people used to believe that birds chose their mates on Valentine's Day. See if you can give Cupid a hand by solving the bird riddle below. (Add and subtract the letters as shown.)

What did one owl, who was playing hard to get, say to the other owl?

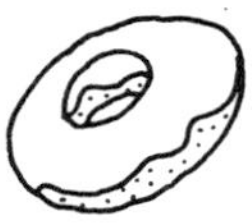

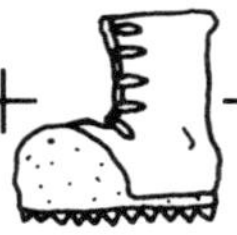

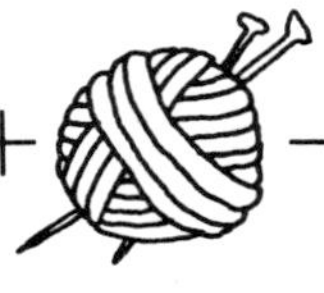

_____   _____   _____

_____   _____

Name: _____

VALENTINE'S DAY

Tussie Mussies

A special valentine greeting that first became popular in England in the 1600s was the *tussie mussie*. A nosegay of flowers and herbs chosen for their special meanings, it could send any message one chose.

Look at the pictures of flowers below and at what each stands for.

THYME—Courage   PANSY—Think of Me   SWEET MARJORAM—Joy

ROSEMARY—Remembrance   RUE—Understanding

ROSE—Love   IVY—Friendship   SAGE—Long Life   DAFFODIL—Regard

Example: (sage and marjoram means—) I wish you long life and joy.

● Can you solve this flower riddle?

_____

What flowers and/or herbs would you put in a tussie mussie in order to send the following messages?

● I offer you my love and regard. _____

● Have courage. I understand. _____

Name: _____

SUSAN B. ANTHONY'S BIRTHDAY

A Brave Woman

From the time she was 17 and a teacher in rural New York, Susan B. Anthony worked for equal rights for women. In 1872, she tried to vote and was arrested for doing so. She devoted her life to getting women the right to vote, but died 14 years before that right was added to the U.S. Constitution in 1920.

    Can you find each of the underlined words in the puzzle below? They may be up, down, across, diagonal, or backwards. Circle each word as you find it.

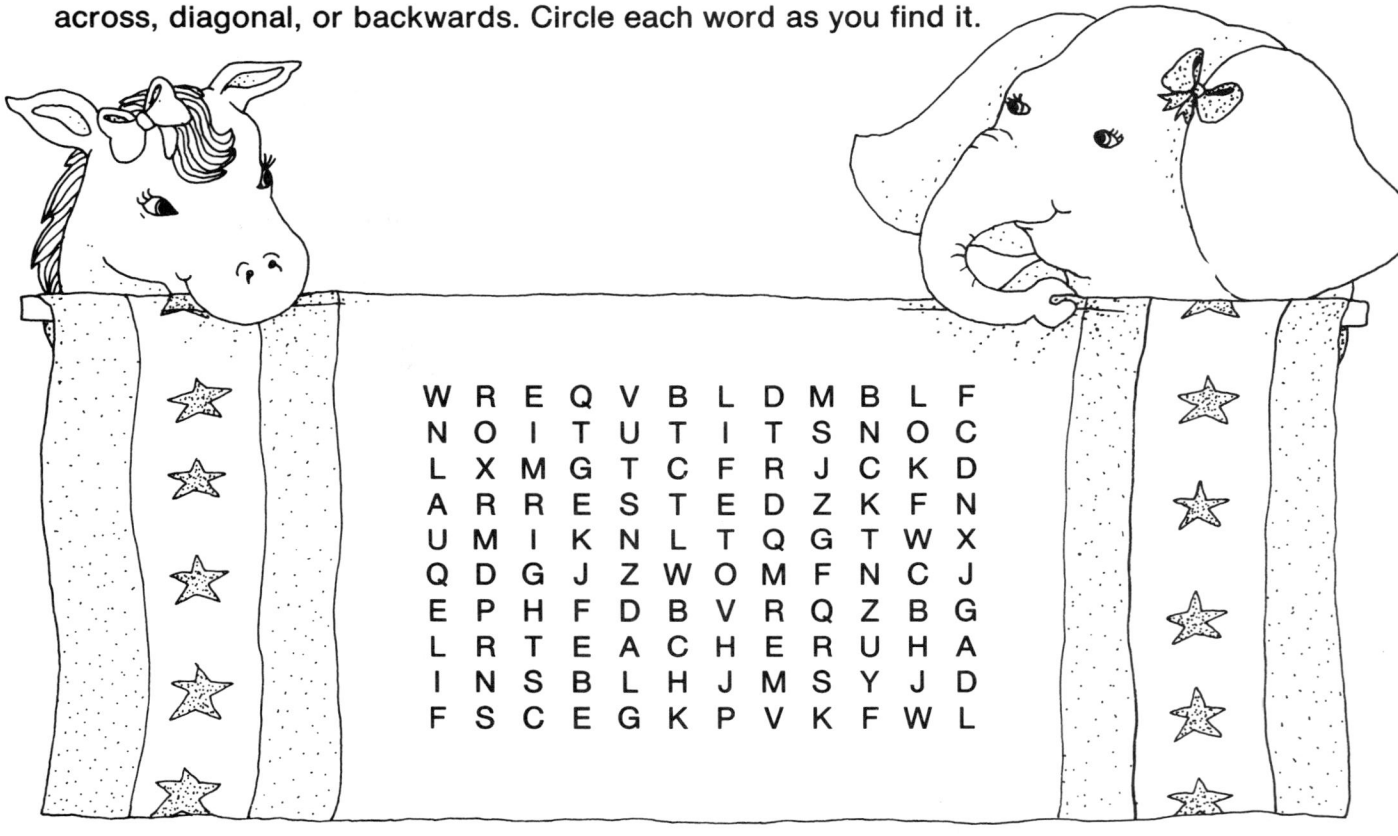

```
W R E Q V B L D M B L F
N O I T U T I T S N O C
L X M G T C F R J C K D
A R R E S T E D Z K F N
U M I K N L T Q G T W X
Q D G J Z W O M F N C J
E P H F D B V R Q Z B G
L R T E A C H E R U H A
I N S B L H J M S Y J D
F S C E G K P V K F W L
```

An Important Right

Can you complete the magic word square below? The answers will be the same across and down.

1	2	3	4
2			
3			
4			

1. To cast a ballot in an election.
2. Opposite of closed.
3. To care for.
4. Last parts of anything.

CANADA'S MAPLE LEAF FLAG

A New Flag

In order to improve relations between the French Canadians and the English Canadians, Parliament adopted a new flag on this day in 1965. A FLAG with Canada's national symbol—the maple leaf—was considered to be the BEST choice.

Can you change the word FLAG into BEST? Change one letter at a time keeping the letter order the same. Each change should result in a new word, until you have changed all four letters and solved the puzzle.

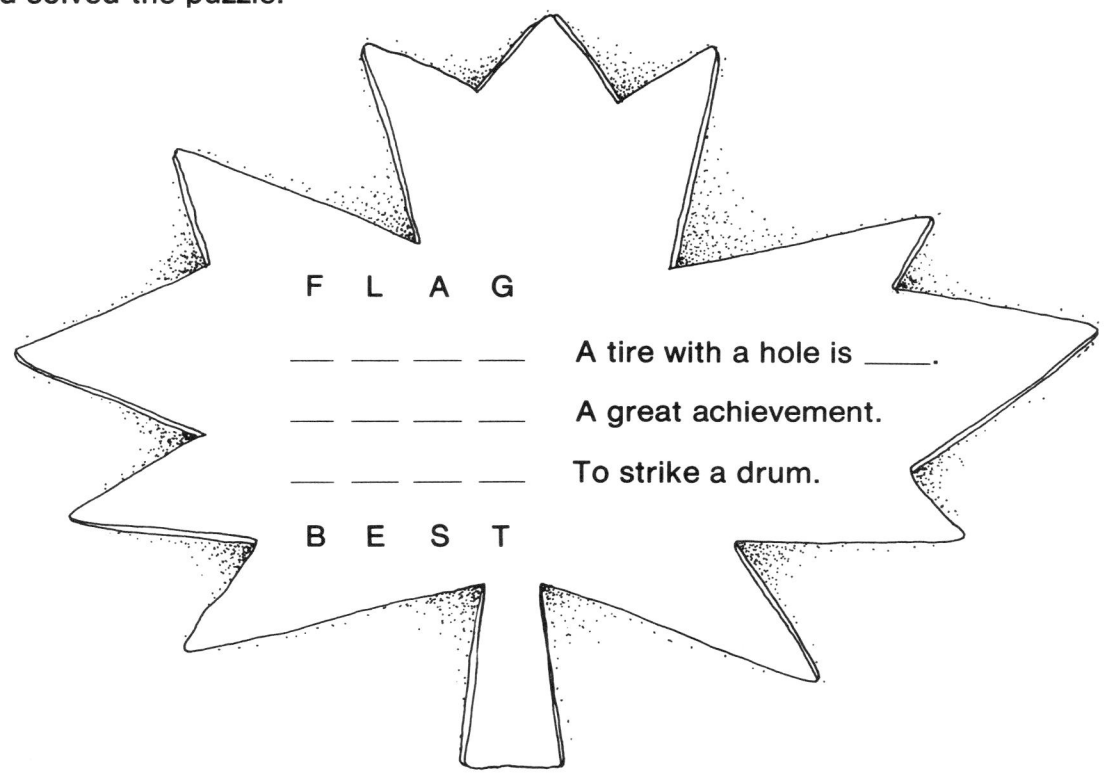

F L A G

__ __ __ __   A tire with a hole is ____.

__ __ __ __   A great achievement.

__ __ __ __   To strike a drum.

B E S T

A Penny for Your Thoughts

The maple LEAF also appears on the back of a Canadian COIN.

Can you change the word LEAF into COIN? Change one letter at a time keeping the letter order the same. Each change should result in a new word, until you have changed all four letters and solved the puzzle.

L E A F

__ __ __ __   To rest against something.

__ __ __ __   To lend.

__ __ __ __   A cut of meat.

C O I N

HERITAGE DAY

Name: _____

Spell the Spirit

Today, Canadians celebrate their own special heritage. They remember the strong pioneer spirit that helped to build their country.

   Celebrate that spirit, too, by completing the puzzle below. See how many smaller words of two letters or more you can find in the word below. (There are at least 40.)

H E R I T A G E

1_____	11_____	21_____	31_____
2_____	12_____	22_____	32_____
3_____	13_____	23_____	33_____
4_____	14_____	24_____	34_____
5_____	15_____	25_____	35_____
6_____	16_____	26_____	36_____
7_____	17_____	27_____	37_____
8_____	18_____	28_____	38_____
9_____	19_____	29_____	39_____
10_____	20_____	30_____	40_____

Quilting Be-Bee

The pioneers could not waste anything and so they often made quilts from small scraps of fabric. Finish stitching the quilt below by filling in the blanks with a homonym for each word. (Remember: A homonym is a word that sounds the same, but is spelled differently and has a different meaning.) One has already been done for you.

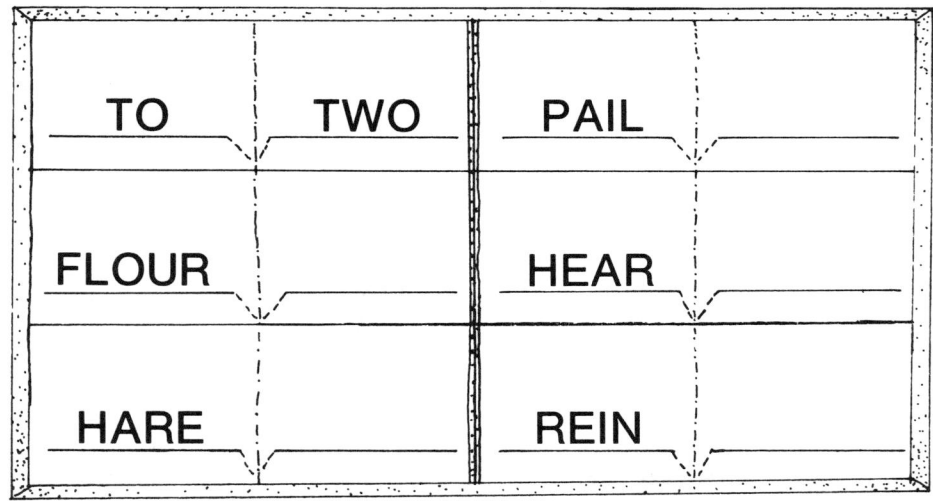

TO   TWO   PAIL _____

FLOUR _____   HEAR _____

HARE _____   REIN _____

Name: _____

GEORGE WASHINGTON'S BIRTHDAY

Early Years

George Washington was born in the state of Virginia on this day in 1732. At an early age, he proved to be very good in mathematics. By 15, he was a land surveyor. He was a soldier and later a farmer. He married his wife, Martha, in 1759.

Can you fit the words underlined in the paragraph above into the puzzle grid? One has already been done for you.

A Fitting Label

Can you solve the cryptogram and learn the special title given to George Washington?

Each number under the blanks below stands for a letter. The numbers that stand for the letters in Washington's name are given to you. Fill in the letters you know, then try to figure out what the others might be.

```
G    E   O   R   G    E        W    A   S   H   I   N   G    T   O   N
14   1   3   6   14   1        15   2   8   9   4   5   14   7   3   5
```

```
__   __   __   __   __   __      __   __      __   __   __      __   __   __   __   __   __   __
10   2    7    9    1    6       3    10      9    4    8       11   3    13   5    7    6    12
```

GEORGE WASHINGTON'S BIRTHDAY

In Command

In 1775, Washington was placed in command of the army. At the end of the American Revolution, in 1789, he was chosen as the first president. In 1797, he retired to his home in Mount Vernon.

　　Can you find each of the words underlined in the paragraph above in the puzzle? They may be up, down, across, diagonal, or backwards. Circle each word as you find it.

```
W  N  D  N  A  M  M  O  C  R
T  A  R  M  Y  X  O  D  K  E
N  K  S  J  R  Q  U  N  J  V
E  B  C  H  Z  L  N  M  B  O
D  F  D  F  I  P  T  V  C  L
I  Z  I  N  O  N  R  E  V  U
S  P  G  R  B  F  G  N  K  T
E  R  W  K  S  D  P  T  B  I
R  M  L  X  P  T  Q  S  O  O
P  D  A  M  E  R  I  C  A  N
```

First in Line

Help President Washington in his FIRST term as the FIRST president of the United States by completing the puzzle. Follow the directions so that each step becomes a new word.

F I R S T

___ ___ ___ ___   Drop a letter.

___ ___ ___   Drop a letter.

___ ___   Drop a letter and reverse those left.

___   Drop a letter.

LEAP YEAR

Name: _____

Look Before You Leap

Julius Caesar discovered that there were actually 365¼ days in the solar year. So that the calendar would not end up being wrong every four years he added an extra day to take care of the problem. February 29 is the extra day and it is observed only every fourth year, which is called Leap Year.

Can you take the leap and complete the magic word square with four words? The answers will be the same across and down.

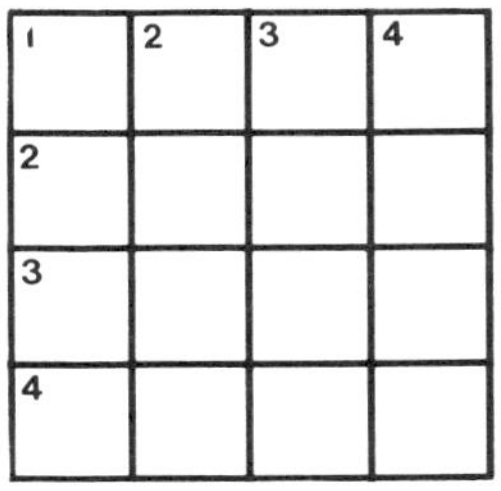

1. To jump.
2. A British nobleman; rhymes with pearl.
3. A space; length $\times$ width = ___.
4. To amuse oneself.

Monthly Reminder

Read the verse below that helps us to remember how many days there are in each month. Then try to fit the underlined words into the puzzle grid below. One is already done for you.

| F | E | B | R | U | A | R | Y |

Thirty days hath September,
April, June, and November,
All the rest have thirty-one,
Excepting February alone,
Which hath but twenty-eight in fine,
Till leap year gives it twenty-nine.

LENT

Name: _____

A Lenten Special

Lent is a period of 40 days (not counting Sundays) that comes before Easter. There is an old tale told about a monk who lived in England over 600 years ago. During Lent, he would bake a special treat to give to the poor. A sweet roll made with raisins and white icing, this treat is popular today. Translate the little poem below to discover its name. (Hint: It is written as a 3-shift cipher. A=D, B=E, C=F, and so on.)

E L Q   Z O L P P   Y R K P,

___ ___ ___   ___ ___ ___ ___ ___   ___ ___ ___ ___

E L Q   Z O L P P   Y R K P.

___ ___ ___   ___ ___ ___ ___ ___   ___ ___ ___ ___

L K B   X   M B K K V,

___ ___ ___   ___   ___ ___ ___ ___ ___

Q T L   X   M B K K V,

___ ___ ___   ___   ___ ___ ___ ___ ___

E L Q   Z O L P P   Y R K P.

___ ___ ___   ___ ___ ___ ___ ___   ___ ___ ___ ___

F C   V L R   E X S B   K L

___ ___   ___ ___ ___   ___ ___ ___ ___   ___ ___

A X R D E Q B O P

___ ___ ___ ___ ___ ___ ___ ___ ___

Q E B K   D F S B   Q E B J

___ ___ ___ ___   ___ ___ ___ ___   ___ ___ ___ ___

Q L   V L R O   P L K P.

___ ___   ___ ___ ___ ___   ___ ___ ___ ___

Flip the Flapjacks

Lent is a time of prayer and fasting for Christians. So, it is a tradition that on the Tuesday before Lent begins, all the butter and fat in the house must be used up. This day has come to be known as "Pancake Tuesday," because the left-over butter is used to make pancakes.

Several places in Europe and the United States have pancake races on this day. In them, a contestant must flip a pancake in a frying pan three times while running.

Enter the Pancake Race and flip your pancake three times by solving the three magic word squares below. (The answers in each puzzle will be the same across and down.)

1. You can fry food in it.

2. A long, long time _____.

3. Didn't is a contraction for did _____.

1. Opposite of lose.

2. Frozen water.

3. Used to catch butterflies.

1. You eat a piece of one for your birthday.

2. A space. (Length x width = _____.)

3. They open doors and start cars.

4. Comfort.

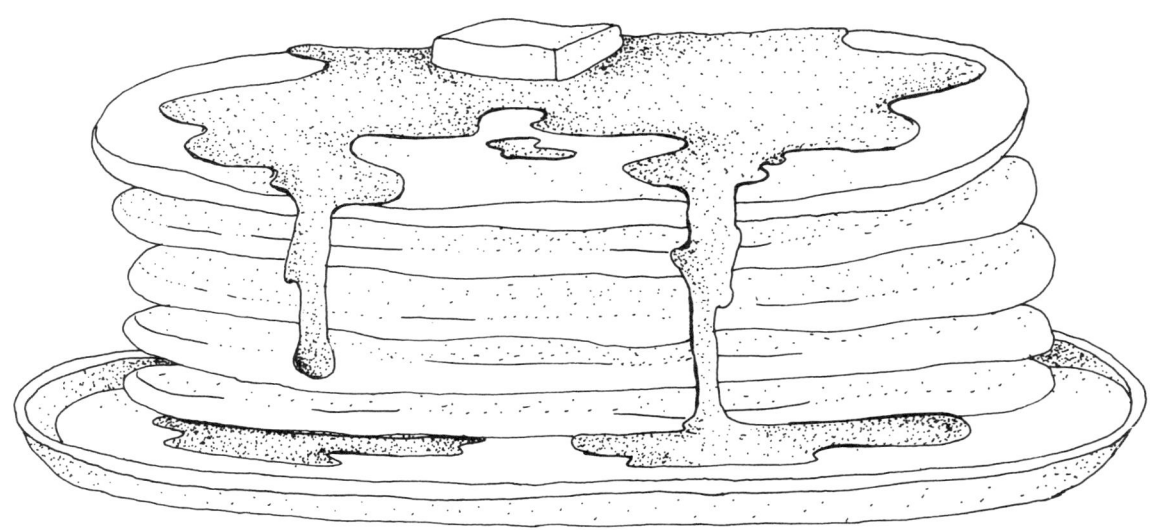

ALEXANDER GRAHAM BELL

Ring the Bell

Born in Scotland on this day in 1847, Alexander Graham Bell was a famous American scientist, inventor of the telephone, and teacher of the deaf.
    Can you fit the words underlined in the sentence above into the puzzle grid? One has already been done for you.

First Phone Message

Can you break the code below and discover what were the first words Bell said to his assistant on his telephone? (Hint: The code is known as a three-shift cipher. A=D; B=E; C=F, and so on.)

T X Q P L K,   Z L J B   E B O B.

___ ___ ___ ___ ___ ___,   ___ ___ ___ ___   ___ ___ ___ ___.

F   T X K Q   V L R.

___   ___ ___ ___ ___   ___ ___ ___.

HINA-MATSURI

Name: _____

That's Peachy!

Hina-Matsuri (pronounced: hee-nah-mah-tsu-ree) is the Japanese Peach Festival. Peach blossoms are used to decorate the family's doll collection. There are about fifteen dolls in a collection, and they include an emperor, an empress, and their attendants. The dolls are displayed only one day each year.

Help to arrange the dolls by solving the word pyramid below. Follow the directions so that each step becomes a new word.

D O L L S

___ ___ ___ ___   Drop a letter.

___ ___ ___ ___   Drop a letter and unscramble; not young.

___ ___ ___   Drop a letter and unscramble; opposite of don't.

___   Drop a letter; 15th letter of the alphabet.

The peach blossoms are everywhere on this day. How many smaller words of three letters or more can you find in the word below. (There are at least ten.)

P E A C H

1. _____   4. _____   8. _____

2. _____   5. _____   9. _____

3. _____   6. _____   10. _____

7. _____

The peach stands for a quality the Japanese admire and hope to achieve. Can you figure out what it is by translating the word below? (Hint: It is written as a 3-shift cipher. A=D, B=E, C=F, and so on.)

M   B   X   Z   B   C   R   I   K   B   P   P

___ ___ ___ ___ ___ ___ ___ ___ ___ ___ ___ ___

Name: _____

KNUTE ROCKNE'S BIRTHDAY

Football Hero

Knute Rockne, born in Norway on this day in 1888, was a famous American college football coach. In 13 years at the University of Notre Dame, his coaching record was 105 wins, 12 losses, and 5 tied games.

Here's your chance to add to the number of wins and carry the ball to victory! Change one letter at a time keeping the letter order the same. Each change should result in a new word, until you have changed all four letters and solved the puzzle.

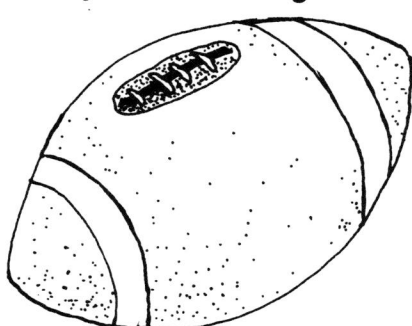

```
B   A   L   L

__  __  __  __

__  __  __  __

__  __  __  __

M   I   N   E
```

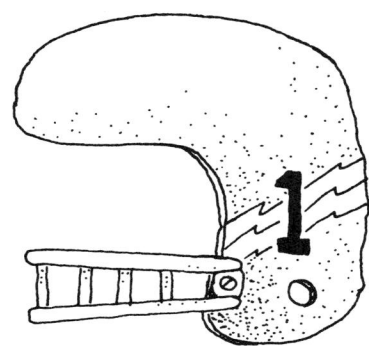

Score!

How many points can you score? See how many smaller words of three letters or more you can find in the word below. (There are at least 21.)

```
T   O   U   C   H   D   O   W   N
```

1. _____   8. _____   15. _____

2. _____   9. _____   16. _____

3. _____   10. _____   17. _____

4. _____   11. _____   18. _____

5. _____   12. _____   19. _____

6. _____   13. _____   20. _____

7. _____   14. _____   21. _____

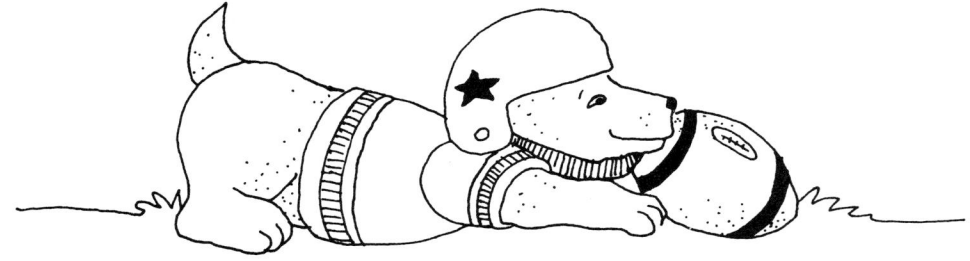

GIRL SCOUTS FOUNDED

Scout Slogan

On this day in 1912, Juliette Gordon Low held the first Girl Scout troop meeting in her home in Georgia. The Girl Guides in Canada, similar to the American Girl Scouts, had been started even earlier in 1910.

Can you solve the puzzle below and figure out the *slogan* of both the Girl Scouts and Boy Scouts of America? The first letter of the name of each picture is a letter in the slogan.

The Girl Scout Law

I will do my best to be honest, to be fair, to help where I am needed, to be cheerful, to be friendly and considerate, to be a sister to every Girl Scout, to respect authority, to use resources wisely, to protect and improve the world around me, and to show respect for myself and others through words and actions.

Can you find each of the words underlined in the Girl Scout Law in the puzzle below? They may be up, down, across, diagonal, or backwards. Circle each word as you find it.

```
I  L  K  G  F  R  I  E  N  D  L  Y
M  U  P  H  J  A  M  Y  S  E  L  F
P  F  S  B  C  U  I  M  P  B  S  R
R  R  Q  E  Z  T  X  R  L  M  X  P
O  E  J  T  K  H  S  M  N  B  C  R
V  E  B  S  W  O  R  L  D  V  R  O
E  H  C  E  D  R  E  S  P  E  C  T
H  C  O  N  S  I  D  E  R  A  T  E
M  E  G  O  F  T  P  V  K  G  Q  C
K  Q  L  H  R  Y  W  R  L  H  M  T
J  R  F  P  H  R  E  T  S  I  S  R
R  E  S  O  U  R  C  E  S  K  G  Q
```

NATIONAL WILDLIFE WEEK

Word Safari

Take a trip to Africa and be on the lookout for many different wild animals. How many animals can you find hidden in the scrambled words below? Unscramble the letters and write the name of each animal correctly in the spaces provided.

F A R I G E F   __ __ __ __ __ __ __

N I L O   __ __ __ __

P E L A N T H E   __ __ __ __ __ __ __ __

B A R E Z   __ __ __ __ __

H I R O N E R O C S   __ __ __ __ __ __ __ __ __ __

Forest Friends

The animals in the forest are shy. They hide when people come by. But if you look very carefully you may be able to spot some.

Find a different wild animal or bird of the forest in each sentence. Underline the word when you find it. (The first one is done for you.)

Mother made Ervin fix the broken window.

Beth, please grab bits of cheese to put in the salad.

Please chop some wood, Chuck.

I ate a whole bowl of cherries.

The team of oxen pulled the wagon.

Name: _____

NATIONAL WILDLIFE WEEK

A Wild Riddle

This riddle is a real wild one! Can you solve it? Add and subtract the letters as shown from the names of the pictures below. If you can figure it out, you're really grrreat!

  —F—T    —M—10

_____   _____   _____

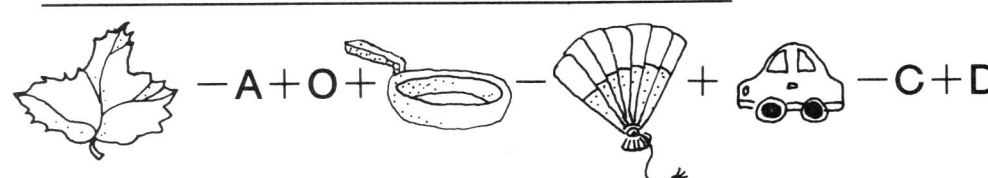

_____   _____   _____

C+ [hat] — [cat] +I+ [deer] —ER

_____

A   [leaf] —A+O+ [pan] — [fan] + [car] —C+D

_____ ?

ANSWER:
 —M—10   [fist]—F—T   [pail]+ [wand] — [pin] —D+ [eyes] —EE

_____   _____

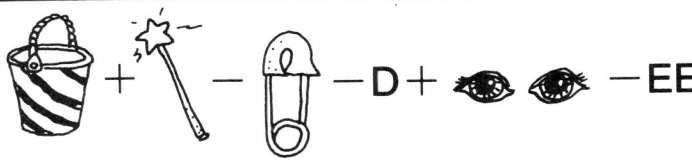

_____ !

Name: _____

ST. PATRICK'S DAY

A Disappearing Act

St. Patrick died on this day in 461 A.D. He was said to have performed many miracles during his life. One of the most famous was supposed to have been when he rid Ireland of snakes. Here's your chance to watch the snakes disappear. Follow the directions by making a new word for each step of the puzzle.

S N A K E S

__ __ __ __ __   Drop a letter and unscramble; word means "to move in a sly way."

__ __ __ __   Drop a letter and unscramble; "what the Titanic did."

__ __ __   Drop a letter; "abbreviation for solution."

__ __   Drop a letter.

__   Drop another letter and you've done it!

Stand Pat

Be a miracle worker and solve this puzzle. Follow the clues and fill in each square with the right letters so that you'll have six new words with pat in them.

☐ PAT   A quarrel.

PAT ☐   A narrow track.

PAT ☐ ☐   Small piece of cloth used to cover a hole.

PAT ☐ ☐ ☐   A regular customer.

PAT ☐ ☐ ☐ ☐   A thing to be copied.

☐ PAT ☐ ☐ ☐   Broad, flat knife used to spread pastes.

PAT ☐ ☐ ☐ ☐   Person who loves and supports own country.

Did you do it? Well, pat yourself on the head!

ST. PATRICK'S DAY

Wearing of the Green

Here's a puzzle that will have you seeing green!

ACROSS:
1. A fruit from a tree that is green before it is ripe.
6. Green, flat parts of a plant.
9. Large, woody plants that have many of #6 ACROSS.
11. A green gem.
12. Clovers.

DOWN:
2. Green citrus fruits.
3. A spicy sauce often used on hot dogs.
4. Stalks of plants.
5. A vegetable that grows in pods (plural).
7. What you see with; some people have green ones.
8. A lawn.
10. A color very popular on St. Patrick's Day.

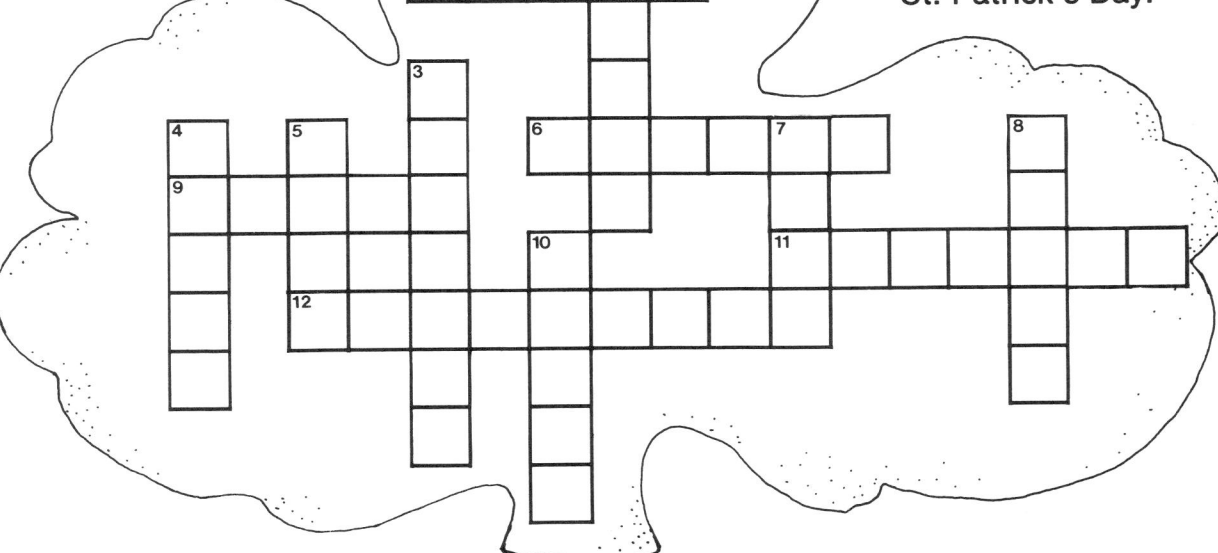

Pot o' Gold

An Irish legend has it that there is a pot of gold at the end of the rainbow. While you're trying to find it, see how many smaller words of three letters or more you can find in

R A I N B O W

1. _____ 6. _____ 11. _____ 16. _____

2. _____ 7. _____ 12. _____ 17. _____

3. _____ 8. _____ 13. _____ 18. _____

4. _____ 9. _____ 14. _____ 19. _____

5. _____ 10. _____ 15. _____ 20. _____

115

PURIM

Name: _____

Feast of Lots

On Purim, Jews everywhere remember the story of how an evil prime minister named Haman cast lots to decide when he would kill all the Jews in Persia. Queen Esther, a Jew herself, was able to turn the plot against Haman and save her people.

    Each of the words below has the word "lot" hidden in it. Can you fill in the blanks with the correct letters?

— L O T   Secret plan.

— L O T __   Slow-moving South American animal that hangs upside down in trees.

L O T __ __ __   Liquid used to soothe skin.

— L O T __ __ __   Garments.

L O T __ __ __ __   Plan to distribute something by lots, or chances.

An Earful

There is a popular pastry shaped in a triangle and filled with poppy seed or prunes that is served at Purim. It is called "Haman's Ear."

    Take a bite of one by solving the magic word square below. (The answers will be the same across and down.)

1. What you hear with.

2. A playing card with a single spot.

3. A color.

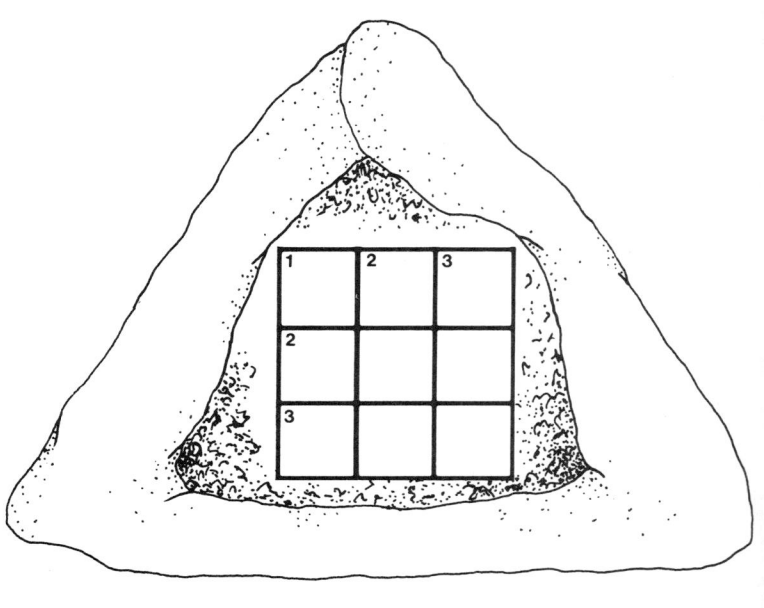

SPRING

Name: _____

Spring Thaw

Melt the snow and go from COLD to WARM with this puzzle.

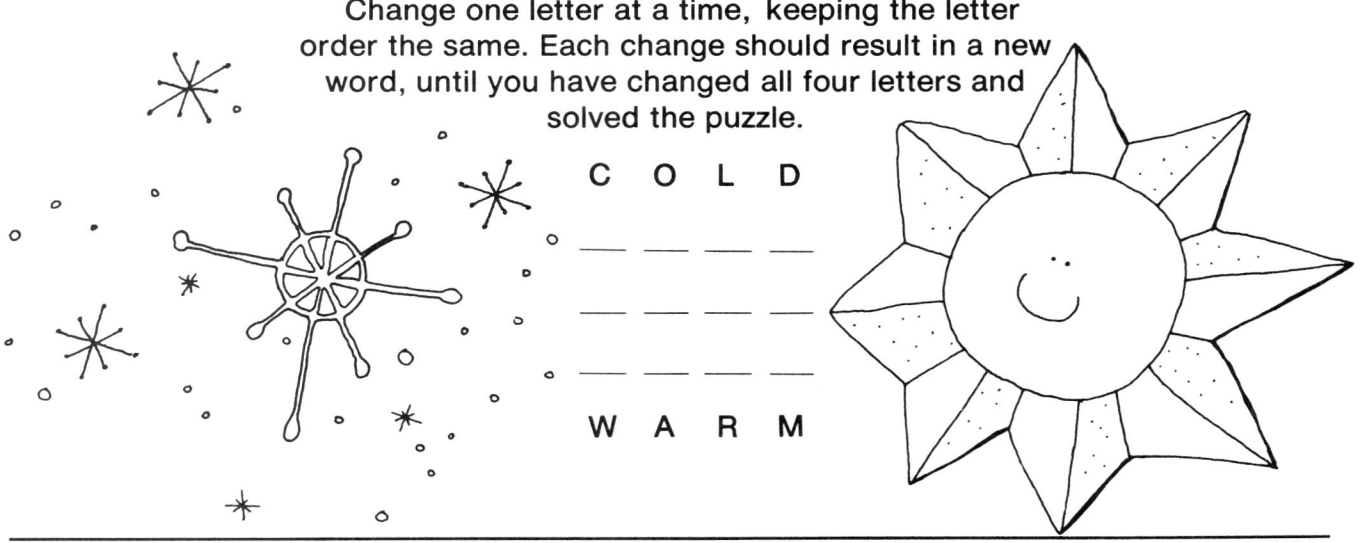

Change one letter at a time, keeping the letter order the same. Each change should result in a new word, until you have changed all four letters and solved the puzzle.

C O L D

___ ___ ___ ___

___ ___ ___ ___

___ ___ ___ ___

W A R M

Happy Birthday!

Lots of animals are having Spring birthdays down on the farm. Can you unscramble the names of the baby animals?

L O A F _____

G L I S N O G _____

F L A C _____

B A L M _____

C I K C H _____

SPRING

Name: _____

Spring Blooms

Can you solve this "bloomin' " puzzle by finding the names of all the flowers listed? They may be up, down, across, diagonal, or backwards. Circle each word as you find it.

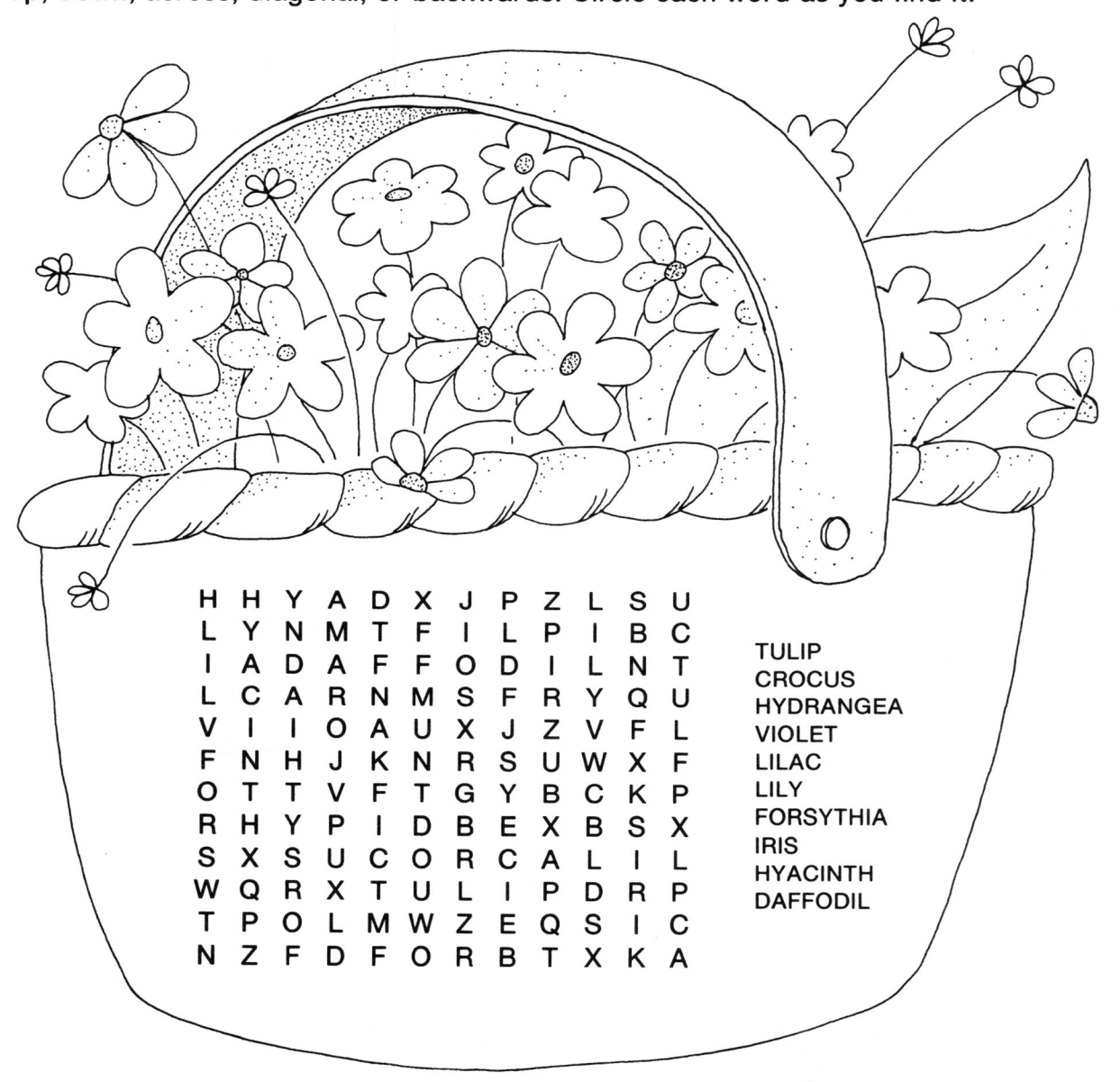

H	H	Y	A	D	X	J	P	Z	L	S	U
L	Y	N	M	T	F	I	L	P	I	B	C
I	A	D	A	F	F	O	D	I	L	N	T
L	C	A	R	N	M	S	F	R	Y	Q	U
V	I	I	O	A	U	X	J	Z	V	F	L
F	N	H	J	K	N	R	S	U	W	X	F
O	T	T	V	F	T	G	Y	B	C	K	P
R	H	Y	P	I	D	B	E	X	B	S	X
S	X	S	U	C	O	R	C	A	L	I	L
W	Q	R	X	T	U	L	I	P	D	R	P
T	P	O	L	M	W	Z	E	Q	S	I	C
N	Z	F	D	F	O	R	B	T	X	K	A

TULIP
CROCUS
HYDRANGEA
VIOLET
LILAC
LILY
FORSYTHIA
IRIS
HYACINTH
DAFFODIL

Flower Riddle

Don't be all wet! Solve this riddle if you can.

If April showers bring May flowers,
what do May flowers bring?

_____

SPRING

Name: _____

Celebrate Spring!

Spring is "bustin' out all over" in the crossword puzzle below. Can you complete the puzzle and say good-bye to Old Man Winter? (This one's a challenge!)

WORD BANK

rain	tulips	birds
maple	blade	bee
plants	to	model
April	balloon	up
ear	seep	rub
peeper	I've	re
grow	pal	see
pt	bat	bus
split	ewe	no
news	pale	bloom
ha	II	baseball
on	we	eve
	lambs	

The crossword grid contains the letters S P R I N G spelling down the center.

ACROSS:

1. Wooden stick used to play baseball.
3. _____ build their nests in the spring.
6. Trees, flowers, and grass are all _____.
9. Short for evening.
11. Opposite of down.
12. Homonym for sea.
13. Name of game mentioned in #1 ACROSS.
16. Opposite of off.
18. Friend.
19. Roman numeral for 2.
20. You can build a _____ boat to sail in a pond; a small copy.
22. The month following March.
23. Abbrev. for part time.
24. Homonym for pail.
25. One of the parts of your body you use to hear.
27. We get syrup in the spring from this tree.
28. To come from a seed.
30. A large vehicle with rows of seats.
31. We need it to make things grow.
32. New information.

DOWN:

1. The flower of a plant.
2. A homonym for two.
3. An insect that makes honey.
4. Contraction of I have.
5. Abbrev. for regarding.
7. Large cup-shaped spring flower. (plural)
8. A banana _____; a dessert.
10. A laugh.
12. To leak slowly.
13. A single piece of grass.
14. The season between winter and summer.
15. A toy rubber sack that can be blown up.
17. Opposite of yes.
18. A tiny frog that makes one of the first sounds of spring.
21. Baby sheep that are born in the spring.
25. A female sheep.
26. To wipe something.
29. You and I.

EARTH DAY

Name: _____

Earth's Bounty

Celebrated on the first day of Spring, Earth Day is a time to remember that we must do our best to preserve Earth's natural resources.

Look at the list of things we must be careful not to use up or to pollute. Then try to fit the underlined words into the puzzle grid opposite.

TREES — for paper, wood.
WATER — for drinking, washing.
METALS — aluminum cans, etc.
CROPS — food for all.
AIR — keep it clean.

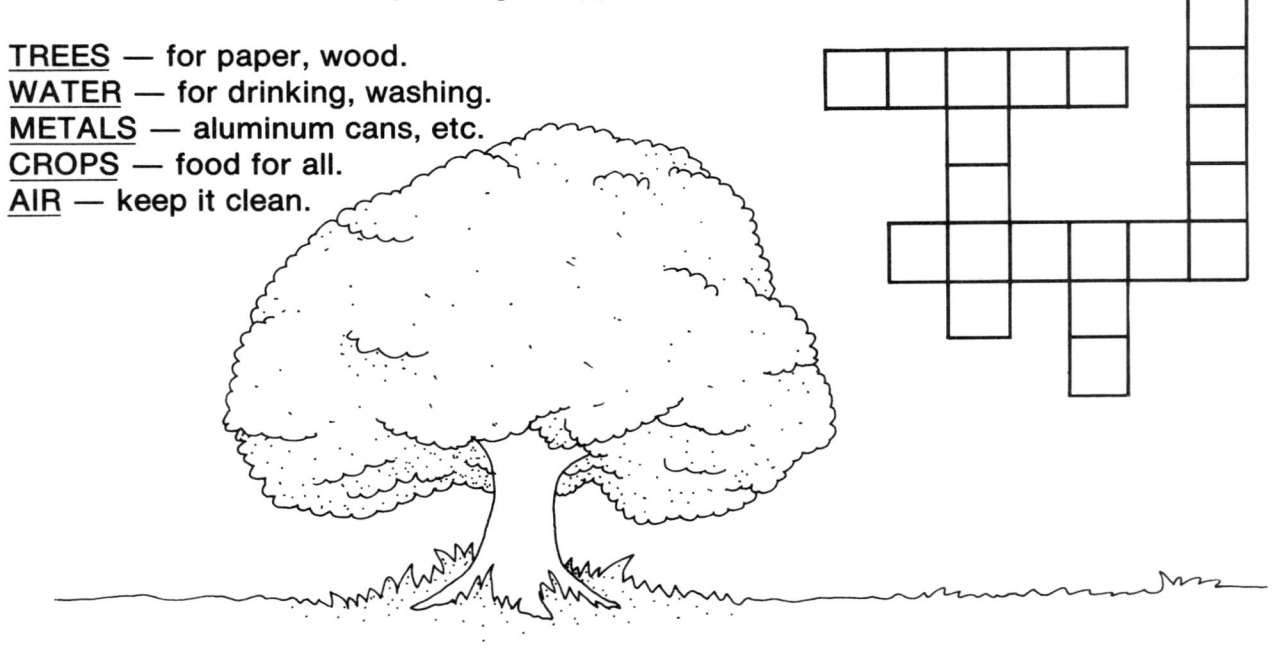

A Word to the Wise

Complete the magic word square below and discover the missing word in the sentence, _ _ _ _ our natural resources. (Hint: The answers will be the same across and down.)

1. To keep from wasting something.
2. A space. (Length × width = _____.)
3. To change direction.
4. What you hear with.

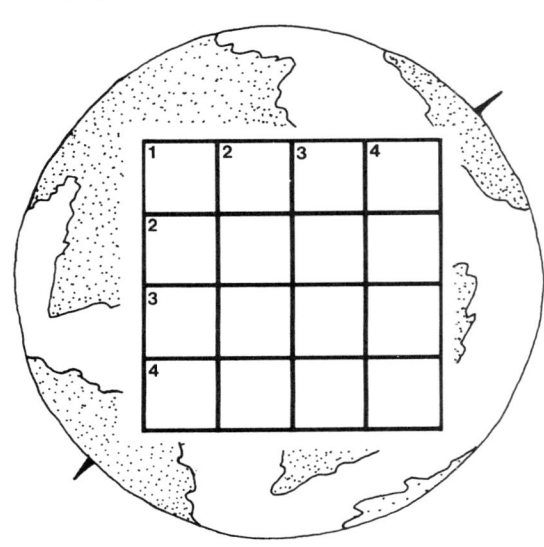

NORUZ

Name: _____

Spring in the New Year

Noruz (pronounced noh-rooz) is Iran's New Year celebration. Begun on March 21, the holiday lasts for 13 days. The evening before Noruz begins, a special meal is prepared. Certain foods are included: colored eggs (to stand for new life), candles, a mirror (to reflect a bright future for everyone), green leaves, roast chicken, fruits, bread, sweets, and rose water.

Can you find the words underlined in the paragraph above in the puzzle? They may be up, down, across, diagonal, or backwards. Circle each word as you find it.

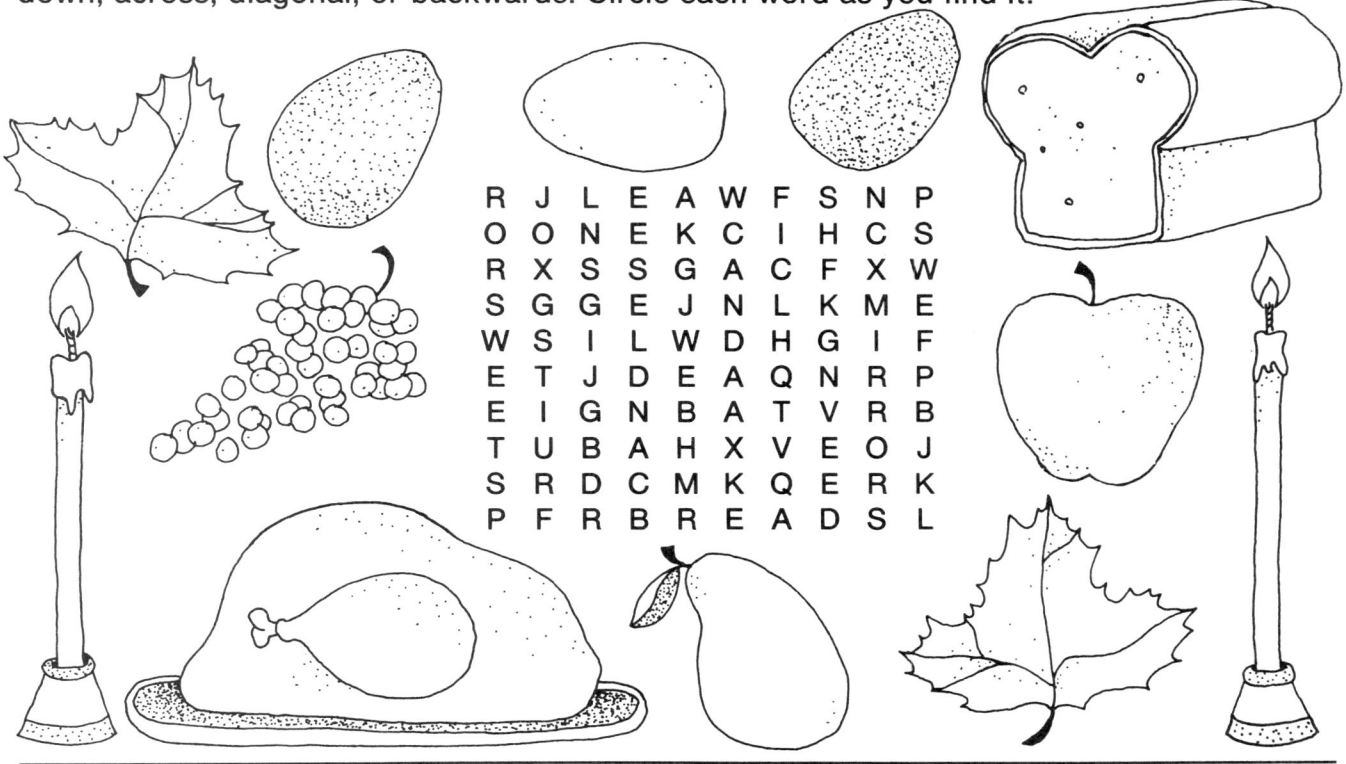

```
R  J  L  E  A  W  F  S  N  P
O  O  N  E  K  C  I  H  C  S
R  X  S  S  G  A  C  F  X  W
S  G  G  E  J  N  L  K  M  E
W  S  I  L  W  D  H  G  I  F
E  T  J  D  E  A  Q  N  R  P
E  I  G  N  B  A  T  V  R  B
T  U  B  A  H  X  V  E  O  J
S  R  D  C  M  K  Q  E  R  K
P  F  R  B  R  E  A  D  S  L
```

Lucky Sprouts

To represent life and good fortune, every family begins to grow green sprouts in a dish or clay jug 15 days before the holiday. On the 13th day of Noruz, the family throws the mass of green sprouts into a stream to represent the throwing away of all bad luck.

Help make the greens grow by following directions in the puzzle below. Each step should form a new word. Start from the bottom up.

__ __	Drop a letter and reverse the remaining letters.
__ __ __	Drop a letter.
__ __ __ __	Drop a letter.
__ __ __ __ __	Drop a letter.
__ __ __ __ __ __	Drop a letter.

S P R O U T S

Name: _____

PASSOVER

Passover Puzzlers

According to Jewish tradition, Passover remembers the time the Pharaoh of Egypt would not free the Jews. As a punishment, the "Angel of Death" killed each Egyptian firstborn son but "passed over" every Jewish home.

Before you pass over these puzzles, try to complete the two magic word squares. The answers to each puzzle will be the same across and down.

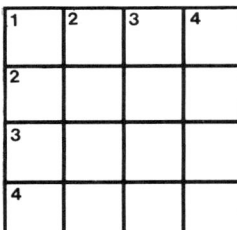

1. To go past.
2. A space; length x width = ___.
3. Sea animal with long body and flippers.
4. Homonym for sail.

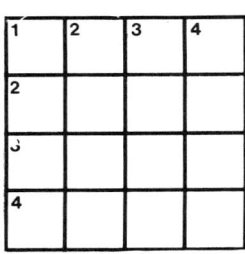

1. Opposite of under.
2. Found on roofs; a weather ___
3. The last parts of anything.
4. Take it easy.

Seder Plate

On the first evening of Passover, a special meal called the "seder" (pronounced say-der) is prepared. Certain foods are placed on a plate and each stands for something.

Roasted <u>lamb bone</u>, roasted <u>egg</u>   =   sacrifices

<u>Horseradish</u>   =   suffering of Jews in Egypt

Mixture of <u>wine</u>, chopped <u>apples</u>, and <u>nuts</u>   =   mortar used by Jewish slaves when building

<u>salt water</u>   =   tears

<u>green vegetable</u>   =   hope and new growth

Find the words underlined in the list opposite in the puzzle below. The words may be up, down, across, diagonal, or backwards. Circle each word as you find it.

```
H O R S F P V S H X P
S K M L X D J W A T L
H S I D A R E S R O H
K A C Z B M X W C R F
N Q P I Q O B I K E G
E N F P K J N N H T G
E T D X L G G E G A R
R N U T S E W V B W P
G B T L A S S H C R C
```

Name: _____

PASSOVER

Holiday Bread

During Passover, the Jewish people eat *matzo* (pronounced: maht-zuh) or unleavened bread. Unleavened means that there is no yeast and so the bread does not rise.

Help to bake the matzo by solving the word pyramid below. Subtract one letter at a time, so that each step makes a new word.

B   R   E   A   D

___ ___ ___ ___   Part of a necklace.

___ ___ ___   Opposite of good.

___ ___   Abbreviation for advertisement.

___   One.

Get-together

Passover is a time for family reunions. Help reunite this family by gathering all the smaller words (of two letters or more) that comprise it! (There are at least ten.)

F A M I L Y

1. _____

2. _____

3. _____

4. _____

5. _____

6. _____

7. _____

8. _____

9. _____

10. _____

Name: _____

EASTER

Easter Lily

Lilies are a favorite flower at Eastertime. Can you complete the magic word square below and make it bloom? (The answers will be the same across and down.)

1. A popular Easter flower.
2. A thought.
3. If it has a hole in it, the roof will _____ when it rains.
4. Long-haired oxen from Tibet.

The Bells Are Ringing

No church bells are rung between Holy Thursday and Easter Sunday. In some countries, children are told that the bells have flown to Rome to visit the Pope.

Can you complete the magic word squares below?

1. What the church bells do *not* do on the three days before Easter.
2. A thought.
3. Where birds lay their eggs.
4. A door in a fence.

5. What the church bells are said to do to get to Rome.
6. To be untruthful.
7. Opposite of no.

Solve the picture puzzle below by adding and subtracting the letters as shown from the names of the pictures. What are the bells supposed to bring when they return on Easter morning?

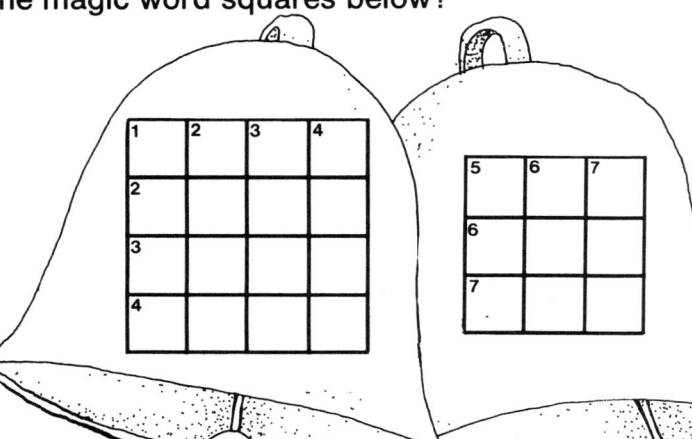

—L + (pig) +N— (safety pin) +S = _____

EASTER

Name: _____

Eggs-tra Colorful

Eggs are a popular Easter symbol because they represent new life. It is the custom in many countries to dye and decorate Easter eggs.

How many different colors can you find hidden in the Easter basket below that you can use to dye your eggs? For each color, you may use the letters given in any order, but only as often as they appear on the eggs. (Hint: There are at least eight colors hidden.)

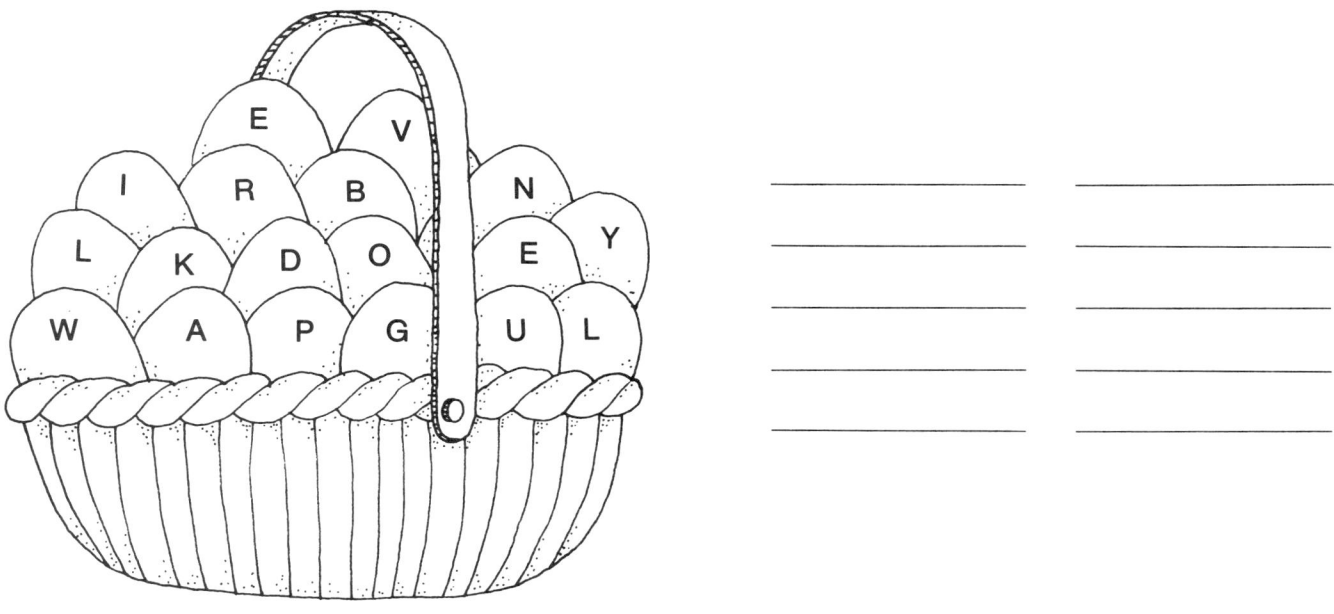

_____ _____

_____ _____

_____ _____

_____ _____

_____ _____

Very Bunny!

Oops, more than eggs are getting colored! Can you unscramble the words of the punchline to get the joke?

What's the fastest way to paint a rabbit?

S E U   R E H A   P A R Y S !

___ ___ ___   ___ ___ ___ ___   ___ ___ ___ ___ ___!

Name: _____

In Your Easter Bonnet

Solve the magic word squares below and you'll have three new hats to wear in the Easter Parade. (The answers in each puzzle will be the same across and down.)

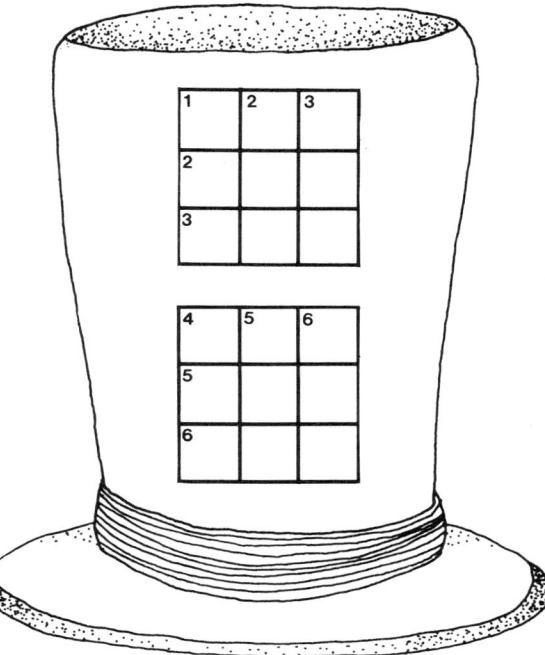

1. Opposite of bottom.
2. Number that comes before two.
3. A dog or cat.

4. A head covering.
5. I am, she is, you ___.
6. A hot drink.

1. A hat worn to play baseball.
2. A gorilla.
3. A vegetable that grows in a pod.

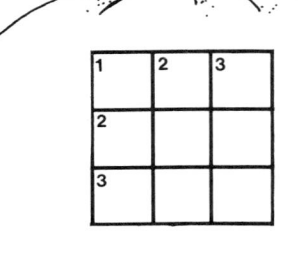

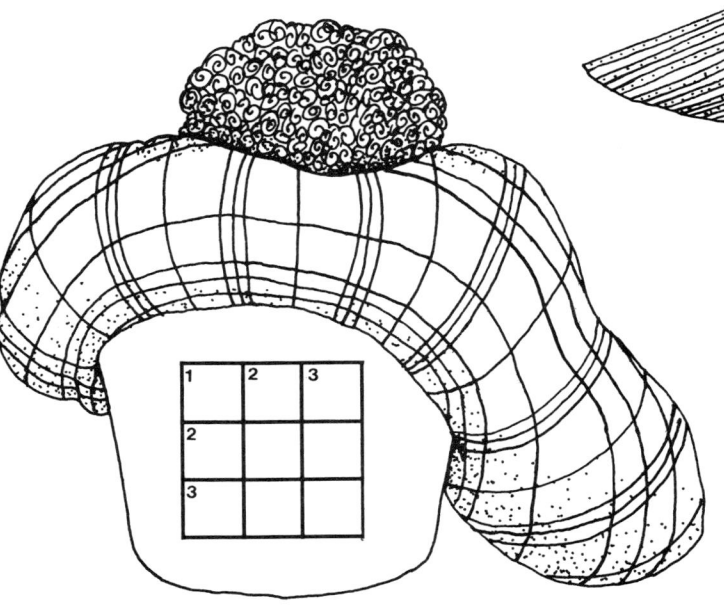

1. A cap of Scottish origin.
2. How old you are.
3. Not women.

Name: _____

NATIONAL HUMOR MONTH

Laugh Lines

Spend this month in a good humor. Get a head start by getting the joke below. Add and subtract the letters from the names of the pictures as shown to learn the punch line.

What is the longest word in the English language?

 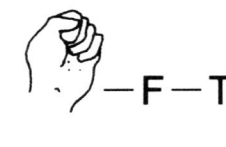

$+$ ___ $-K+A+$ ___ $-$ ___   T+ ___ $-N+RE$ ___ $-F-T$

_____ .   _____

A   ___ $-K+E$ ___ $+2+G-$ ___ $+E+$ ___ $-H$

_____   _____   _____

$+$ ___ $-N$ ___ $-D+$ ___ $-FT+P+9-$ ___ $+$ ___ $-R$

_____   _____

___ $-H$ ___ $-H+D$

_____   _____ .

Name: _____

APRIL FOOL'S DAY

No Fooling!

Did you know that on April Fool's Day you can only play a joke before noon? If you play one after noon, *you* become the fool! ("April Fool's gone past; you're the biggest fool at last.")

   Don't let anyone make you the fool. Figure out the joke below by adding and subtracting the letters as shown from the names of the objects pictured.

W +    (fist) − F − T   R + (bed) − B   (witch) − C

_____ _____ _____ _____

(bag) − SE + (flag) − O   S + 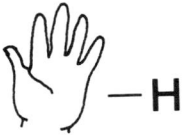   (hand) − H    − T

_____ _____ _____ _____

1   H + (sun) + (dress) − SSS + D   L + (eggs) − G

_____   _____   _____?

ANSWER:

(eye)   (doughnut) − U   K + (snowflakes) − S   (bus) − S + T

_____ _____ _____ _____

 − 10 − M + S   (crab) + (well) − (bell) + L + (ring) − R

_____ _____

1 − E   Y + 4 − F    − G + (tack) + G − (tag) !

_____ _____

APRIL FOOL'S DAY

Holiday Riddle

Can you solve the cryptogram and get a chuckle? Each number under the blanks below stands for a letter. The numbers for some letters have been given to you. Fill in the letters you know, then try to figure out what the others might be.

Y O U R   A P R I L   F O O L'S   D A Y   J O K E
10 11 5 2   7 18 2 16 19   15 11 11 19 8   12 7 10   1 11 20 14

Why are you so tired on April Fool's Day?

10 11 5   1 5 8 4   9 7 12   7   6 7 2 3 9   11 15

—

4 9 16 2 4 10   11 17 14   12 7 10 8.

Gone Fishing

In France, you are called a *Poisson d'Avril* (pwah-sohn dahv-reel) or "April Fish" if you are fooled by a joke today. Chocolate fish are a special treat on this holiday.

Catch your own April Fish by solving the magic word square below. (The answers will be the same down and across.)

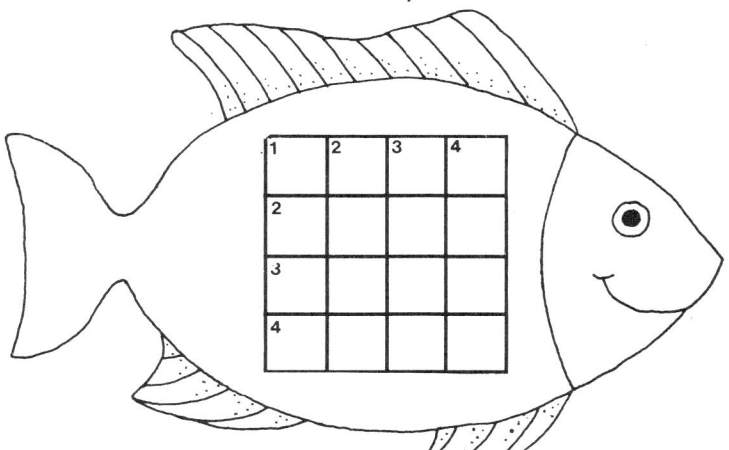

1. An animal with fins and gills that lives in water.
2. A thought.
3. Looked at.
4. Part of the arm below wrist.

Name: _____

HANS CHRISTIAN ANDERSEN

Fairy Tale Maker

Hans Christian Andersen, Denmark's greatest author, was born on this day in 1805. He wrote many of the world's favorite fairy tales. Some of these tales are listed below. But you must break the code in order to read them. (Hint: They are written as 3-shift ciphers. A=D, B=E, C=F, and so on.)

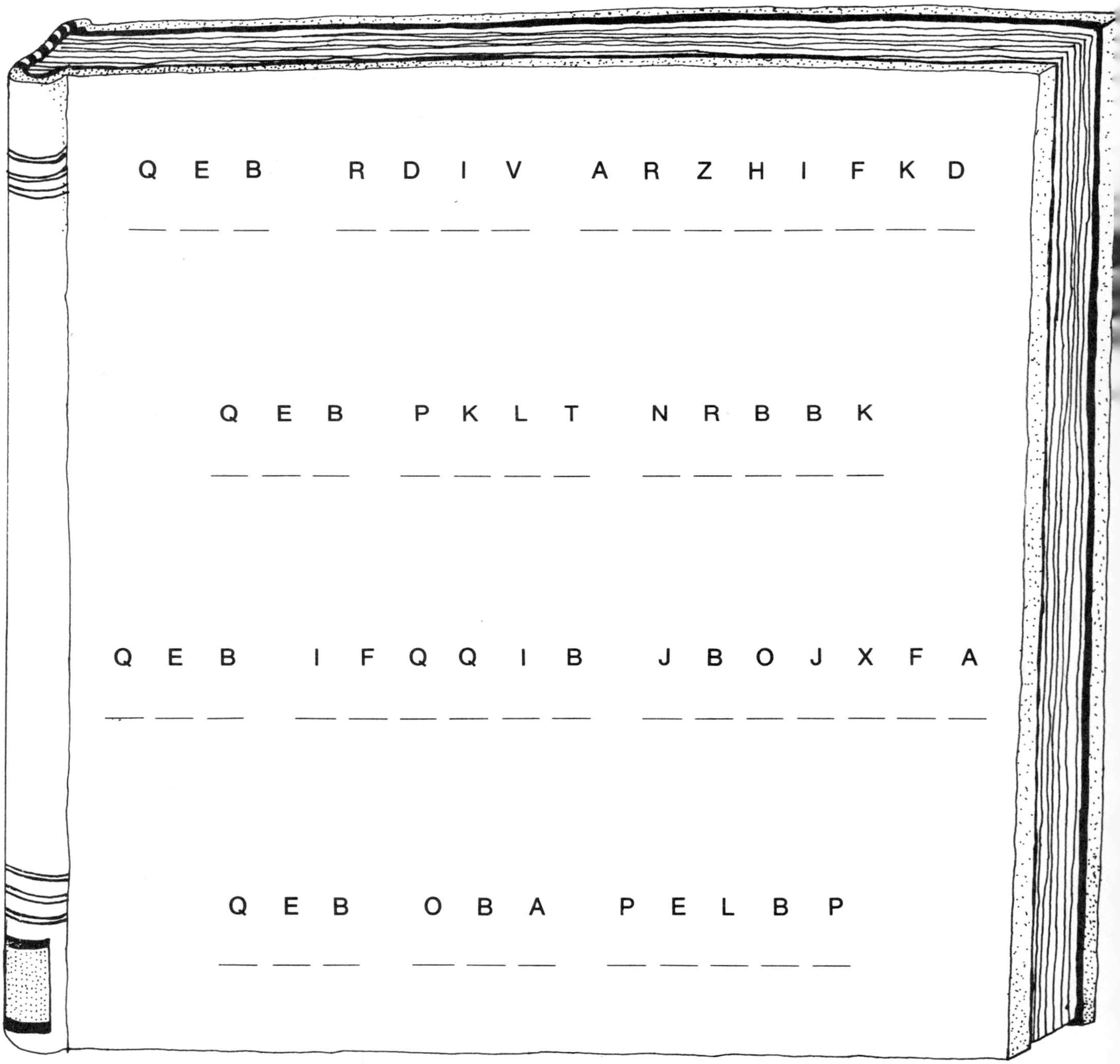

Q E B   R D I V   A R Z H I F K D

_ _ _   _ _ _ _   _ _ _ _ _ _ _ _

Q E B   P K L T   N R B B K

_ _ _   _ _ _ _   _ _ _ _ _

Q E B   I F Q Q I B   J B O J X F A

_ _ _   _ _ _ _ _ _   _ _ _ _ _ _ _

Q E B   O B A   P E L B P

_ _ _   _ _ _   _ _ _ _ _

Name: _____

FIRST MODERN OLYMPIC GAMES

Go for the Gold

The first Olympic games were held in ancient Greece. They were nothing like the modern games we now know, which were begun on this day in 1896.

The puzzle below includes many of the sports that make up the modern Summer Olympics. Can you complete the puzzle and win the gold medal?

WORD BANK

track	arrow
yes	horseback
box	swimming
td	be
lift	ago
oat	re
gas	se
ti	caps
AAA	co.
basketball	soccer
gymnastics	bicycle
go	cb
ha	ET
oar	mi
do	la
it	or
lt	to
no	XI

DOWN:
1. A game in which a ball is tossed through a basket.
2. Either, ____.
3. A water sport.
4. Abbrev. for company.
5. Small hats.
6. A favorite movie alien.
7. Type of riding done on a horse.
9. Abbrev. for regarding.
13. Musical note that comes after *re*.
14. Ready, set, ____!
15. Citizen's Band radio.
18. Musical note that comes after *ti*.
20. Opposite of no.
21. Musical note that comes after *so*.
23. Roman numeral for eleven.
26. Initials of Automobile Association of America.
27. What is used to row a boat.
29. Musical note that comes after *la*.
30. A thing.
31. Homonym for two.

ACROSS:
3. A ball game in which hands and arms cannot be used.
8. Something shot from a bow in archery.
10. A cereal plant.
11. Opposite of yes.
12. Abbrev. for southeast.
14. Physical exercises that include tumbling, the balance beam, and the rings.
16. To be or not to ____.
17. Abbrev. for touchdown. (Football is not yet an Olympic sport.)
19. Vehicle used in cycling.
22. To fight with fists wearing gloves.
24. A laugh.
25. Needed to power a car.
28. Abbrev for left.
31. Footraces that involve running around a ____.
32. An athlete may ____ weights while training.
33. A long, long time ____.

FIRST MODERN OLYMPICS

Carrying the Torch

Every four years, the Olympic torch is lit by the eternal Olympic flame in Greece and carried by runners to the country where the games will be held.

   Help to carry the torch by solving the word pyramid. Follow the directions and make a new word for each step.

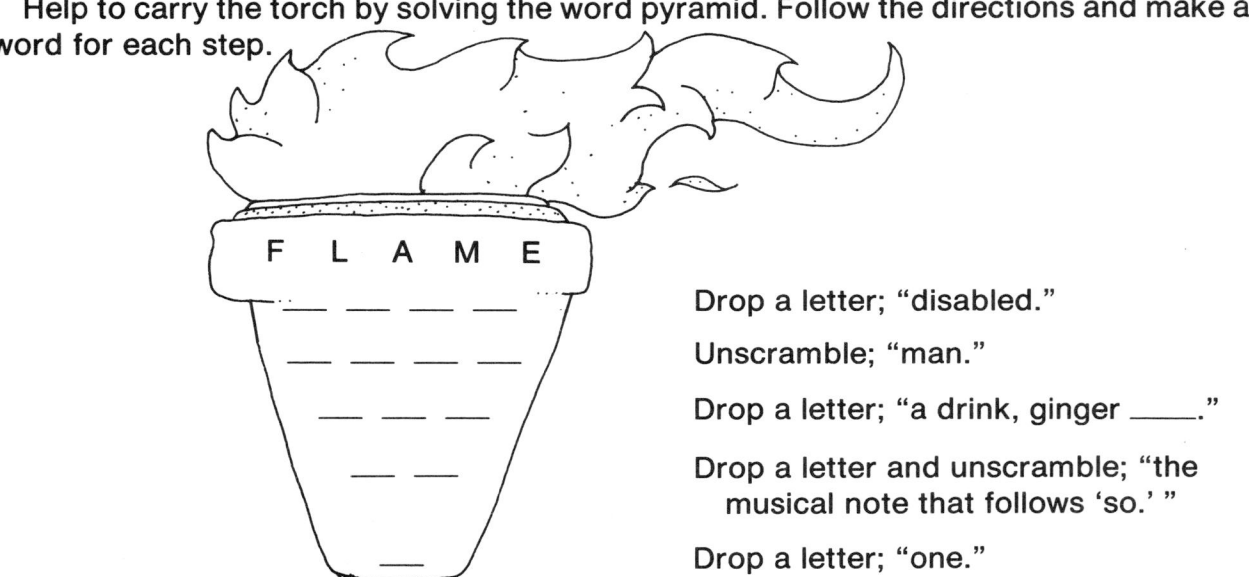

F L A M E

Drop a letter; "disabled."

Unscramble; "man."

Drop a letter; "a drink, ginger _____."

Drop a letter and unscramble; "the musical note that follows 'so.'"

Drop a letter; "one."

Raise the Flag

The Olympic flag contains five rings—one to represent each of the five continents. Complete the magic word square below. The answers will be the same across and down.

1. A circle around something.
2. Used to press out wrinkles in clothing.
3. A star that suddenly explodes.
4. A tiny insect.

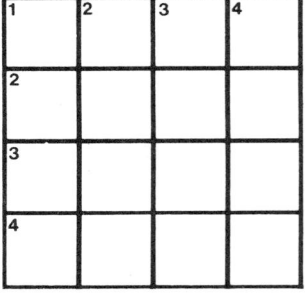

When the Olympic FLAG is unfurled, people from all over the world have a chance to MEET. To solve the puzzle, change one letter at a time, keeping the letter order the same. Each change should result in a new word until you have changed all four letters.

F L A G

_ _ _ _

_ _ _ _

_ _ _ _

M E E T

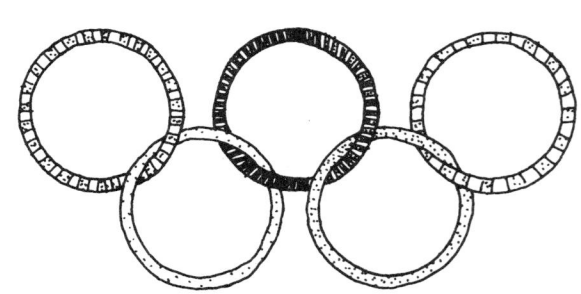

Name: _____

BUDDHA'S BIRTHDAY

A Holy Man

Many Asian countries celebrate the birthday of Buddha (pronounced Bood-uh), the founder of Buddhism, at this time of year. Born around 563 B.C. in northern India, Buddha's real name was Siddhartha Gautama. Buddha was a special title.

To learn the meaning of Buddha, do the math shown under the blanks and then use the answers as a code to fill in the letters.

4＝D   6＝G   1＝N   8＝H   9＝I   7＝O   2＝T   5＝L   3＝E

"___ ___ ___ ___ ___ ___ ___ ___ ___ ___ ___ ___"
2+1 6−5 3+2 5+4 7−1 4+4 3−1 2+1 6−5 2+1 6−2

___ ___ ___
4+3 6−5 2+1

Meaning of Life

According to legend, Buddha had a vision that helped him to understand the meaning of life. Complete the magic word square below and solve one of "life's" riddles. (The answers are the same down and across.)

1. The state of being alive.
2. A thought.
3. Feeling of fright.
4. What you hear with.

BE KIND TO ANIMALS WEEK

Animal Friends

It was on April 10, 1866 that the American Society for Prevention of Cruelty to Animals (or A.S.P.C.A.) was founded. Be a friend to animals by taking good care of your pets. Look at the list of pets below and try to fit each word into the puzzle grid.

SNAKE
DOG
HORSE
CAT
PARAKEET
PARROT
RABBIT
FISH
MOUSE
HAMSTER

Hidden Pets

There is a pet hidden in each of the words below. Can you make six new words by filling in the blank spaces? Try solving the puzzle first without looking at the clues opposite.

__ __ __ PET	Pull its strings to make it move.
PET __ __	Part of a flower.
PET __ __ __	Small.
__ __ __ PET	Rug.
PET __ __ __ __	A flower.
PET __ __ __ __ __ __	Oil.

134

BE KIND TO ANIMALS WEEK

Animal Riddles

Can you break the code in the riddles below and figure out the punch lines? (Hint: The code is a 3-shift cipher: A=D; B=E; C=F, and so on.)

What do gerbils have that no other animals have?

Y　X　Y　V　　D　B　O　Y　F　I　P

___ ___ ___ ___　___ ___ ___ ___ ___ ___ ___.

Why did the mother pig tell the baby pig to eat all his dinner?

Y　B　Z　X　R　P　B　　E　B　　J　R　P　Q　　J　X　H　B

___ ___ ___ ___ ___ ___ ___　___ ___　___ ___ ___ ___　___ ___ ___ ___

X　E　L　D　　L　C　　E　F　J　P　B　I　C

___ ___ ___ ___　___ ___　___ ___ ___ ___ ___ ___ ___ ___.

What happened when the cat licked a lemon?

F　Q　　Y　B　Z　X　J　B　　X　　P　L　R　O　M　R　P　P

___ ___　___ ___ ___ ___ ___ ___　___　___ ___ ___ ___ ___ ___ ___ ___.

What animal can tell time?

X　　T　X　Q　Z　E　A　L　D

___　___ ___ ___ ___ ___ ___ ___ ___.

135

Name: _____

ARBOR DAY

Plant a Tree

The first Arbor Day was held in Nebraska on this day in 1872. Arbor Day is celebrated on different days in different places—usually at the best time for planting in that area. Trees are planted on this day each year.

Plant some trees of your own by solving the three magic word squares below. (The answers in each puzzle will be the same across and down.)

1. A tree. Also, what is left after a fire.

2. Ocean; homonym for see.

3. A head covering.

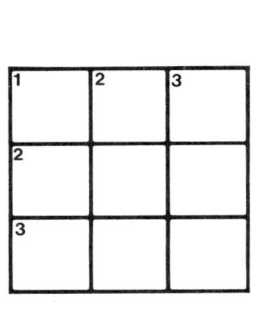

1. A shade tree.

2. A Hawaiian flower necklace.

3. To stir cake batter.

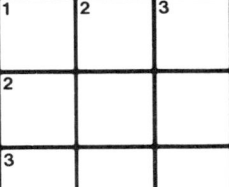

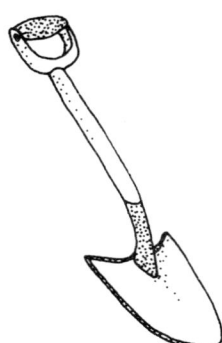

1. A tree; grows from an acorn.

2. I am, he is, you _____.

3. Used to open a door.

Tree-hee-hee!

Want to get the joke below? Translate the punch line and you will. (Hint: It is written as a 3-shift cipher. A=D, B=E, C=F, and so on.)

How far can you walk into a forest?

Q L   Q E B   J F A A I B — X C Q B O

___ ___   ___ ___ ___   ___ ___ ___ ___ ___ ___ — ___ ___ ___ ___ ___

Q E X Q   V L R   X O B

___ ___ ___ ___   ___ ___ ___   ___ ___ ___

T X I H F K D   L R Q!

___ ___ ___ ___ ___ ___ ___   ___ ___ ___!

Name: _____

BEVERLY CLEARY'S BIRTHDAY

Reading Is Fun!

Beverly Cleary, a well-loved children's author, was born on this day in 1916. To learn the titles of some of her most popular books, solve the puzzles below. The first letter of the name of each picture is a letter in the title of a book. (The first one is already done.)

R A M O N A   T H E   P E S T

NATIONAL LIBRARY WEEK

Dewey's Code

The *Dewey Decimal System,* a way of arranging all non-fiction books in the library into ten groups, was invented in 1876 by a librarian named Melvil Dewey.

Can you find the underlined words in the list below in the puzzle?

General Works   000-099
Philosophy and
   Psychology   100-199
Religion and
   Mythology   200-299
Social Sciences   300-399
Language   400-499
Science   500-599
Technology   600-699
Fine Arts and
   Recreation   700-799
Literature   800-899
History, Geography
   and Biography   900-999

```
G L H L Y H P O S O L I H P
E Y B I O G R A P H Y R F S
N G T T S S T R A E N I F X
F O E E C T N O I G I L E R
R L C R I S O Q B A C W G F
V O H A E D O R M U K B J I
Q N M T N S N C Y G Q H L N
T H C U C O D L I N C T U F
M C L R E C V R G A H V M A
G E N E R A L F V L L I T E
B T P W G U K B Q D J S X C
X K R R E C R E A T I O N D
```

Words may be up, down, across, diagonal, or backwards. Circle each word as you find it.

Got References?

What reference books would you go to in order to find the answers to the questions below? Write the name of the correct book next to each question.

DICTIONARY: what words mean and how to spell and pronounce them.

ATLAS: maps that show location of cities, countries, lakes etc.

ALMANAC: current information about populations, laws, sports records, etc.

ENCYCLOPEDIAS: brief facts about events, places, people, animals, plants, etc.

1. What is a sturgeon? _____

2. Who was Thomas Edison? _____

3. Who won the Super Bowl? _____

4. How many people live in Cleveland? _____

5. Where is Ouagadougou? _____

WILLIAM SHAKESPEARE'S BIRTHDAY

Happy Birthday, Will!

William Shakespeare, English playwright and poet, was born today in the year 1564. The world's most popular author, he is also considered to be perhaps the greatest writer of plays and poetry in the English language.

Read the lines below from one of his plays, *As You Like It.* Then try to fit each of the underlined words into the puzzle grid below. (One is already done for you.)

"All the world's a stage
And all the men and women merely players:
They have their exits and their entrances;
And one man in his time plays many parts. . . ."

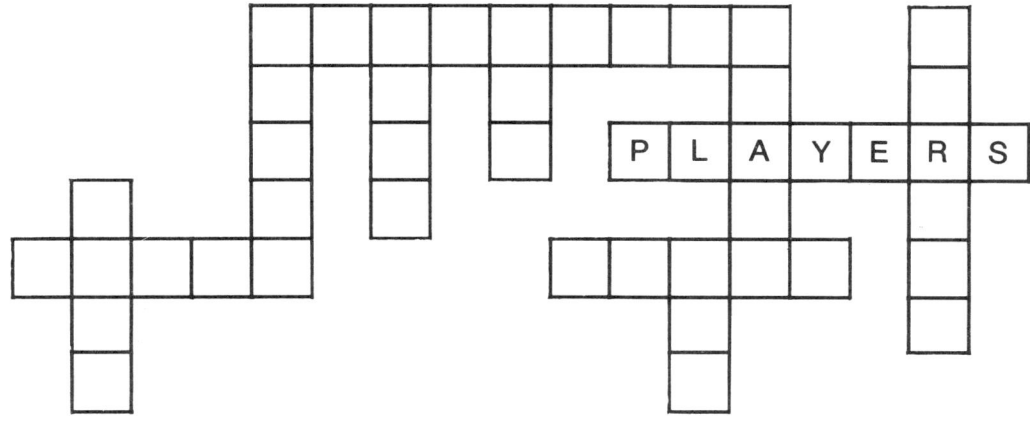

Living Language

Shakespeare created many words and phrases that are now part of our everyday speech. Some examples: fair play, catch cold, assassination, bump, and lonely.

Can you find the words and phrases underlined above in the puzzle? They may be up, down, across or backwards. Circle each word as you find it.

```
F  A  I  P  K  G  H  S  B  V  C  W  X
F  Y  Z  M  P  R  L  J  G  Q  S  M  T
A  S  S  A  S  S  I  N  A  T  I  O  N
I  M  V  Z  J  K  G  S  R  F  L  E  F
R  G  B  L  C  A  T  C  H  C  O  L  D
P  M  U  B  Z  F  D  W  M  Q  N  Q  Z
L  H  D  M  V  H  R  P  B  N  E  M  S
A  F  C  Q  R  J  Y  R  Z  J  L  E  G
Y  S  W  X  D  K  V  K  M  S  Y  L  H
```

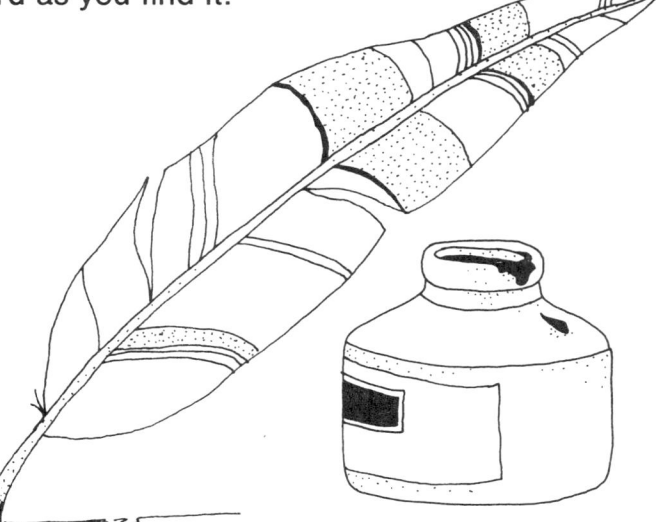

BIRD DAY

Name: _____

Be a Bird Watcher

Bird Day is celebrated on the birthday of John James Audubon, a famous expert on the birds of North America.

Get out your binoculars and see how many different birds from the list below you can spot in the puzzle. The words may be up, down, across, diagonal, or backwards. Circle each word as you find it.

TERN   WREN
HUMMINGBIRD   THRUSH
WOODPECKER   BLUEBIRD
CROW   WARBLER
ORIOLE   SPARROW
CARDINAL   PIGEON

```
K T J T H R U S H G K
G Q O N O E G I P W J
L P R R N F S X L O P
H U M M I N G B I R D
R S Z V D O K H X C U
E P C W Q M L S B V J
L A B H R N R E T Y F
B R E K C E P D O O W
R R K X Z R N H P J G
A O B L U E B I R D L
W W C A R D I N A L B
```

Happy Bird Day!

Can you translate the answers to each riddle below to learn what kind of birds have got the giggles? (Hint: The answers are written as 3-shift ciphers. A=D, B=E, C=F, and so on.)

What bird likes to play a flute on the beach?

P X K A M F M B O

_ _ _ _ _ _ _ _ _

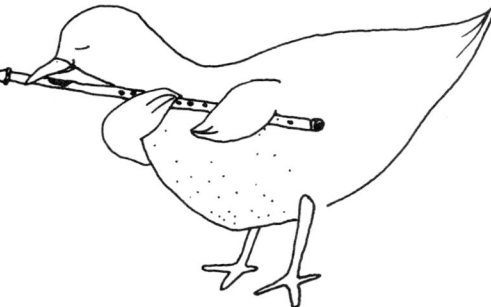

What bird was caught in the act of stealing something?

O L Y F K

_ _ _ _ _

What bird knows what to do when a ball is thrown at it?

A R Z H

_ _ _ _

BIRD DAY

Name: _____

A Bird in the Hand. . .

In honor of Bird Day, can you solve the three magic word squares below? (The answers in each puzzle will be the same across and down.) A bird is hidden in each puzzle.

1. A bird in the pigeon family that stands for peace.
2. Opposite of closed.
3. To sell or peddle.
4. Last parts of anything.

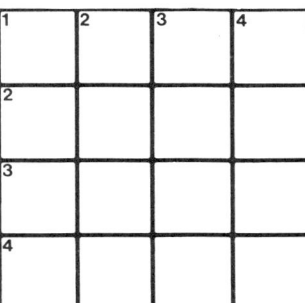

1. This bird hoots and hunts at night.
2. A path or road.
3. Used to make soap; a homonym for lie.

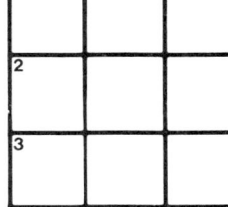

1. A chattering, brightly colored bird; a blue_____.
2. A monkey.
3. Opposite of no.

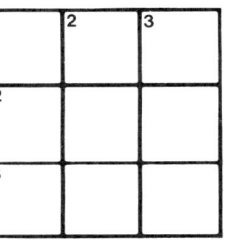

Name: _____

SAMUEL F. B. MORSE'S BIRTHDAY

Dots and Dashes

Samuel F. B. Morse, born today in the year 1791, contributed to the invention of the telegraph. He also developed the Morse Code, a system of dots and dashes used to send messages over the telegraph.

The International Morse Code

A	B	C	D	E	F	G	H	I	J	K	L	M
.-	-...	-.-.	-..	.	..-.	--.	....	..	.---	-.-	.-..	--

N	O	P	Q	R	S	T	U	V	W	X	Y	Z
-.	---	.--.	--.-	.-.	...	-	..-	...-	.--	-..-	-.--	--..

Solve the riddle below by reading the Morse Code Message.

.-- .... .- -   -.. ---   .-. --- ..-   -.-. .- .-.. .-..

- .-- ---   - . .-.. . --. .-. .- .--. ....

--- .--. . .-. .- - --- .-. ...   ..-. .-. --- --

-.-. --- .-.. --- .-. .- -.. ---   .-- .... --- --. . -

-- .- .-. .-. .. . -..?

ANSWER:

.- .-. --- -.-. -.-   -- --- ..- -. - .- .. -.   ..- -. .. --- -.!

Name: _____

OLDER AMERICANS' MONTH

A Golden Age

Old age . . . has so great authority,
that this is of more value than
all the pleasure of youth.
Cicero (ancient Roman writer)

During the month, Americans honor their older citizens and the many achievements that they
have made.

Can you figure out who each of the famous senior citizens are who are described below?
(Hint: Their names are written as 3-shift ciphers. A=D, B=E, C=F, and so on.)

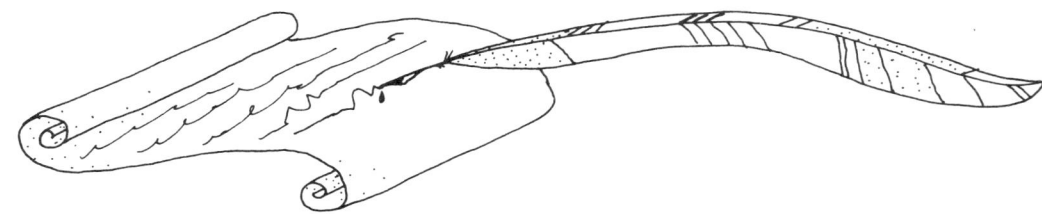

He was 81 years old when he helped to create the Constitution of the United States.

Y   B   K   G   X   J   F   K   C   O   X   K   H   I   F   K

___   ___   ___   ___   ___   ___   ___   ___   ___   ___   ___   ___   ___   ___   ___   ___

She first began painting at age 78 and continued until she was more than 100 years old.

D   O   X   K   A   J   X   J   X   O   V   J   L   P   B   P

___   ___   ___   ___   ___   ___   ___   ___   ___   ___   ___   ___   ___   ___   ___   ___

He won an Academy award for his acting in a movie when he was 80 years old.

D   B   L   O   D   B   Y   R   O   K   P

___   ___   ___   ___   ___   ___   ___   ___   ___   ___   ___

Go A-Maying

Let's go "a-maying" today to collect branches, greens, and flowers to decorate the *maypole*. In many countries, the maypole is also hung with ribbon streamers so that people can dance around it to celebrate spring.

Decorate your own maypole by completing the two magic word squares below. (Hint: the answers in each puzzle will be the same across and down.)

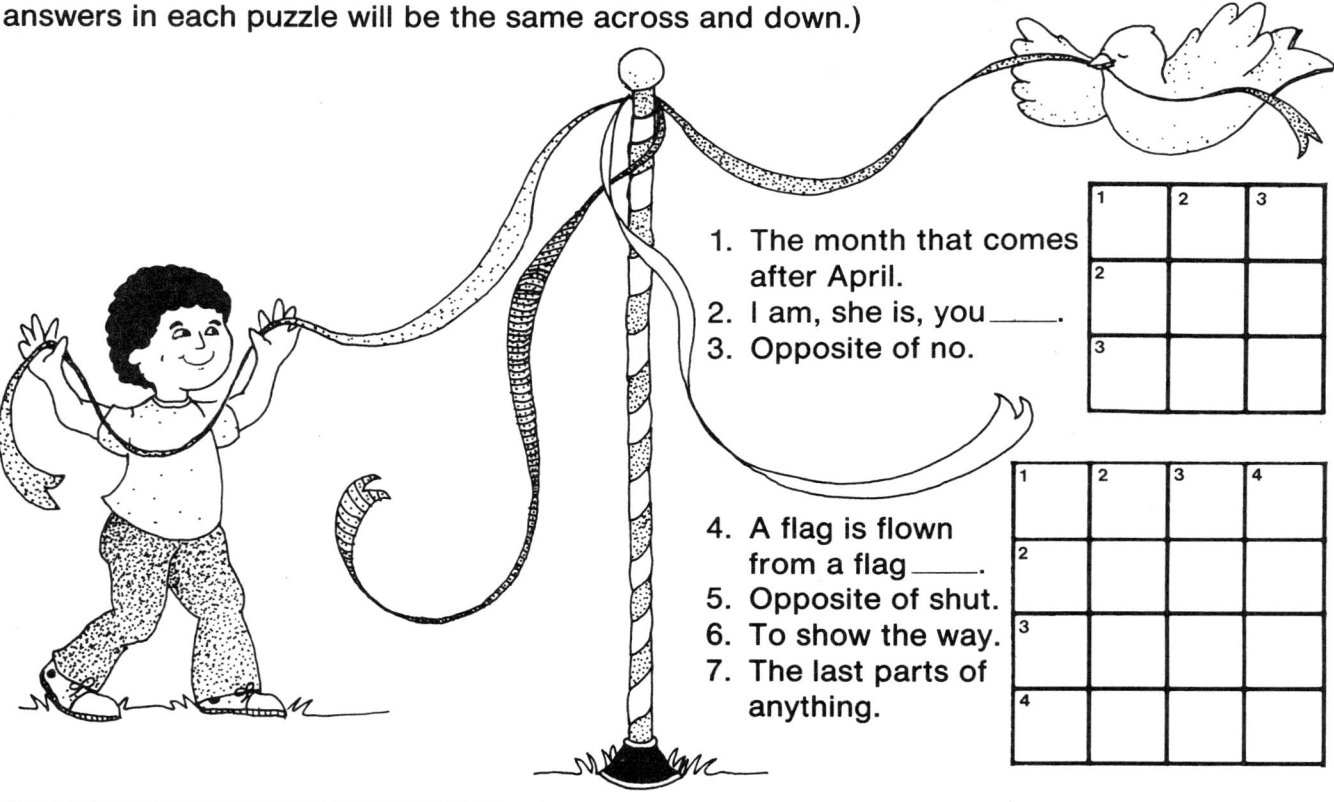

1. The month that comes after April.
2. I am, she is, you ____.
3. Opposite of no.

4. A flag is flown from a flag ____.
5. Opposite of shut.
6. To show the way.
7. The last parts of anything.

May Flowers

In England, some people still follow the old custom of wearing wreaths of flowers or carrying chains of flowers they have woven together.

See if you can weave a flower chain by completing the word pyramid below. Follow the directions so that each step becomes a new word.

F L O W E R S

__ __ __ __ __ __   Drop one letter.

__ __ __ __ __   Drop two letters; to move in a stream.

__ __ __   Drop one letter; opposite of high.

__ __   Drop one letter; a cry of pain.

__   Drop one letter; 15th letter of the alphabet.

Law Day

In the United States, Law Day is celebrated on May 1. On this day, Americans are reminded that in order to protect their freedom, they must make good laws.

Be a good citizen and solve the magic word square below. (The answers will be the same across and down.)

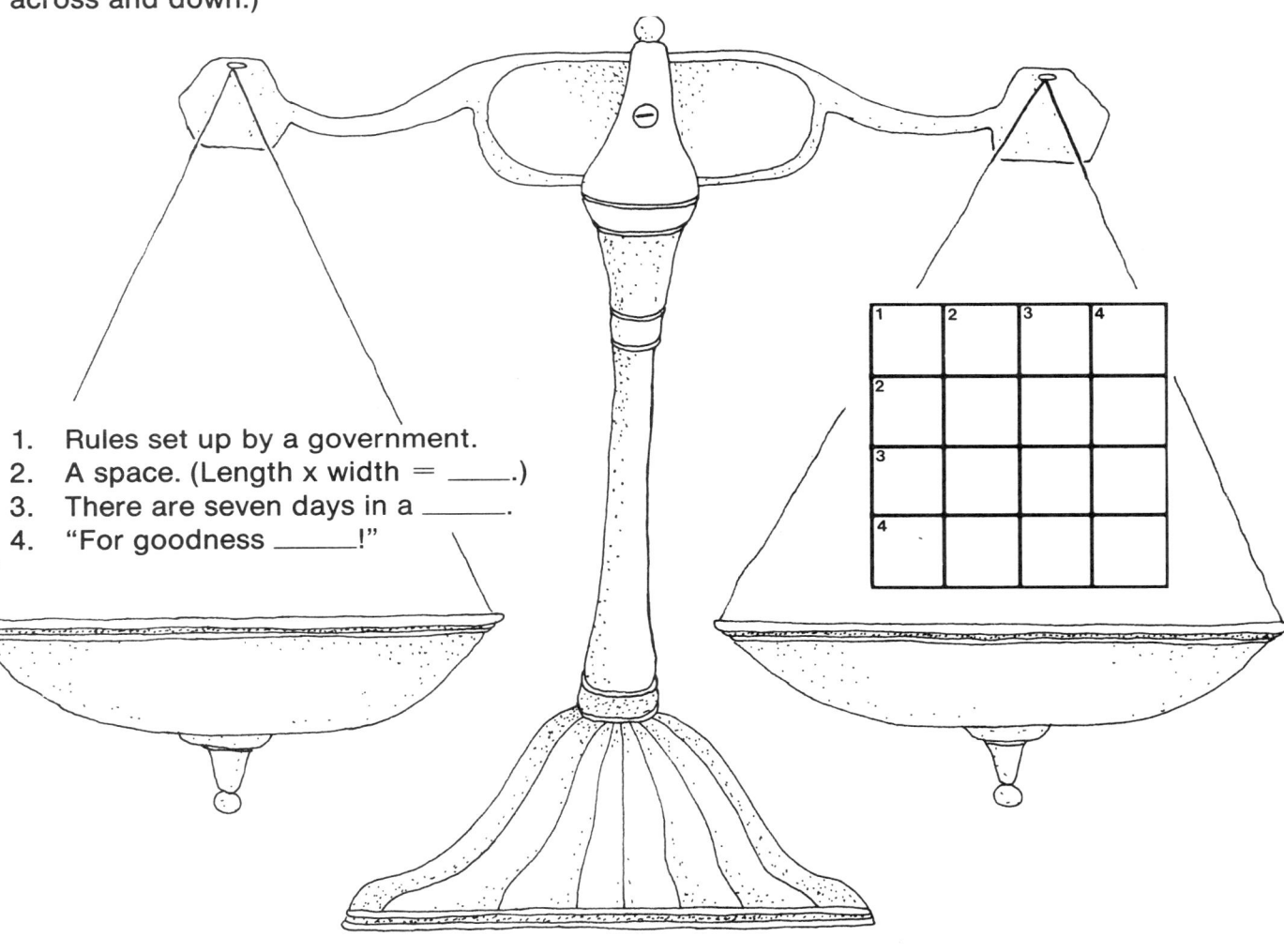

1. Rules set up by a government.
2. A space. (Length x width = _____.)
3. There are seven days in a _____.
4. "For goodness _____!"

Letter of the Law

The word *law* is part of each of the words below. Can you fill in the blanks to complete them? If you have trouble, take a look at the clues opposite.

___ L A W	A nail on the foot of a lion.
L A W ___	Grass.
___ ___ ___ L A W	A bandit.
L A W ___ ___ ___	Person trained in the law; attorney.
___ ___ ___ ___ ___ ___ ___ - ___ ___ - L A W	Sister of one's husband or wife.

Name: _____

TANGO-NO-SEKKU

Go Fly a Kite

Tango-no-Sekku (pronounced tahn-goh-noh-sek-koo) is a Japanese Kite Festival. Children fly all kinds of kites on this day, especially ones that look like a fish called a carp. Boys, in particular, will hang their fish kites on bamboo poles outside their homes.

Fly your own kite by completing the three magic word squares below. (Hint: The answers in each puzzle will be the same across and down.)

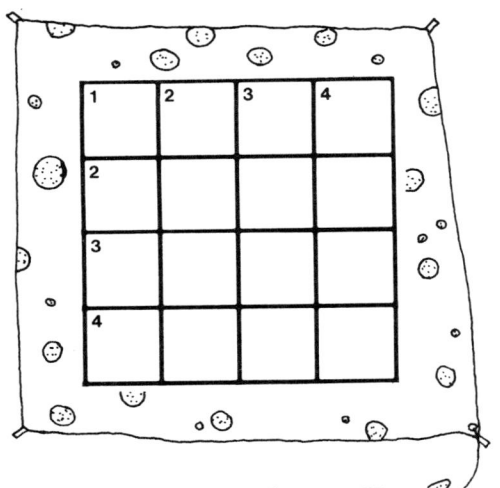

1. A water animal that has fins and gills.
2. A thought.
3. A sea animal with a round head, fur, and flippers.
4. One of two equal parts.

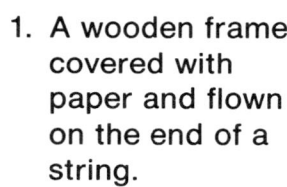

1. A wooden frame covered with paper and flown on the end of a string.
2. Use to press out wrinkles.
3. Stated.
4. The last parts of anything.

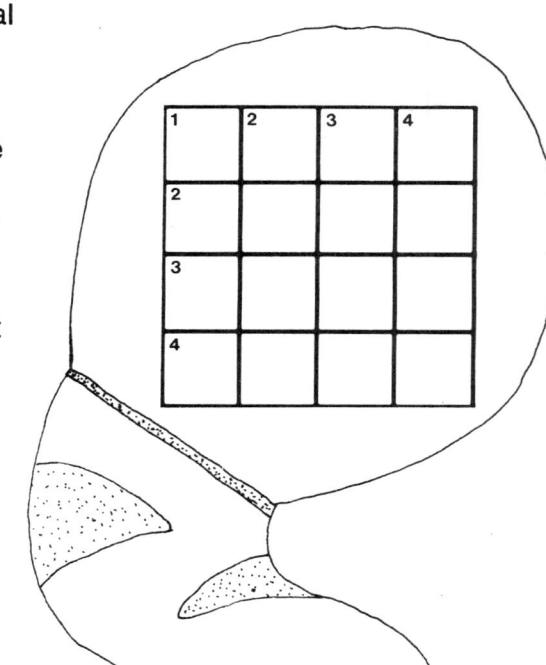

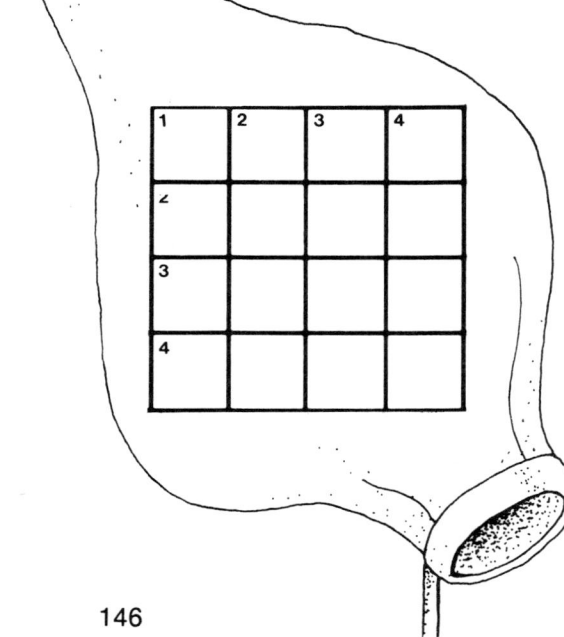

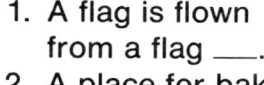

1. A flag is flown from a flag ___.
2. A place for baking.
3. To give something on condition it will be returned.
4. The last parts of anything.

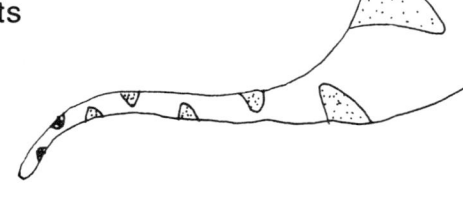

CINCO DE MAYO

A Special Date

On this day in 1862, Mexican soldiers were able, for a time, to prevent an invasion of their country by the French. *Cinco de Mayo* is Spanish for May 5th. If you successfully complete the magic word squares below, you will find this special date hidden in them. (The answers will be the same across and down.)

1. Three plus two equals _____.
2. A thought.
3. To change direction.
4. What you hear with.

5. The month that comes before June.
6. How old you are.
7. A desire or craving.

Good Neighbors

Because there are many Mexican-Americans in Southern California, this holiday is celebrated on both sides of the border. Join in the fiesta, too, and see how many good neighbors you can make by finding as many smaller words of two letters or more as you can from the word below. (There are at least 35.)

NEIGHBORS

1_____	10_____	19_____	28_____
2_____	11_____	20_____	29_____
3_____	12_____	21_____	30_____
4_____	13_____	22_____	31_____
5_____	14_____	23_____	32_____
6_____	15_____	24_____	33_____
7_____	16_____	25_____	34_____
8_____	17_____	26_____	35_____
9_____	18_____	27_____	

NATIVE AMERICAN DAY

Tribute to the First Americans

Today we pay tribute to the people who made their homes in North America long before the European settlers first came. Called Native Americans, they made up many different tribes.

Can you find the name of each tribe listed in the puzzle below? The names may be up, down, across, diagonal, or backwards. Circle each name as you find it.

SENECAS
KIOWAS
SEMINOLES
SIOUX
COMANCHES
CREEKS
APACHES
UTES
CHEROKEES
NAVAJOS

```
S  U  K  N  A  V  A  J  O  S
E  J  T  S  R  D  B  F  K  J
M  C  H  E  R  O  K  E  E  S
I  G  R  N  S  G  I  M  N  E
N  I  M  E  X  U  O  I  S  M
O  C  N  C  E  V  W  P  L  I
L  A  V  A  R  K  A  J  D  B
E  B  P  S  F  G  S  H  V  D
S  F  A  P  A  C  H  E  S  Q
L  C  O  M  A  N  C  H  E  S
```

Follow the Buffalo

One tribe of Native Americans, the Sioux, lived on the Great Plains, where the buffalo also roamed. They followed the herds, using buffalo hides to cover their houses (called tepees) and to make into clothing. For food, they ate pemmican (buffalo meat dried, pounded, and mixed with hot fat and berries and stuffed into animal skin).

Can you fit each of the underlined words from the paragraph above into the puzzle grid? (One has already been done for you.)

NATIVE AMERICAN DAY

Totems

A totem is a way of signing your name in picture form. Can you match the names to the totems? Draw a line from the name to the totem that correctly matches it.

Crazy Horse

Flying Eagle

Sun Woman

Striped Wolf

Mountain Flower

Singing-Long-Time

Many Moons

Native American tribes figured the months by the moon. Each month had a special name to describe it. The names below were used by the woodland Indians. Read the names given. Then fill in the blanks with the correct names from the list below.

JANUARY

_____

FEBRUARY

The Hunger Moon

MARCH

The Crow Moon

APRIL

The Green Grass Moon

MAY

_____

JUNE

The Rose Moon

JULY

The Thunder Moon

AUGUST

_____

SEPTEMBER

The Hunting Moon

OCTOBER

_____

NOVEMBER

The Mad Moon

DECEMBER

The Long Night Moon

The Green Corn Moon   The Planting Moon   The Snow Moon   The Falling Leaf Moon

Name: _____

FLORENCE NIGHTINGALE'S BIRTHDAY

A Famous Nurse

Florence Nightingale, the founder of modern nursing, was born on this day in 1820. As a nurse during the Crimean War, she became famous for her care of the sick and wounded. She was the first woman to receive the British Order of Merit.

   Can you find each of the underlined words in the paragraph above in the puzzle? They may be up, down, across, diagonal or backwards. Circle each word as you find it.

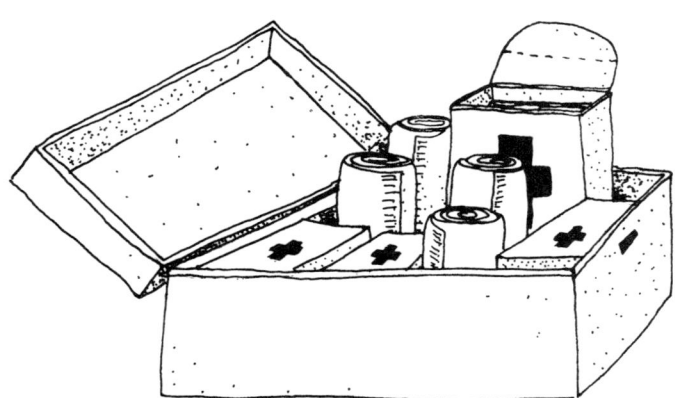

```
T  I  R  E  M  K  F  J  H  P  W
E  S  G  K  S  D  L  G  N  E  O
S  L  I  Q  V  K  O  X  M  N  U
R  B  K  C  F  I  R  S  T  G  N
U  D  L  M  K  Q  E  P  Z  C  D
N  I  G  H  T  I  N  G  A  L  E
C  Z  N  F  G  N  C  R  Q  N  D
K  B  C  R  I  M  E  A  N  F  B
W  O  M  A  N  M  O  W  G  D  R
J  C  D  B  R  I  T  I  S  H  N
P  X  O  R  D  E  R  S  F  B  X
```

A Bright Light

Because she believed that a nurse's work and care never ended, night or day, Florence Nightingale was given a special name. Unscramble the letters below to learn what it was.

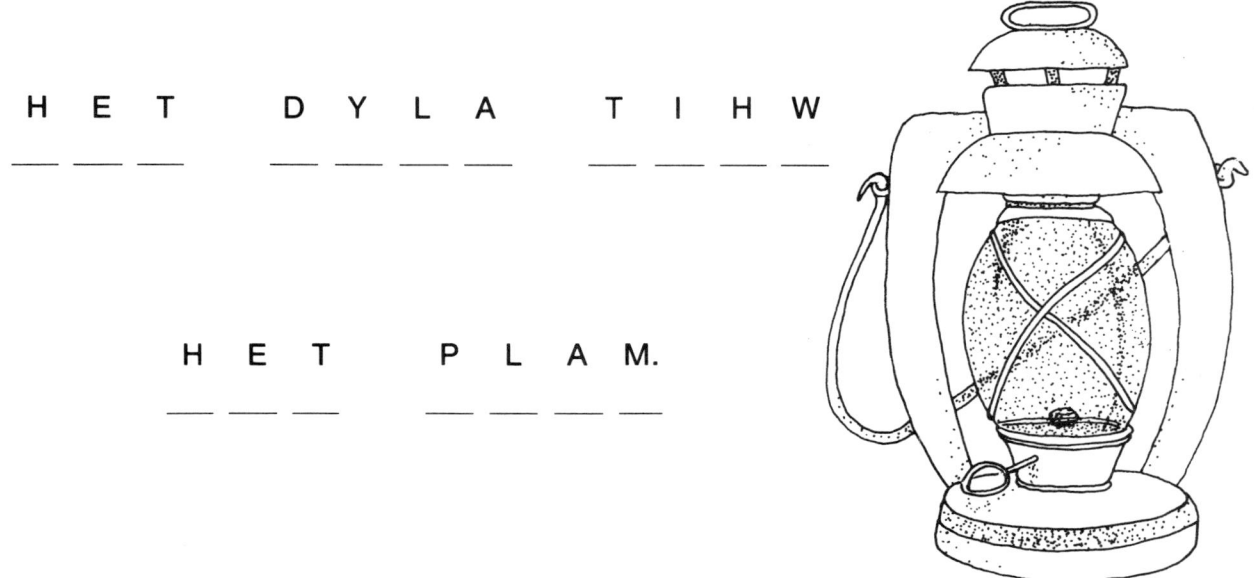

H E T   D Y L A   T I H W

___ ___ ___   ___ ___ ___ ___   ___ ___ ___ ___

H E T   P L A M.

___ ___ ___   ___ ___ ___ ___

MOTHER'S DAY

A Flower for Mom

At first, Anna M. Jarvis encouraged the idea of a "Mother's Day" in the United States to honor her own mother who died in May of 1905, but later she wanted it to honor all mothers.

Because her mother liked a certain flower, it became a custom to wear it in honor of one's own mother on this day.

Solve the picture puzzle to learn what kind of flower it is. Add and subtract the letters as shown from the names of the pictures.

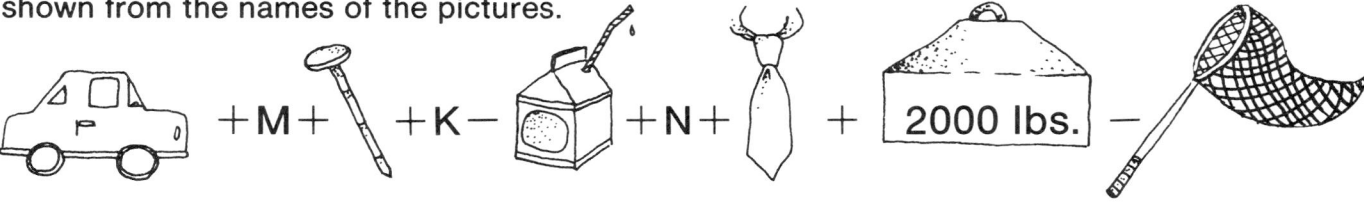

_____

To Go A-Mothering

In old <u>England</u>, <u>Mothering Sunday</u>, the fourth Sunday in Lent, was a popular holiday with <u>servants</u>, who were allowed to visit their <u>homes</u> on this day. The <u>eldest</u> son would bring a "mothering cake," a <u>plum</u> cake, to his mother and share it with the family.

Can you fit each of the underlined words in the paragraph above into the puzzle grid?

MOTHER'S DAY

With Love

When President Wilson proclaimed the first national Mother's Day in 1914, he called the celebration "a public expression of our love. . .for the mothers of our country."

Can you complete the two magic word squares below and pay tribute to mothers everywhere? The answers in each puzzle will be the same across and down.

1. Mother.
2. Less than two.
3. What a kitten says.

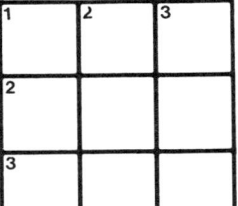

1. Mother.
2. Alike; related.
3. A place where money is produced.
4. Small insects that live in tunnels.

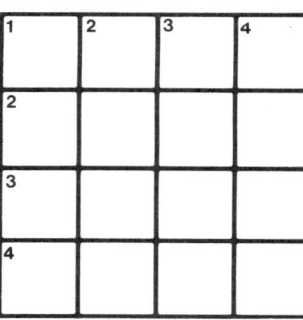

Can you fill in the word square opposite using only the following clues: two two-letter words, one of which is another name for mother?

Mom's Day

How many smaller words of two letters or more can you find hidden in the word . . .
MOTHER?   (There are at least 12.)

1. _____   5. _____   9. _____

2. _____   6. _____   10. _____

3. _____   7. _____   11. _____

4. _____   8. _____   12. _____

Name: _____

INTERNATIONAL PICKLE WEEK

A Pickled Puzzle

Can you fit each word from the list of ingredients used to make pickles into the puzzle grid below? (One is already done for you.)

   Now don't get in a pickle! It's easier than it looks.

Ingredients for making pickles:

cucumbers

salt

water

garlic

dill

vinegar

A Green Giggle

Don't be a picklepuss. Solve the joke below and get a chuckle! (Hint: It is written as a 3-shift cipher. A=D, B=E, C=F, and so on.)

What is green and half a mile high?

Q E B   B J M F O B   P Q X Q B

___ ___ ___   ___ ___ ___ ___ ___ ___   ___ ___ ___ ___ ___

M F Z H I B

___ ___ ___ ___ ___ ___

ARMED FORCES DAY

Atten-tion!

On this day we celebrate the men and women of the U.S. Armed Forces: the army, navy, air force, marines, and coast guard.

   Decode the answers to the riddles below and get into the military spirit! (Hint: The answers are written as 4-shift ciphers. A=E, B=F, C=G, and so on.)

What's the first thing a sailor does when he or she falls overboard?

  C   A   P   O   S   A   P.

__ __ __ __   __ __ __

What did the soldier say when the armored car stopped to pick
  him up?

  P   W   J   G   U   K   Q.

__ __ __ __   __ __ __

Why did the pilot fly over the mountain?

  X   A   Y   W   Q   O   A   O   D   A

__ __ __ __ __ __ __   __ __ __

  Y   K   Q   H   Z   J'   P   B   H   U

__ __ __ __ __ __ __   __ __ __

  Q   J   Z   A   N   E   P.

__ __ __ __ __   __ __

Name: _____

VICTORIA DAY

Fit for a Queen

The birthday of Queen Victoria is a holiday celebrated in Great Britain and in Canada. Victoria, "Queen of Great Britain and Ireland and Empress of India," was born on this day in 1819.

Here's a royal puzzle to solve. Subtract one letter at a time, keeping the letter order the same, and make a different word for each step of the puzzle.

C R O W N

_ _ _ _

_ _ _

_ _

_

What's in a Name?

The name Victoria is Latin for "victorious."

Here are some other names. Can you match each with its meaning? Draw a line from the name in the first column to its correct meaning in the second column.

Angela	A flower
Leo	A dweller at the ford near the cliff
Joy	Heavenly messenger
Noel	The lion
Carol	The break of day
Glen	Christmas
Dawn	Delight
Clifford	A gem
Opal	Of the valley
Flora	Song of joy

Name: _____

SALLY RIDE'S BIRTHDAY

Blast Off!

Sally Ride, born on this day in 1951, was the first U.S. woman in space. Together with the rest of the crew of the space shuttle *Challenger*, she blasted off on June 18, 1983.

Head for outer space yourself by solving the puzzle below. How many different names of things in outer space can you discover hidden in the puzzle? For each name, you may use the letters given in any order, but only as often as they appear in the star. (There are at least five.)

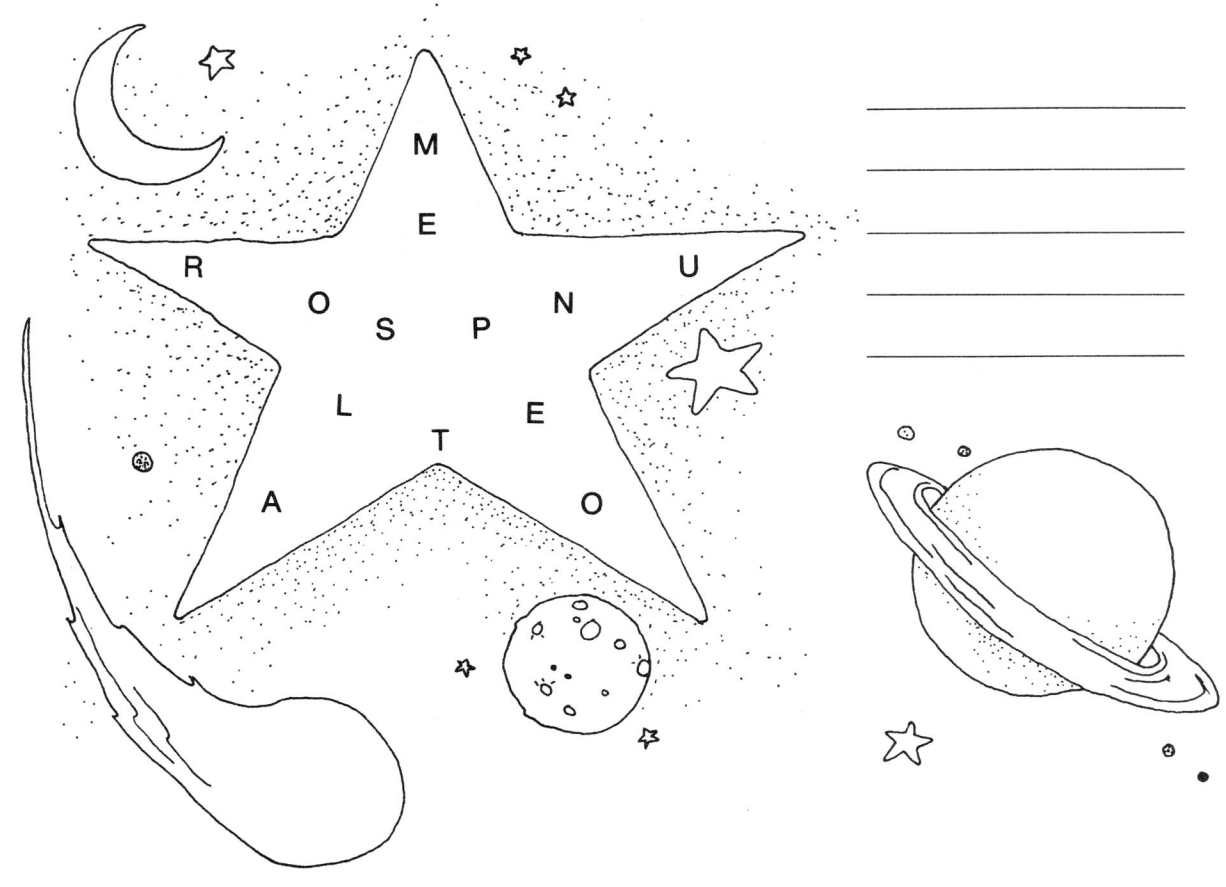

_____

_____

_____

_____

_____

Exploring Space

Unscramble the letters in each of the words below to make a brand new word. (The first is already done.)

Can you find some rodents hidden in STAR?   _____RATS_____

Can you find a valentine in EARTH?   _____

Can you find some male sheep in MARS?   _____

Can you find several coats without sleeves in SPACE?   _____

MEMORIAL DAY

Name: _____

Remembering

Memorial Day was first celebrated in 1868. Then it was called "Decoration Day" because people decorated the graves of Civil War soldiers to honor and remember them.

Help to honor all war heroes. Find as many words of three letters or more as you can in the word below. (There are at least 50.)

D E C O R A T I O N

1. _____	13. _____	26. _____	39. _____
2. _____	14. _____	27. _____	40. _____
3. _____	15. _____	28. _____	41. _____
4. _____	16. _____	29. _____	42. _____
5. _____	17. _____	30. _____	43. _____
6. _____	18. _____	31. _____	44. _____
7. _____	19. _____	32. _____	45. _____
8. _____	20. _____	33. _____	46. _____
9. _____	21. _____	34. _____	47. _____
10. _____	22. _____	35. _____	48. _____
11. _____	23. _____	36. _____	49. _____
12. _____	24. _____	37. _____	50. _____
	25. _____	38. _____	

Symbol of Hope

Red silk or paper poppies are sold at this time of year in order to raise money to aid disabled veterans. Poppies are a symbol of hope because they bloomed in the European fields destroyed by World War I.

Complete the magic word square below. The answers will be the same across and down.

1. Color of the poppies.
2. A period of time.
3. The last Monday in May is Memorial _____.

Name: _____

JEFFERSON DAVIS'S BIRTHDAY

Dixie Land

Jefferson Davis, born on this day in 1808, was an American statesman and President of the Confederacy. The Confederacy was made up of 11 states that left the U.S. government in 1860-61. On April 12, 1861, civil war broke out between these states ("the South") and "the North."

How many of the Confederate states listed below can you find in the puzzle? They may be up, down, across, diagonal, or backwards. Circle each word as you find it.

SOUTH CAROLINA
MISSISSIPPI
FLORIDA
ALABAMA
GEORGIA
LOUISIANA
TEXAS
ARKANSAS
NORTH CAROLINA
VIRGINIA
TENNESSEE

```
S  O  U  T  H  C  A  R  O  L  I  N  A  K
O  L  K  G  J  X  B  D  F  N  A  M  R  Q
U  Q  R  P  C  D  P  N  X  Y  N  S  K  G
T  J  L  S  A  S  N  A  K  R  A  T  A  B
F  P  V  M  I  S  S  I  S  S  I  P  P  I
R  T  I  J  K  G  P  S  B  F  S  C  D  F
N  O  R  T  H  C  A  R  O  L  I  N  A  K
B  Q  G  B  J  L  X  G  V  O  U  M  I  W
S  L  I  C  D  F  T  H  I  R  O  P  G  D
T  E  N  N  E  S  S  E  E  I  L  X  R  C
E  K  I  R  H  Z  J  K  X  D  F  L  O  M
N  J  A  A  M  A  B  A  L  A  H  N  E  R
N  G  D  S  R  C  S  J  G  K  S  P  G  Q
E  M  P  Q  H  T  B  H  L  R  T  U  Z  V
```

The Dividing Line

During the Civil War, the Mason-Dixon Line was thought by many to be the point that divided the North from the South.

The line was actually the boundary between two states. Do you know which states? To find out, unscramble the words below.

N E P Y N S L A V A I N

___ ___ ___ ___ ___ ___ ___ ___ ___ ___ ___ ___

Y A R M D L A N

___ ___ ___ ___ ___ ___ ___ ___

KAMEHAMEHA DAY

Hawaiian Feast

In 1795, Kamehameha (pronounced: kah-may-hah-may-hah) founded the Kingdom of Hawaii when he united the islands for the first time. To celebrate this occasion, come to the special feast called a luau (loo-ow).

　　The main dish at a luau is usually roast pork. A fat, young <u>pig</u> is stuffed with <u>hot</u> lava <u>stones</u> and <u>wrapped</u> in a blanket of native ti-plant <u>leaves</u>. It is then laid on a bed of hot <u>coals</u>, covered in <u>dirt</u>, and <u>baked</u> underground for many hours.

Can you fit each of the underlined words from the paragraph above into the puzzle grid? (One is already done for you.)

Tropical Delights

Along with roast pork, there are many other special dishes often served at a luau. How many of them can you find in the puzzle below? The words may be up, down, across, diagonal, or backwards. Circle each word as you find it.

Sweet POTATOES
Raw FISH
KELP (from the ocean)
BANANAS
BREADFRUIT
PAPAYA
COCONUT Milk
PINEAPPLE Juice

```
F  C  O  C  Q  N  V  P  X  J  G
R  I  K  L  D  C  B  K  N  V  T
U  R  S  E  O  T  A  T  O  P  I
I  K  R  H  L  S  N  G  B  I  U
P  M  B  P  A  P  A  Y  A  N  R
K  N  C  D  R  L  N  J  K  E  F
J  D  F  G  H  M  A  Q  V  A  D
G  F  S  Z  D  Y  S  X  B  P  A
H  K  N  C  M  P  G  L  Q  P  E
C  O  C  O  N  U  T  J  X  L  R
M  U  W  H  R  P  S  D  C  E  B
```

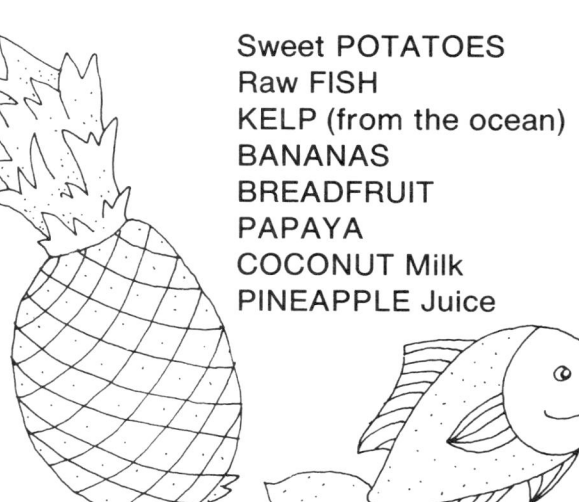

159

FLAG DAY

Name: _____

Red, White, and Blue

Why does the American flag look the way it does? According to George Washington, "We take the <u>star</u> from <u>Heaven</u>, the <u>red</u> from our <u>mother</u> <u>country</u>, separating it by <u>white</u> <u>stripes</u>, thus showing that we have <u>separated</u> from her, and the white stripes shall go down. . .representing <u>liberty</u>."

Can you find each of the underlined words in the puzzle below? They may be up, down, across, diagonal, or backwards. Circle each word as you find it.

```
S  T  A  B  N  M  Q  L  P  Y
R  E  S  K  D  G  S  F  S  T
W  H  I  T  E  D  M  X  E  R
H  N  L  Z  A  E  O  Q  P  E
I  S  E  P  I  R  T  S  A  B
F  Y  J  B  S  C  H  J  R  I
X  M  C  G  F  M  E  H  A  L
D  C  O  U  N  T  R  Y  T  J
P  R  M  Z  N  E  V  A  E  H
K  Q  T  S  L  F  B  C  D  G
```

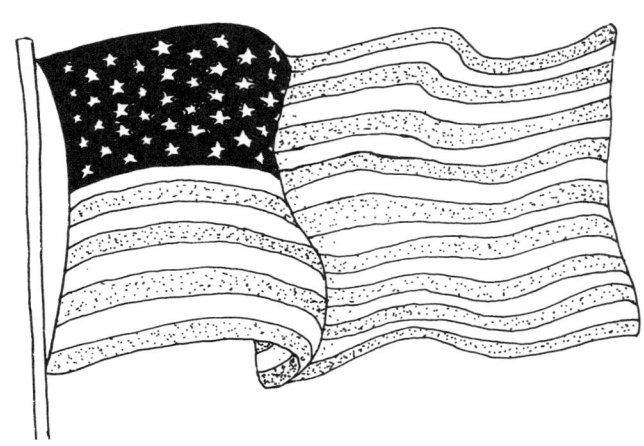

A Musical Salute

Do you know the name of a song that was written about the American flag? To find out what it is solve the puzzle below.

   Look at the pictures. Put the name of what you see in the spaces below each picture. The numbers under the spaces are a code that will help you learn the tune.

__ __ __ __   __ __ __   __ __ __   __ __ __ __   __ __ __ __
7 1 9 8   10 2 6   11 13 3   12 2 1 5   4 2 9 4

__ __ __   __ __ __ __
4 7 2   3 4 1 5

__ __ __ __ __ __   __ __ __ __ __
3 12 1 9 6 10   2 8 11 1 9 9 2 5

FLAG DAY

Name: _____

A Grand Old Flag

Can you fit the underlined words of the Pledge of Allegiance into the puzzle grid below? (One has already been done.)

I pledge allegiance to the flag of the United States of America and to the Republic for which it stands, one nation under God, indivisible, with liberty and justice for all.

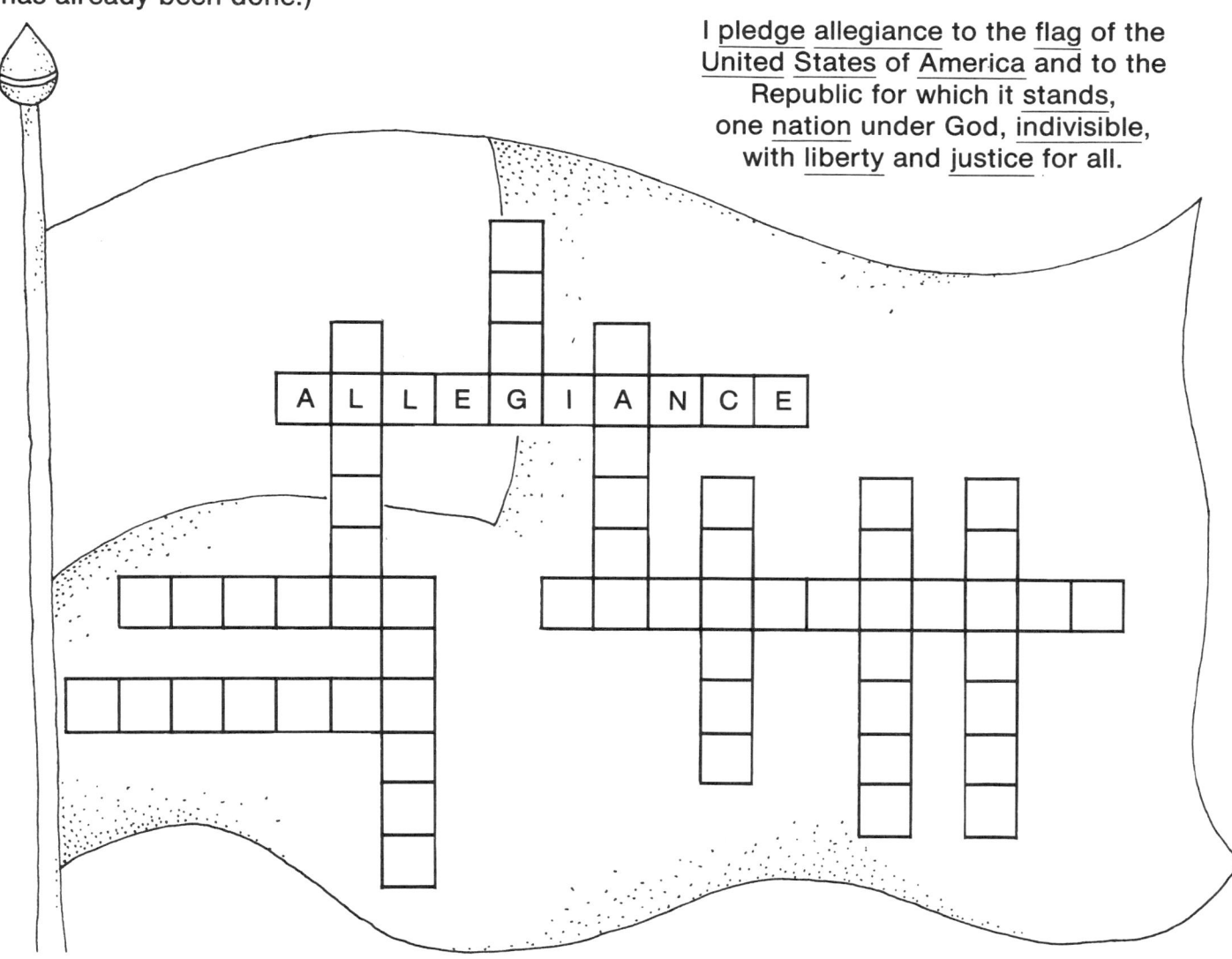

The Stars and Stripes

Legend has it that George Washington asked someone to make the first flag of the United States. Unscramble the letters in the name below to see who that person was.

S E T B Y   S O R S

___ ___ ___ ___ ___   ___ ___ ___ ___

Name: _____

CHILDREN'S DAY

Flower Children

Today is the day many Protestant churches dedicate to the interests of boys and girls. Originally, this day was called Rose Day. It probably began when children brought flowers to church for May Day. Since more flowers were available in June, the holiday was moved.

Can you complete the magic word square and have it coming up roses? (The answers will be the same across and down.)

1. A flower the children carried on this day.
2. Not closed.
3. To make something go somewhere else.
4. The last parts of anything.

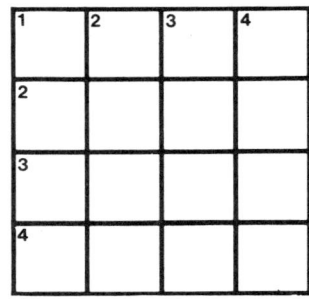

Counting the Kids

Try to find at least 21 smaller words of three letters or more in the word

C H I L D R E N

1. _____
2. _____
3. _____
4. _____
5. _____
6. _____
7. _____

8. _____
9. _____
10. _____
11. _____
12. _____
13. _____
14. _____

15. _____
16. _____
17. _____
18. _____
19. _____
20. _____
21. _____

162

FATHER'S DAY

Hip, Hip, Hooray!

On the third Sunday in June every year, we take time out to honor fathers. Here's your chance to give three cheers for dad by doing the three magic word squares below. Each puzzle has a different name for father hidden in it. (The answers in each puzzle will be the same across and down.)

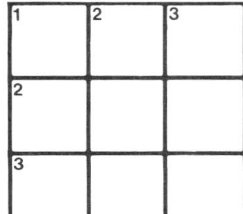

1. Father.
2. I am, he is, you _____.
3. A lion lives in one.

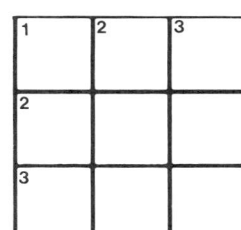

1. Father; also the noise a cork makes coming out of a bottle.
2. A single thing.
3. A dog or cat.

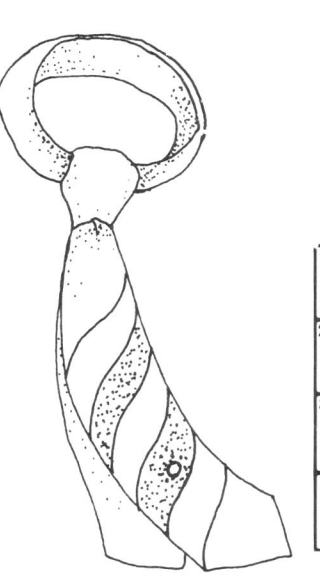

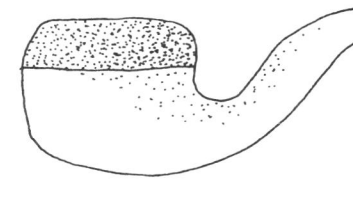

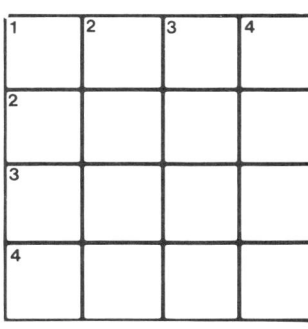

1. Father.
2. Alike, related.
3. Two of these equal a quart.
4. Tiny insects that live in tunnels.

Dad's Day

How many smaller words of three letters or more can you find hidden in the word FATHER? (There are at least 20.)

F   A   T   H   E   R

1. _____   6. _____   11. _____   16. _____

2. _____   7. _____   12. _____   17. _____

3. _____   8. _____   13. _____   18. _____

4. _____   9. _____   14. _____   19. _____

5. _____   10. _____   15. _____   20. _____

FATHER'S DAY

Name: _____

Famous Fathers

Can you figure out who the "fathers" are in the riddles below?
   Look at the pictures. Put the name of what you see in the spaces below each picture. The numbers under the spaces are a code that will help you learn the answers.

$\overline{\ \ }\ \overline{\ \ }\ \overline{\ \ }\ \overline{\ \ }\ \overline{\ \ }$
7 8 14 17 18

$\overline{\ \ }\ \overline{\ \ }\ \overline{\ \ }$
15 1 13

$\overline{\ \ }\ \overline{\ \ }\ \overline{\ \ }\ \overline{\ \ }$
3 14 16 13

$\overline{\ \ }\ \overline{\ \ }\ \overline{\ \ }\ \overline{\ \ }$
12 9 11 10

$\overline{\ \ }\ \overline{\ \ }\ \overline{\ \ }$
10 5 19

$\overline{\ \ }\ \overline{\ \ }\ \overline{\ \ }$
2 5 4

$\overline{\ \ }\ \overline{\ \ }\ \overline{\ \ }\ \overline{\ \ }$
6 9 17 8

(Santa Claus) $\overline{\ \ }\ \overline{\ \ }\ \overline{\ \ }\ \overline{\ \ }\ \overline{\ \ }\ \overline{\ \ }\ \ \overline{\ \ }\ \overline{\ \ }\ \overline{\ \ }\ \overline{\ \ }\ \overline{\ \ }\ \overline{\ \ }\ \overline{\ \ }\ \overline{\ \ }\ \overline{\ \ }$
6 1 18 8 5 16   3 8 16 9 17 18 12 1 17

(The Old Year) $\overline{\ \ }\ \overline{\ \ }\ \overline{\ \ }\ \overline{\ \ }\ \overline{\ \ }\ \overline{\ \ }\ \ \overline{\ \ }\ \overline{\ \ }\ \overline{\ \ }\ \overline{\ \ }$
6 1 18 8 5 16   18 9 12 5

(A spider-like insect) $\overline{\ \ }\ \overline{\ \ }\ \overline{\ \ }\ \overline{\ \ }\ \overline{\ \ }\ \text{-}\ \overline{\ \ }\ \overline{\ \ }\ \overline{\ \ }\ \overline{\ \ }\ \overline{\ \ }\ \overline{\ \ }\ \overline{\ \ }\ \overline{\ \ }$
4 1 4 4 19   11 14 13 7 11 5 7 17

(Pennsylvania at the Post Office) $\overline{\ \ }\ \overline{\ \ }$
15 1

Pop Goes the Puzzle

Follow the clues and fill in the blanks with four different words that have a pop in them.

P O P __ __   (A flower.)

P O P __ __ __   (A tree.)

P O P __ __ __ __   (A snack.)

P O P __ __ __ __ __ __ __   (The total number of people living in an area.)

SUMMER

Name: _____

Buzz Words

How many insects can you find "buzzing around" this summer puzzler? The words may be up, down, across, diagonal, or backwards. Circle each word as you find it.

```
C A T E R P H T F N R P
T A N G B C T H H M O T
X K T S U C O L P O R M
G Z E E B W M X Z S J K
N L R F R Y T E R Q M I
A O M Z Q P M B Z U S M
P N I R N A I F K I U O
X E T B C A T L J T V S
K J E C G R Q Y L O G Z
G M N V O J L P S A W V
H B C E D F W X A M R T
R T E R N I P F G K H Z
```

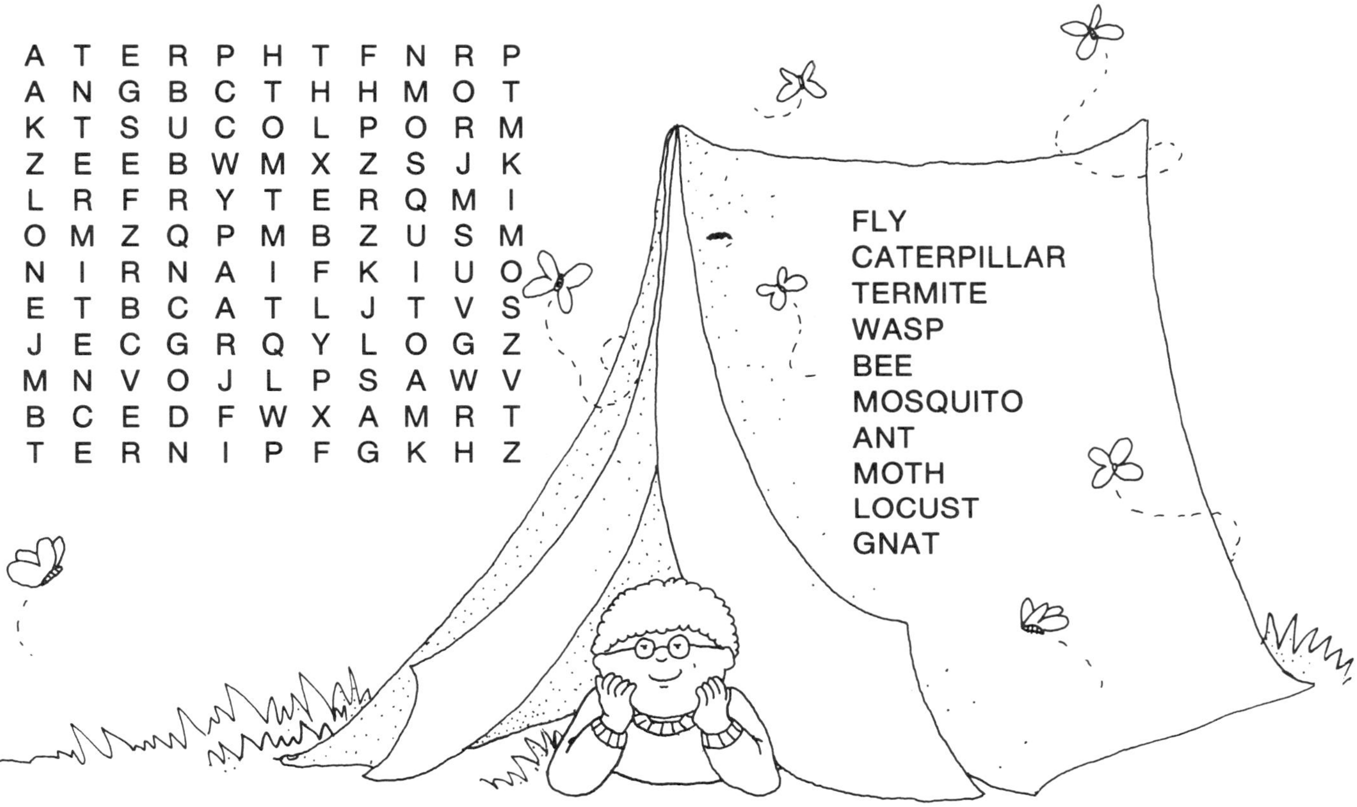

FLY
CATERPILLAR
TERMITE
WASP
BEE
MOSQUITO
ANT
MOTH
LOCUST
GNAT

A Zinger!

Add and subtract the letters as shown from the picture puzzle below to—ouch!—get the joke.

What did the camper say to the mosquito?

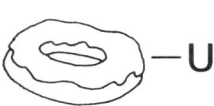 −U   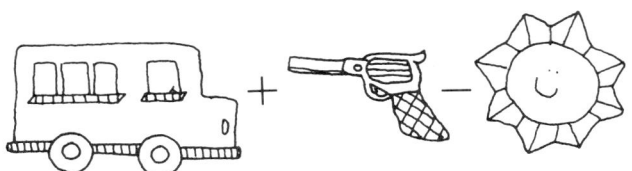   C+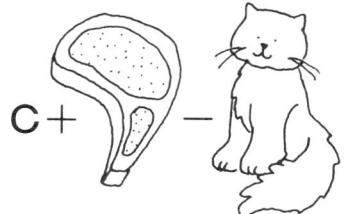

_____   _____   _____

Name: _____

SUMMER

Let the Sunshine In

Add one letter at a time to form a new word for each step and really get things "glowing"!

I
_ _
_ _ _
_ _ _ _
SHINE

Ahoy There!

How many kinds of boats can you find hidden in the puzzle below? There are at least five.

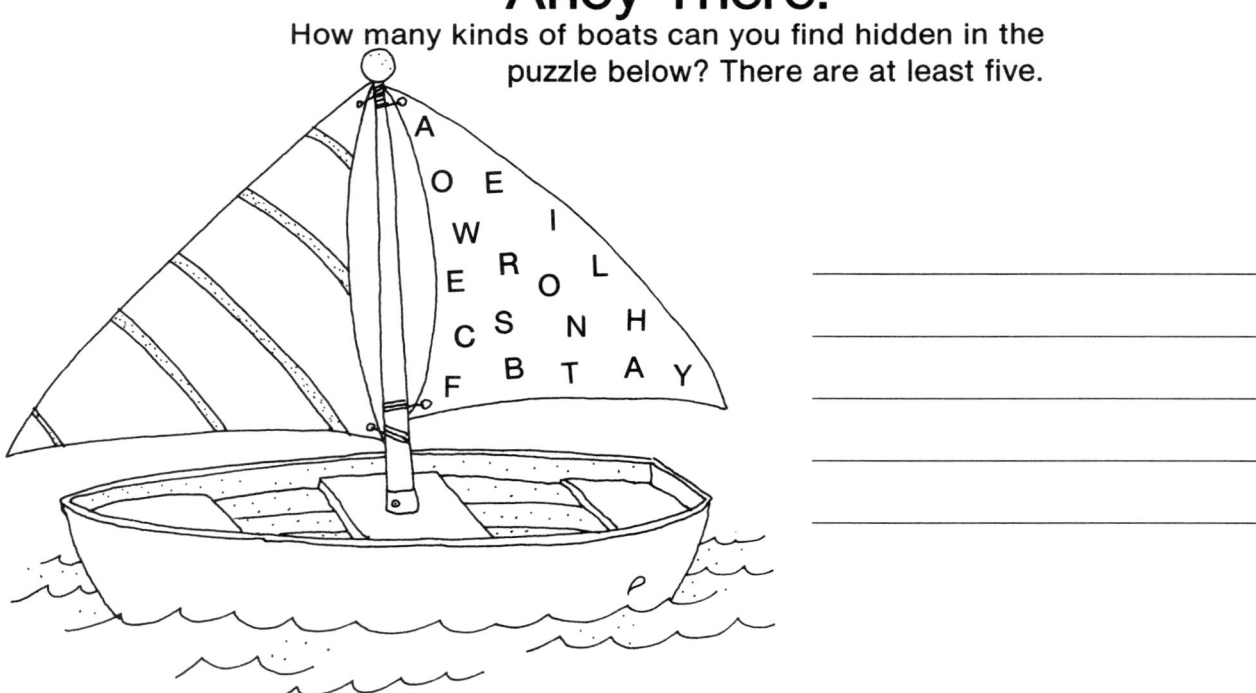

_____

_____

_____

_____

SUMMER

Name: _____

Summer Fun

Have a "hot time in the old town" with this super summer crossword puzzle!

(Crossword grid with letters S, U, M, M, E, R filling column 15)

WORD BANK

green	she	sunny
warmer	ada	pools
rose	funny	east
yard	on	daisies
tan	ft	spry
pt	ah	soar
rn	daylight	yo
KM	wow	TR
ad	eve	op
swimmer	ski	sea
ash	sod	ho
loan	its	er

ACROSS:

1. Flowers that have a yellow center and white petals.
6. You swim in these.
9. A notice used to sell something.
10. An exclamation.
11. Abbrev. for operation.
12. In summer, a person might bar-b-que in his/her back_____.
14. A body of salt water.
15. A glider can _____ through the sky.
17. Abbrev. for feet.
18. The nicest summer days are clear and _____.
19. Of or belonging to it.
22. Initials of the king with the golden touch.
23. Color of healthy grass.
25. A person who passes through the water by using legs and arms.
28. Registered Nurse.
29. A hearty laugh.
30. To make the skin brown by exposing it to the sun.
31. The way a soldier says "present."
32. Summer days are usually _____ than spring days.

DOWN:

1. During summer, there are more hours of _____.
2. A girl's name.
3. Grass and the layer of soil just underneath it.
4. The sun rises in the _____.
5. He and _____.
6. Abbrev. for part time.
7. To lend.
8. Active, nimble.
13. A popular flower that has thorns.
15. The season that comes between spring and autumn.
16. Opposite of off.
17. Amusing; makes one laugh.
18. You can do this on water or snow.
20. Initials of Theodore Roosevelt.
21. A shade tree.
24. A person that sings is a sing_____.
26. An exclamation.
27. The evening or day before a holiday.

Name: _____

MIDSUMMER'S DAY

Salute the Sun

At dawn on this day, the ancient Celtics would hold a special ceremony to salute the rising sun. At night, people would light a chain of bonfires across the hilltops to frighten away evil spirits.

   Help to light one of the fires by seeing how many smaller words of two letters or more you can find in the word below. (There are at least 24.)

B O N F I R E S

1._____   7._____   13._____   19._____

2._____   8._____   14._____   20._____

3._____   9._____   15._____   21._____

4._____   10._____   16._____   22._____

5._____   11._____   17._____   23._____

6._____   12._____   18._____   24._____

Jump the Flame

In France, it is an ancient belief that crops will grow as high as a person can jump over a bonfire on this day.

   The little poem below is all about someone who is very good at this trick. Can you translate it? (Hint: It is written as a 3-shift cipher. A=D, B=E, C=F, and so on.)

G X Z H   Y B   K F J Y I B

__ __ __ __   __ __   __ __ __ __ __ __

G X Z H   Y B   N R F Z H

__ __ __ __   __ __   __ __ __ __ __

G X Z H   G R J M   L S B O

__ __ __ __   __ __ __ __   __ __ __ __

Q E B   Z X K A I B P Q F Z H.

__ __ __   __ __ __ __ __ __ __ __ __ __ __.

Name: _____

HELEN KELLER'S BIRTHDAY

Talking with Your Hands

Helen Keller was born today in the year 1880. Blind and deaf from early childhood, she had to learn a special way to communicate. Annie Sullivan, her teacher, taught her the *manual alphabet* by spelling the names of familiar objects into her hand.

Take a look at the manual alphabet below. Now try to read the answers to the riddles.

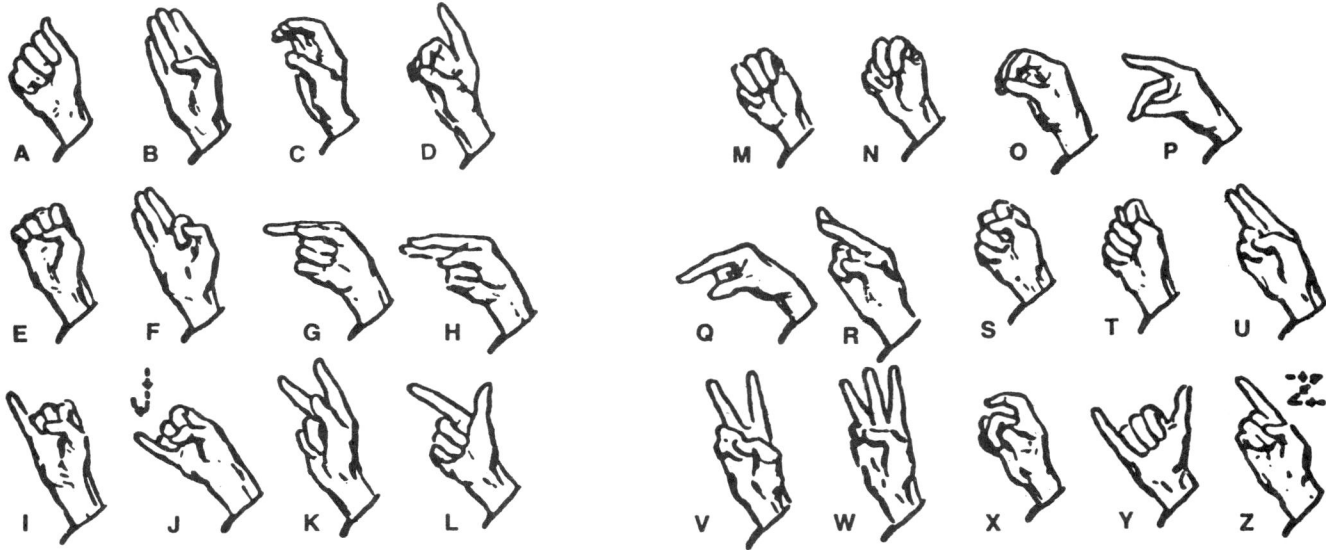

What five-letter word has six left when you take two away?

_____

When is a piece of wood like a king?

____ ____ ____ ____

What bird is found at every meal?

____ ____

Name: _____

GREEN CORN CELEBRATION

A Magic Bundle

Each year at this time, the Seminole Indians of Florida gather to celebrate the Green Corn Festival. An important part of the celebration is when the tribe's medicine man brings the "Magic Medicine Bundle" from its hiding place in the swamp. The "Bundle" holds objects that are sacred to the tribe: magic <u>stones</u>, magic <u>powder</u>, dried <u>roots</u> and <u>herbs</u>, bits of <u>horn</u> and <u>bone</u>, <u>feathers</u>, and <u>snake fangs</u>.

   The medicine man must check to see that none of the objects are missing. Help him by finding each of the words underlined above in the puzzle. They may be up, down, across, diagonal, or backwards. Circle each word as you find it.

```
H  S  Q  M  V  J  G  R  K  N
O  K  T  X  G  B  X  N  C  D
R  B  P  O  W  D  E  R  F  G
M  C  D  R  N  E  N  O  B  H
G  R  F  F  P  E  K  H  M  Z
R  Q  M  L  A  D  S  E  A  V
K  O  E  K  A  N  S  R  G  W
L  S  O  G  P  C  G  B  I  R
F  E  A  T  H  E  R  S  C  L
K  T  Y  N  S  J  L  M  Q  P
```

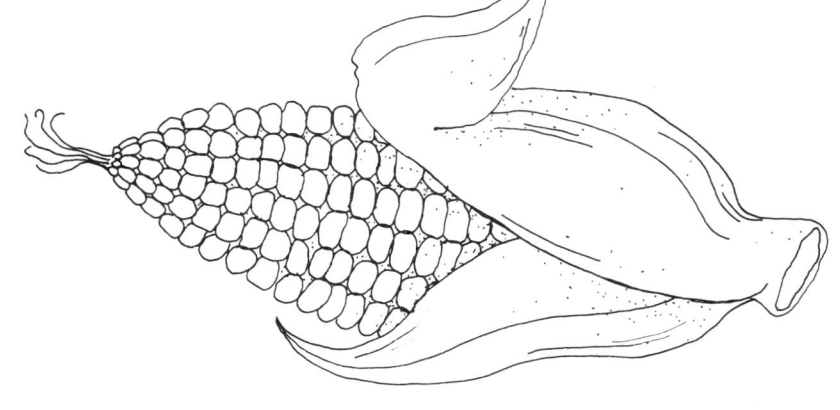

Dances

The "Magic Bundle" is placed near the great campfire and the people dance around it. Seminole dances imitate nature. There are the <u>Buffalo</u> Dance, the <u>Chicken</u> Dance, the <u>Alligator</u> Dance, the <u>Catfish</u> Dance, and the <u>Green Corn</u> Dance.

   Can you fit each of the underlined words in the puzzle grid?

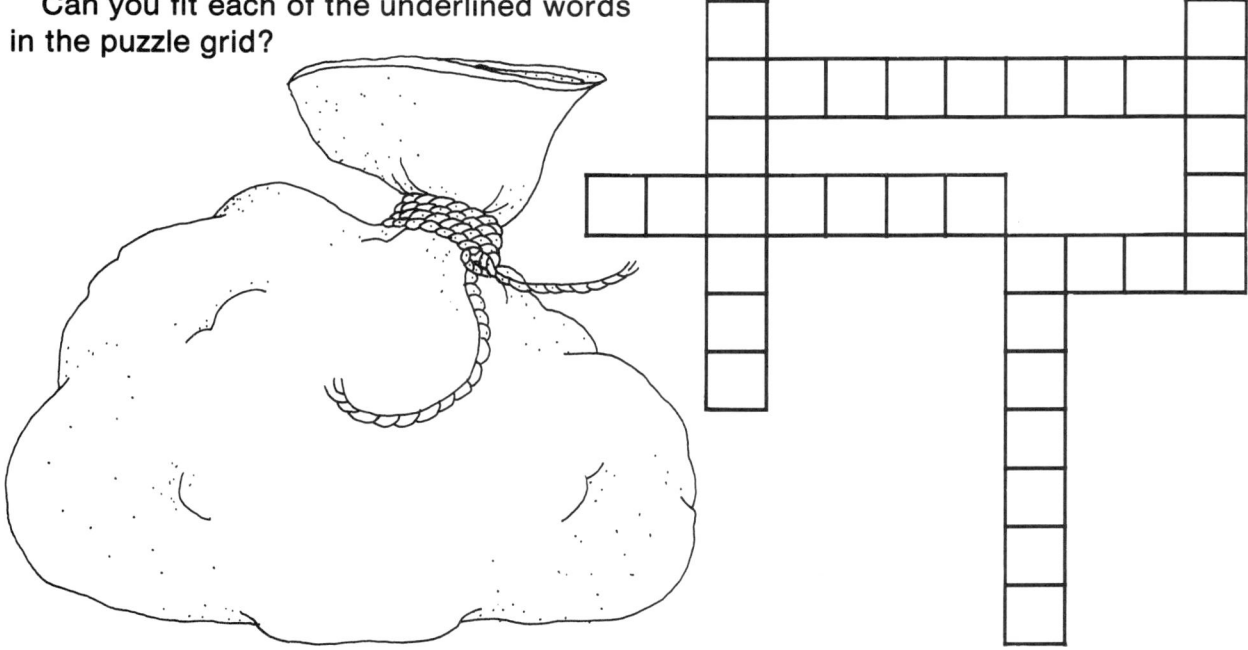

CANADA DAY

Name: _____

O' Canada!

On this day in 1867, the first four provinces of Canada were united to form the Dominion of Canada.

Listed below are the 10 provinces and two territories that make up Canada today. Can you find each of them in the puzzle? The names may be up, down, across, diagonal, or backward. Circle each name as you find it.

NEWFOUNDLAND
NOVA SCOTIA
NEW BRUNSWICK
PRINCE EDWARD ISLAND
QUEBEC
ONTARIO
MANITOBA
SASKATCHEWAN
ALBERTA
BRITISH COLUMBIA
YUKON (Territory)
NORTHWEST (Territory)

```
C  O  N  T  A  P  Q  S  G  M  H  J  K  L  B
N  N  E  W  F  O  U  N  D  L  A  N  D  P  I
E  N  O  V  Q  J  M  L  G  V  H  B  C  R  S
W  O  C  K  Y  U  K  O  N  R  T  A  S  I  L
B  R  G  F  D  C  E  B  M  J  K  I  A  N  A
R  T  S  A  T  R  E  B  L  A  G  T  B  C  N
U  H  U  G  S  O  H  B  E  F  J  O  O  E  D
N  W  N  L  K  N  O  R  V  C  S  C  T  E  K
S  E  P  B  F  T  N  Z  B  F  H  S  I  D  J
W  S  A  S  K  A  T  C  H  E  W  A  N  W  B
I  T  B  G  V  R  A  Q  G  M  N  V  A  A  F
C  X  D  M  W  I  Y  L  P  B  R  O  M  R  M
K  L  A  B  M  O  V  A  S  C  O  N  T  D  R
B  R  I  T  I  S  H  C  O  L  U  M  B  I  A
M  X  G  P  R  L  K  C  D  F  Z  H  Y  B  V
```

Canada's Breadbasket

How many words of three letters or more can you find in Canada's greatest wheat-growing region? (There are at least 40. Use the back of this page to complete your list.)

S A S K A T C H E W A N

1. _____ 7. _____ 13. _____ 19. _____

2. _____ 8. _____ 14. _____ 20. _____

3. _____ 9. _____ 15. _____ 21. _____

4. _____ 10. _____ 16. _____ 22. _____

5. _____ 11. _____ 17. _____ 23. _____

6. _____ 12. _____ 18. _____ 24. _____

FIRST REGULAR TV TELECASTS

A First TV Show

In 1936, RCA (which owned NBC) installed TV sets in 150 homes in the New York City area. NBC began broadcasting to these homes. To learn the name of the first TV show they saw, solve the puzzle below.

Look at the pictures. Put the name of what you see in the spaces below each picture. The numbers under the spaces are a code that will help you discover the answer.

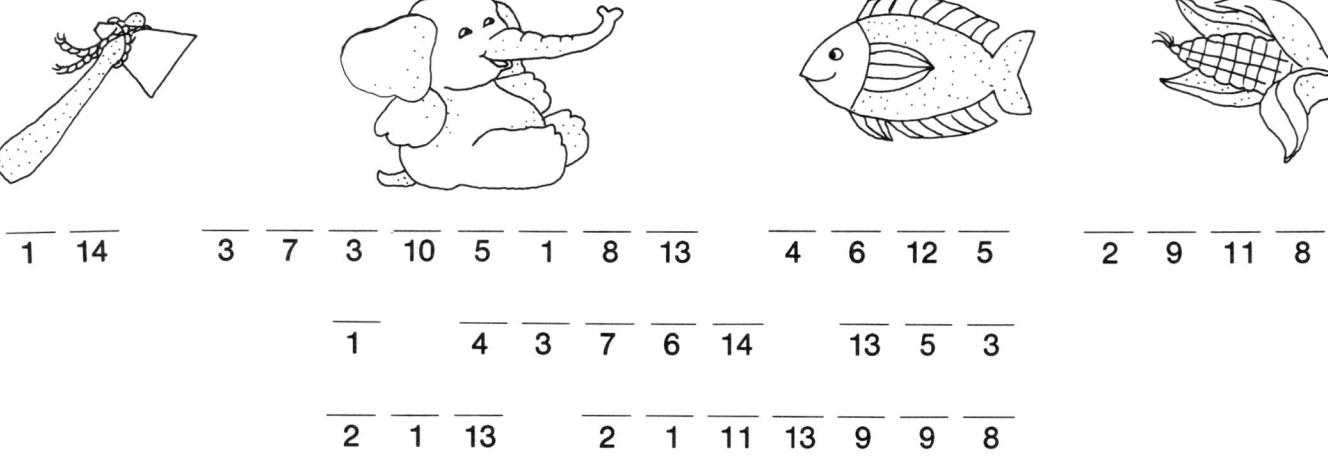

    ___ ___   ___ ___ ___ ___ ___ ___   ___ ___ ___ ___   ___ ___ ___ ___
     1   14   3   7   3   10   5   1   4   6   12   5   2   9   11   8

                     ___   ___ ___ ___ ___ ___ ___   ___ ___ ___
                      1   4   3   7   6   14   13   5   3

                     ___ ___ ___   ___ ___ ___ ___ ___ ___ ___ ___
                      2   1   13   2   1   11   13   9   9   8

TV Tee-Hee

In what room could a lion watch television?

_____

The People's Choice

In the early days of television, comedy and variety shows were very popular. Milton Berle, the comedian, was the first big TV star. In 1951, "I Love Lucy," starring Lucille Ball, was a big hit. Also very popular were professional wrestling matches and quiz shows.

```
T E L F S W O H S M W Z
L M R P Q Z T S J V R S
M I L T O N B E R L E P
K C O E M P D F G N S L
J H V L X L U C Y W T D
G Q Z E Q S X L J V L N
P B U V B J B F A A I G
H C P I R A T S S R N B
W Q N S Z C N H G I G P
Z Q M I C G F L P E T P
T R C O M E D Y U T N R
P N L N H C N X M Y V G
```

Can you find each of the underlined words in the paragraph above in the puzzle grid? They may be up, down, across, diagonal, or backwards. Circle each word as you find it.

Name: _____

INDEPENDENCE DAY

Celebrate History!

On July 4, 1777, the people of Philadelphia, Pennsylvania, held the first anniversary celebration of the signing of the Declaration of Independence. Bells rang, cannons boomed, and there were bonfires and fireworks.

Join in the celebration by completing the magic word squares below. (The answers in each puzzle will be the same across and down.)

1. The bells ____ loud and clear on July 4, 1777.
2. A space. (Length × width = ____.)
3. Opposite of sloppy.
4. A door in a fence.

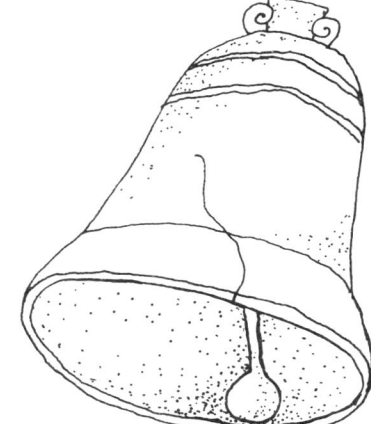

1. The loud noise a cannon makes.
2. A fairy tale monster.
3. Having to do with the mouth; brushing teeth is part of ____ hygiene.
4. The warm sun will ____ the snow.

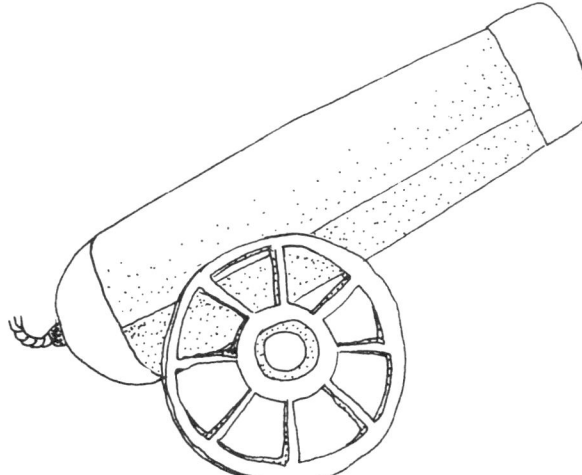

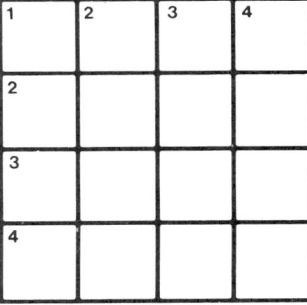

1. Heat and light made by burning; bon ____ and ____ works.
2. Used to press out wrinkles.
3. A street.
4. The last parts of anything.

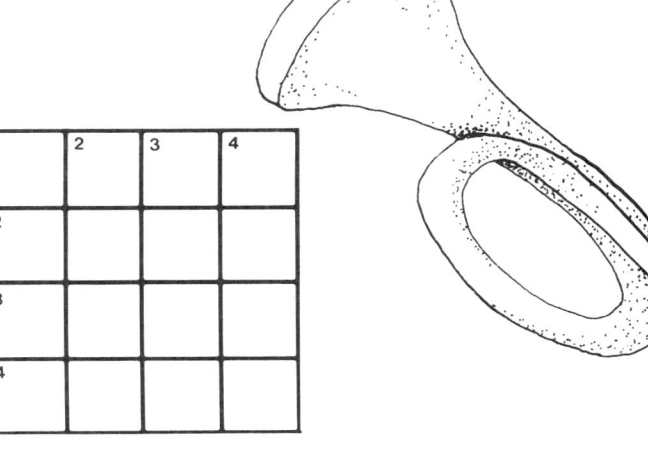

INDEPENDENCE DAY

Liberty Bell

The Liberty Bell was rung at noon on July 8, 1776 to announce the signing of the Declaration of Independence four days before. The bell originally had a different name. To learn that name, you must break the code in the puzzle below. (Hint: It is a 4-shift cipher. A=E, B=F, C=G, and so on.)

L N K R E J Y A   X A H H

_ _ _ _ _ _ _ _   _ _ _ _

Message of Freedom

Discover part of the inscription engraved on the Liberty Bell by translating the sentence below. (It is a 4-shift cipher.)

"L N K Y H W E I   H E X A N P U

_ _ _ _ _ _ _ _   _ _ _ _ _ _ _

P D N K Q C D K Q P

_ _ _ _ _ _ _ _ _ _

W H H   P D A   H W J Z..."

_ _ _   _ _ _   _ _ _ _...

Name: _____

INDEPENDENCE DAY

Fun on the Fourth

You'll get a bang out of this puzzle! See how many smaller words of two letters or more you can find hidden in the word below. (There are at least 20.)

FIREWORKS

1._____   6._____   11._____   16._____

2._____   7._____   12._____   17._____

3._____   8._____   13._____   18._____

4._____   9._____   14._____   19._____

5._____   10._____   15._____   20._____

Boom!

Don't let your brain explode trying to solve this puzzle!

   To learn the answer to the joke, do the math shown under the blanks and then use the answers as a code to fill in the letters.

What did one firecracker say to the other firecracker?

	2 P	14 E	11 R	1 G	
9 A					12 S
10 N					8 H
4 O					7 T
					13 I
	5 B	3 Y	6 M	15 U	

$$\overline{}\ \overline{}\quad \overline{}\ \overline{}\ \overline{}$$
$$8-2\ \ 5-2\quad\ \ 5-3\ \ 8-4\ \ 5-3$$

$$\overline{}\ \overline{}$$
$$7+6\ \ 7+5$$

$$\overline{}\ \overline{}\ \overline{}\ \overline{}\ \overline{}\ \overline{}$$
$$6-1\ \ 7+6\ \ 3-2\ \ 3-2\ \ 8+6\ \ 6+5$$

$$\overline{}\ \overline{}\ \overline{}\ \overline{}$$
$$9-2\ \ 4+4\ \ 5+4\ \ 6+4$$

$$\overline{}\ \overline{}\ \overline{}\ \overline{}\quad \overline{}\ \overline{}\ \overline{}$$
$$5-2\ \ 8-4\ \ 8+7\ \ 6+5\quad\ \ 5-3\ \ 8-4\ \ 5-3$$

Name: _____

P.T. BARNUM'S BIRTHDAY

No Ordinary Circus

Phineas Taylor Barnum, the great American showman, was born on this day in 1810. He is most famous for the circus he started in 1871 in Brooklyn, New York, which went on to become world famous. Barnum gave his circus a special title. Can you figure out what it is? Add and subtract the letters as shown from the names of the pictures in the puzzle below.

T+  −N

_____

_____

 − E+W   1−E   +TH

_____   _____   _____

In the Center Ring . . .

Take a look under the big top and see some of the performers from Barnum's circus. Do you know who they are? Unscramble the letters in each word to see the show!

N O W L C   Makes us laugh. __ __ __ __ __

G E L J U G R   Amazes us by keep- __ __ __ __ __ __ __
                  ing three balls
                  moving in the
                  air at once.

N I L O M E A R T Bravely faces __ __ __ __ __ __ __ __ __
                    wild animals.

C R A B O A T   Does fantastic __ __ __ __ __ __ __
                  tumbling tricks.

Name: _____

P.T. BARNUM'S BIRTHDAY

Circus Star

The main attraction of P.T. Barnum's famous circus was a 6½ ton African elephant he bought from the London Zoo. To learn the name of Barnum's elephant, solve the puzzle below. Look at the pictures. Put the name of what you see in the spaces below each picture. The numbers under the spaces are a code that will help you learn the name.

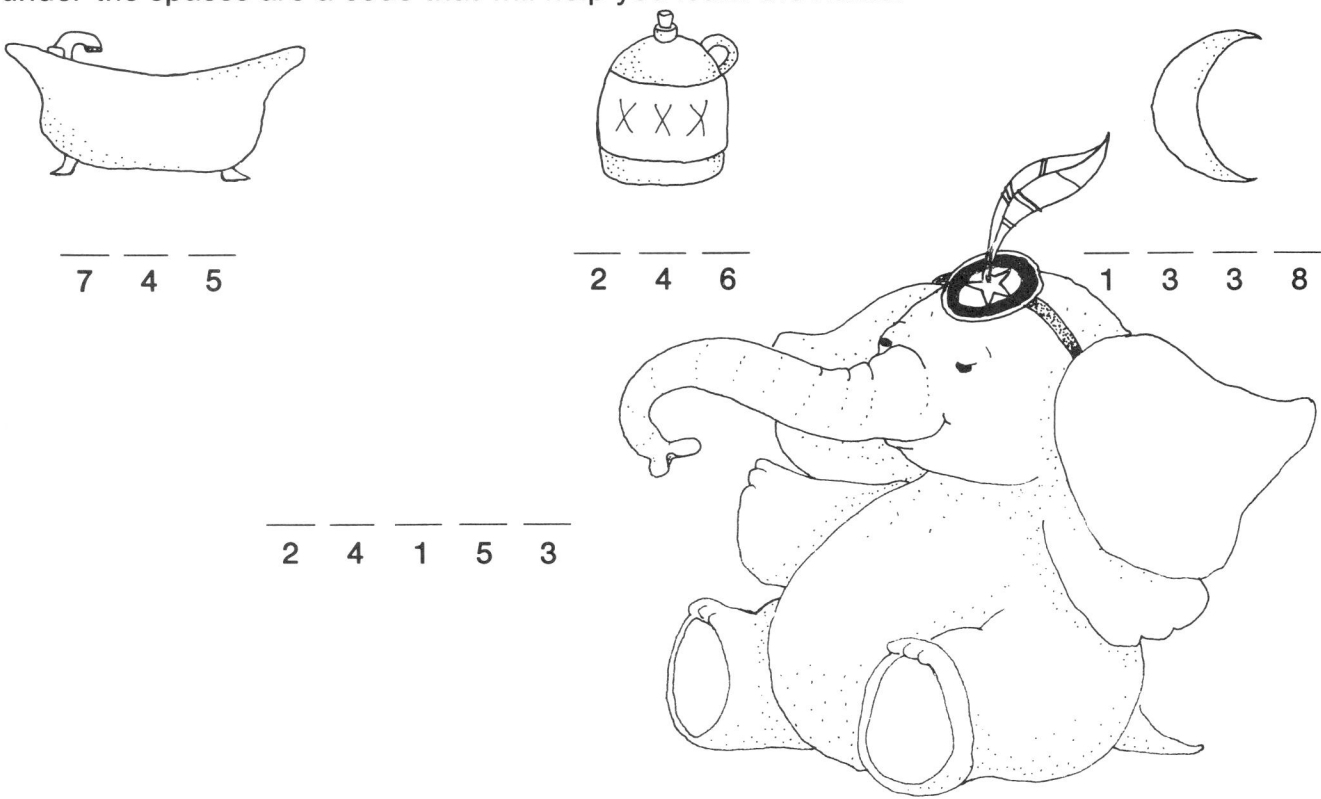

___ ___ ___
7 4 5

___ ___ ___
2 4 6

___ ___ ___ ___
1 3 3 8

___ ___ ___ ___ ___
2 4 1 5 3

Elephant Jokes

Here's your chance to get some "elephant-size" laughs! Translate the punch lines to the jokes below. (Hint: They are written as 3-shift ciphers. A=D, B=E, C=F, etc.)

What did Barnum do when his elephant sneezed?

E B   D L Q   L R Q   L C   Q E B   T X V!

___ ___   ___ ___ ___   ___ ___ ___   ___ ___   ___ ___ ___   ___ ___ ___

How did Barnum always know where his elephant was?

E B   Z L R I A   P J B I I   Q E B

___ ___   ___ ___ ___ ___ ___   ___ ___ ___ ___ ___   ___ ___ ___

M B X K R Q P   L K   F Q P   Y O B X Q E.

___ ___ ___ ___ ___ ___ ___   ___ ___   ___ ___ ___   ___ ___ ___ ___ ___ ___.

BASTILLE DAY

Name: _____

The Spirit of '89

A national holiday in France, today celebrates the day in 1789 when the people of Paris seized the Bastille (an old prison) in their fight for freedom.

Can you complete the word pyramid below? Follow the directions, making a new word for each step.

S P I R I T

___ ___ ___ ___ ___

___ ___ ___ ___ ___

___ ___ ___ ___

___ ___ ___

___

Drop one letter and unscramble; word means "voyages."
Drop one letter; "tears or shreds."

Drop one letter and unscramble; "to drink little by little."
Drop one letter and unscramble; "I am, you are, he ____."
Drop one letter, "me."

Freedom Words

Today marked the beginning of the French Revolution. Can you find the motto of the Revolution hidden in the puzzle below?

Go around the box three times and count off every third letter. Print the letter as you come to it in the space below and circle it in the puzzle to learn the message. (The first two letters are circled.)

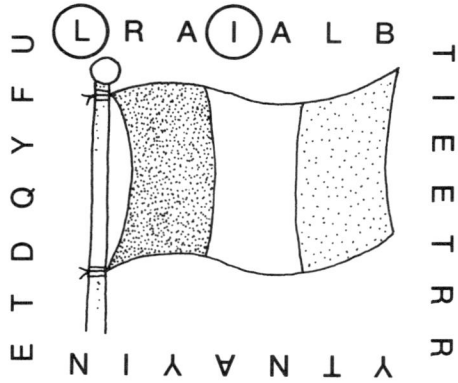

"LI_____"

Name: _____

U.S. LANDING ON THE MOON

Moon Men

American astronauts Neil Armstrong and Buzz Aldrin became the first men on the moon on this day in 1969.

You can help them land their Apollo spaceship by solving the two magic word squares below. (The answers in each puzzle will be the same across and down.)

1. To bring a spaceship to the ground.
2. A space. (Length × width = ____.)
3. Opposite of far.
4. To mend a sock.

1. Where the moon is. Outer ____.
2. Boiled water is cleaner and ____ than river water.
3. A place usually in an enclosed stadium, where ball games and shows are held.
4. A quarter equals 25 ____.
5. To rub out.

Famous Words

Break the code and discover what astronaut Neil Armstrong's first words were as he stepped onto the surface of the moon. (Hint: The code is a 4-shift cipher. A=E, B=F, and C=G, and so on.)

"K J A   O I W H H   O P A L
__ __ __   __ __ __ __ __   __ __ __ __

B K N   I W J
__ __ __   __ __ __

K J A   C E W J P   O P A L
__ __ __   __ __ __ __ __   __ __ __ __

B K N   I W J G E J Z."
__ __ __   __ __ __ __ __ __ __

U.S. LANDING ON THE MOON

Ball of Fire

Ancient peoples thought that the moon was a giant mirror or a huge, turning ball of fire.
    Can you turn the word BALL into the word FIRE? Change one letter at a time keeping the letter order the same. Each change should result in a new word, until you have changed all four letters and solved the puzzle.

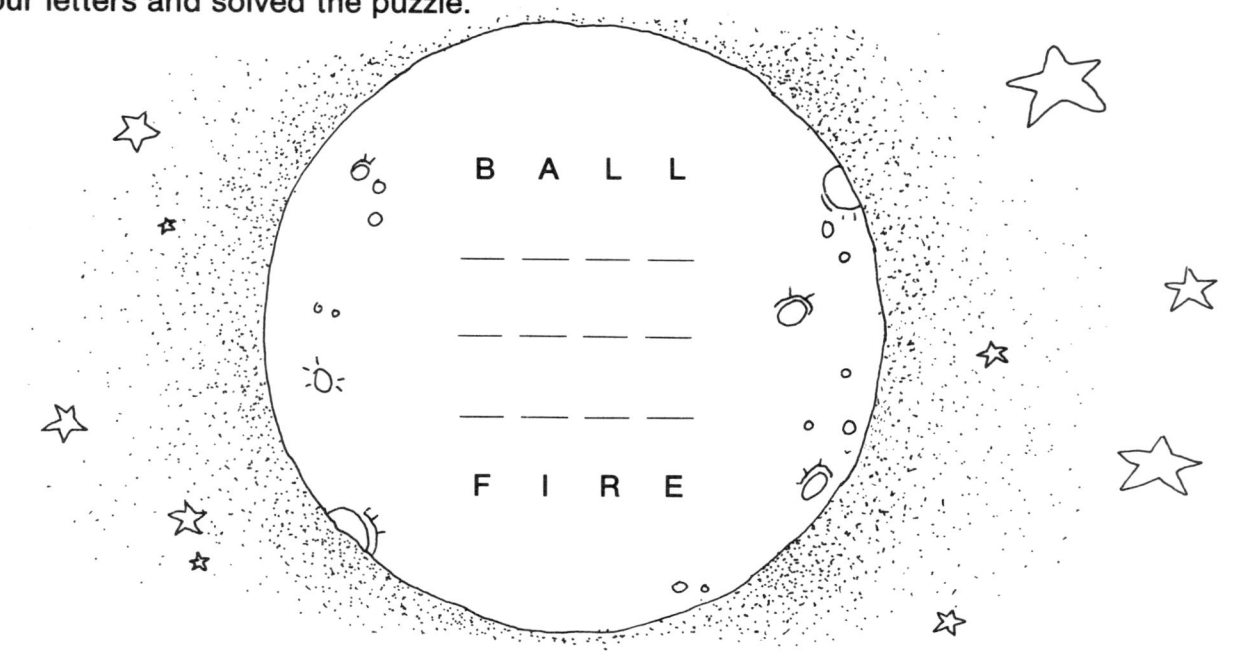

B A L L

_ _ _ _

_ _ _ _

_ _ _ _

F I R E

Green Cheese

Is the <u>moon</u> made of green cheese as the old story claims? The astronauts that landed there discovered that the moon's <u>soil</u> is made of <u>ground</u> <u>up</u> rock, <u>bits</u> of <u>glass</u>, and larger <u>chunks</u> of <u>rocks</u>. <u>Nothing</u> <u>grows</u> or lives on the moon.
    Set out on your own trip to the moon by fitting each of the underlined words from the paragraph above into the puzzle grid below. (One has already been done for you.)

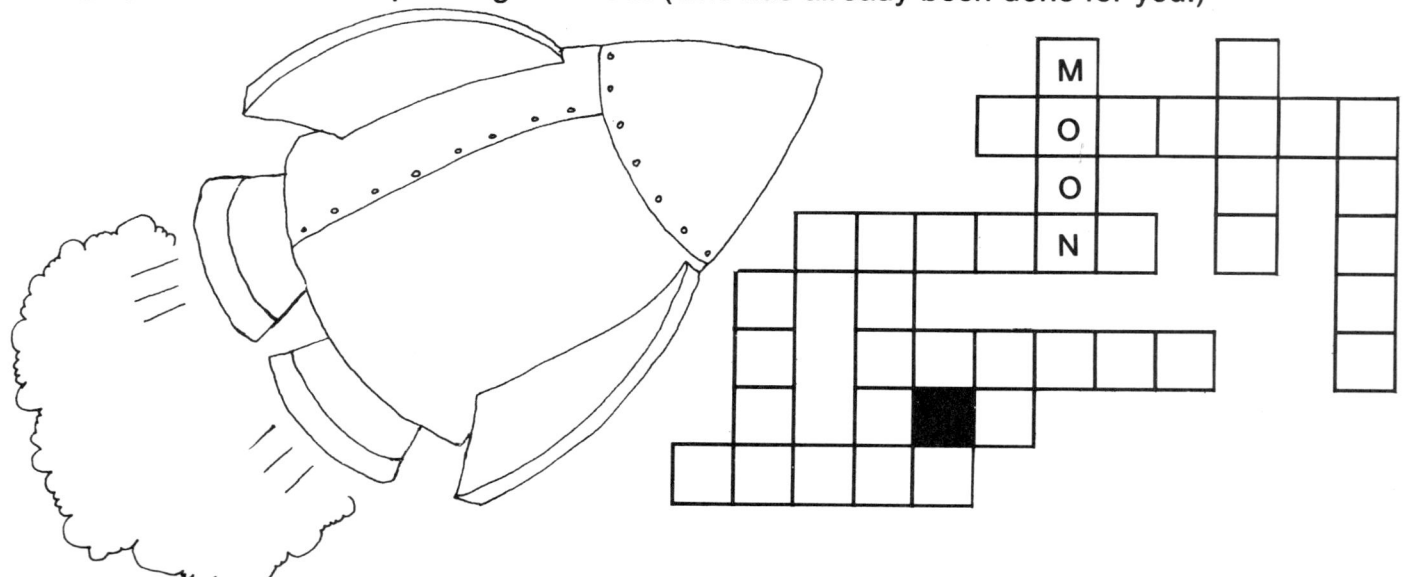

PUERTO RICO'S CONSTITUTION DAY

Friendly Nations

Puerto Rico became a commonwealth—a self-governing territory of the United States—on this day in 1952 when its constitution was signed.

Can you translate the special message shared by both Puerto Rico and the United States? If you don't know Spanish, unscramble the words below to learn the message.

Somos amigos.

E W   R A E   D E R I F N S

___ ___   ___ ___   ___ ___ ___ ___ ___ ___ ___

Magic Island

Constitution Day is celebrated with parades, singing and dancing. Read the words (translated from the Spanish) of a favorite song sung by children on this day.

The island. . .where I was born
Is a garden of flowers of magic beauty.
A sky always clear
Serves as its canopy
And the placid ocean
Murmurs around it.

On the day long ago,
When Columbus arrived in
its harbor,
He exclaimed full of admiration
'Oh! Oh! Oh!
This is the beautiful island
For which I have been seeking.'

Try to fit each of the underlined words in the song into the puzzle grid below. One has already been done.

Name: _____

FIRST AMERICA'S CUP RACE

Racing the Waves

The America's Cup is the world's most famous sailboat race. A boat from another country challenges the New York Yacht Club for the cup (trophy) that was first won by the schooner *America* in 1851.

Take a look at the names of the five different kinds of sailboats. Can you fit each of them into the puzzle grid opposite?

CATBOAT (smallest, with one sail)
SLOOP (two sails)
YAWL (Three sails)
KETCH (three or more sails)
SCHOONER (largest, with many sails)

PARTS OF A <u>SAILBOAT</u>
(A Sloop)

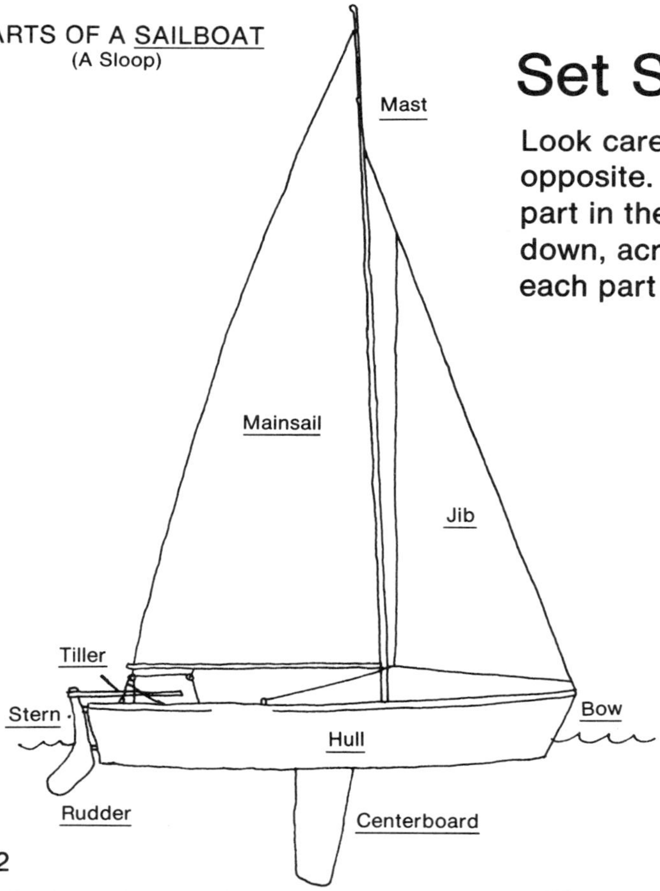

Mast

Mainsail

Jib

Tiller

Stern

Hull

Bow

Rudder

Centerboard

Set Sail

Look carefully at the diagram of a sailboat opposite. Can you find the names of each underlined part in the puzzle? The names may be up, down, across, diagonal, or backwards. Circle each part as you find it.

```
S  M  R  U  D  D  G  P  B  C  X
A  A  L  T  M  T  I  L  L  E  R
I  I  I  V  T  Q  S  J  K  N  E
F  N  E  L  S  T  E  R  N  T  D
B  S  C  L  B  I  J  D  F  E  D
Q  A  H  U  G  O  H  V  T  R  U
K  I  B  H  T  S  A  M  M  B  R
G  L  W  O  D  R  P  T  L  O  F
J  X  K  M  W  J  R  V  L  A  G
H  N  Q  U  Z  M  K  B  D  R  E
D  Y  L  J  Y  S  P  N  W  D  L
```

Name: _____

19th AMENDMENT

A Special Victory

Almost fifty years after Susan B. Anthony tried to vote and was arrested for doing so, American women finally won the right to vote. On this day in 1920, the 19th Amendment was added to the Constitution of the United States. It read:
The <u>right</u> of <u>citizens</u> of the <u>United States</u> to <u>vote</u> shall <u>not</u> be <u>denied</u> or <u>abridged</u> by the <u>United States</u> or by any state on account of <u>sex</u>.

Can you fit each of the underlined words from the paragraph above into the puzzle grid? (One has already been done for you.)

U N I T E D S T A T E S

Fighting for the Right

Can you unscramble the name of one Western nation in which women were granted the right to vote in general elections only as late as 1971?

The years women received
the right to vote:
New Zealand — 1893
Australia — 1902
Canada — 1917
   (Quebec — 1940)
United States — 1920
Brazil — 1934
Philippines — 1937
France — 1945
Belgium — 1946
Mexico — 1946

R E W Z I T S D A L N

— — — — — — — — — — —

	Name: _____
# YOUR BIRTHDAY	

The Birthday Child

Read the poem below and fill in the blanks by using the pictures as a code. Put the name of what you see in the spaces below each picture. The numbers under the spaces are the code that will help you complete the poem.

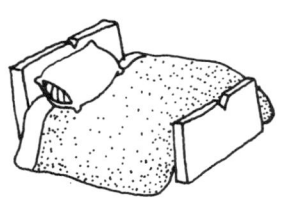
‾2‾ ‾5‾ ‾4‾

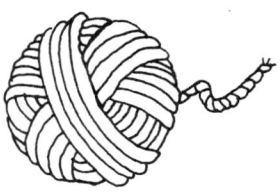
‾20‾ ‾1‾ ‾14‾ ‾12‾

‾6‾ ‾9‾ ‾15‾ ‾8‾

‾13‾ ‾19‾ ‾11‾

‾8‾ ‾9‾ ‾18‾ ‾5‾

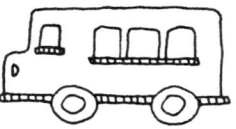
‾2‾ ‾17‾ ‾15‾

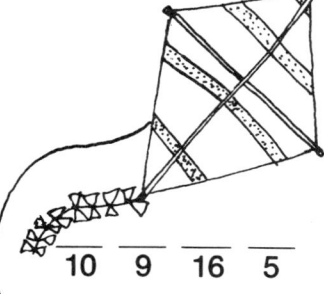
‾10‾ ‾9‾ ‾16‾ ‾5‾

‾4‾ ‾13‾ ‾7‾

‾3‾ ‾1‾ ‾16‾

Monday's child is ‾6‾ ‾1‾ ‾9‾ ‾14‾ ‾13‾ ‾6‾ ‾6‾ ‾1‾ ‾3‾ ‾5‾ ,

Tuesday's child is ‾6‾ ‾17‾ ‾11‾ ‾11‾ ‾13‾ ‾6‾ ‾7‾ ‾14‾ ‾1‾ ‾3‾ ‾5‾ ,

Wednesday's child is ‾6‾ ‾17‾ ‾11‾ ‾11‾ ‾13‾ ‾6‾ ‾19‾ ‾13‾ ‾5‾ ,

Thursday's child has ‾6‾ ‾1‾ ‾14‾ ‾16‾ ‾13‾ ‾7‾ ‾13‾ ,

Friday's child is ‾11‾ ‾13‾ ‾18‾ ‾9‾ ‾12‾ ‾7‾ and ‾7‾ ‾9‾ ‾18‾ ‾9‾ ‾12‾ ‾7‾ ,

Saturday's child ‾19‾ ‾13‾ ‾14‾ ‾10‾ ‾15‾ ‾8‾ ‾1‾ ‾14‾ ‾4‾ for a living,

And the child that is born on the Sabbath Day,

Is ‾2‾ ‾13‾ ‾12‾ ‾12‾ ‾20‾ and blithe, ‾7‾ ‾13‾ ‾13‾ ‾4‾ and gay.

184

YOUR BIRTHDAY

Good Wishes

In ancient times, it was believed that a birthday party protected a person from evil spirits. Having friends and family around, giving gifts, and wishing the person well was considered to be good luck.

Can you think of a story that tells how a good fairy's birthday wish protected a baby from evil?

Solve the puzzle to learn the title of the story. The first letter of the name of each picture is a letter in the title?

Fortune Cake

Did you know that some birthday cakes were able to tell your fortune? Mixed into the batter would be a <u>coin</u>, a <u>button</u>, a <u>ring</u>, and a <u>thimble</u>. The person who found the coin in his/her piece would be rich; the one to get the button, poor; the ring meant you would marry one day; the thimble meant you would not.

Can you find all four of the underlined items in the puzzle "cake"? The words may be up, down, across, diagonal, or backwards. Circle each word as you find it.

<table>
<tr><td></td><td></td><td align="right">Name: _____</td></tr>
</table>

YOUR BIRTHDAY

Piñata

In Mexico, many children think the best part of a party is the piñata.

How to make a piñata:

A clay bowl is filled with <u>treats</u>, covered with papier-mâché (<u>wet</u>, pulpy <u>paper</u>), and <u>molded</u> into shape. Then it is covered with frilled strips of colored paper in order to look like a <u>bird</u> or <u>animal</u>. Someone then <u>hangs</u> the piñata from the ceiling.

Try to fit each of the underlined words from the paragraph above into the puzzle grid. (One is already done for you.)

A Shower of Goodies

Each child at the party takes a turn trying to hit the piñata hard enough to <u>break</u> it open. A <u>blindfold</u> is placed over the child's eyes, and he or she is given a <u>stick</u>. If the child is <u>lucky</u> enough to hit it just right, a <u>shower</u> of goodies (<u>candies</u> and <u>toys</u>) tumbles out and all the children <u>scramble</u> to <u>pick</u> them up.

Can you find each of the underlined words from the paragraph above in the puzzle? They may be up, down, across, diagonal, or backwards. Circle each word as you find it.

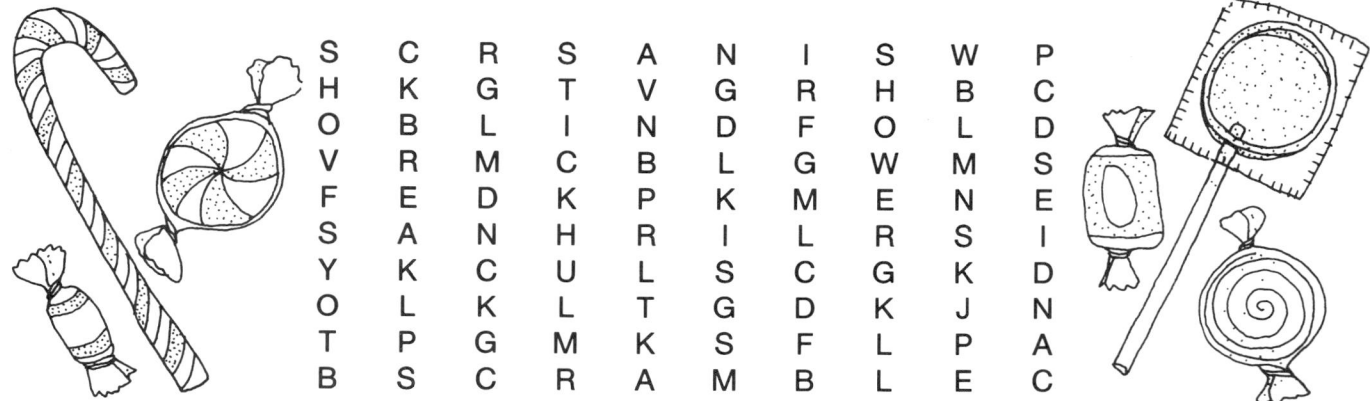

```
S  C  R  S  A  N  I  S  W  P
H  K  G  T  V  G  R  H  B  C
O  B  L  I  N  D  F  O  L  D
V  R  M  C  B  L  G  W  M  S
F  E  D  K  P  K  M  E  N  E
S  A  N  H  R  I  L  R  S  I
Y  K  C  U  L  S  C  G  K  D
O  L  K  L  T  G  D  K  J  N
T  P  G  M  K  S  F  L  P  A
B  S  C  R  A  M  B  L  E  C
```

186

Key To Answers

7— 2. farmer; 3. dancer; 4. dentist; 5. teacher; 6. carpenter; 7. actor; 8. chef. Baseball, sail, roller-skate, camp out, fish, surf, sunbathe, picnic; a lot of fun

8— tea, each, eat, ate, at, cheat, heat, hat, hate, cat

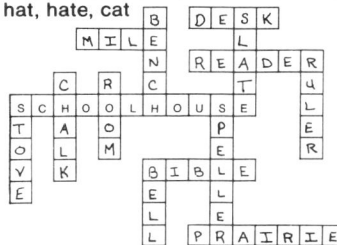

9— geography, social studies, mathematics, language arts, science; smart! Snappy answers!

10— gap, gape, grand, grape, ran, rap, rare, rent, and, ant, are, ape, art, asp, nag, nap, drag, drape, dare, dent, par, pad, pear, pare, pant, pants, peg, pan, pander, parents, parent, ear, ere, end, tag, tan, trap, ten, tar, tend, tear, tap, star, stare, stand, sang, strap, stag, pendant, strand

11— mother, father, brother, sister, aunt, uncle, cousin, grandmother, grandfather; your grandmother; your grandfather

12—

surf; turf

13— George Washington; James Madison

14—

15— You'd have three! Emmie, see the bee? Oh, yes, Abie, I see the bee. It's easy to see the bee.

16—

17—
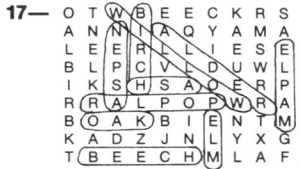
bus, fly, star, kite; by its bark

18—

glow, blow, blot, boot, boat

19—
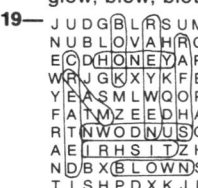
May you be inscribed and sealed for a good year.

20— horn, born, bore, bare, bake

21—
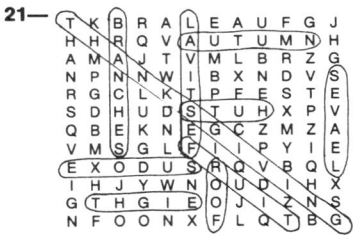
shut, huts, chute, hutch, shutter

22— shooting stars; a half moon, a full moon is lighter; sun beams

23—

24—

1. Call fire department from outside building; 2. Give address and name; 3. Never go back into a burning building.

25— burn, born, bore, core, cope
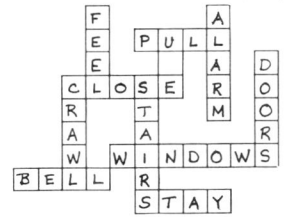

26— Nothing, it just waved; his step; someone was always sitting on the deck.

27— candle, bus, pot, grapes, ham, violin, jar; Bahamas; Puerto Rico; Virgin Islands; Jamaica; South America.

28— Great Land; bed, sock, ax, ring, web; Seward's ice box; kayak

29—
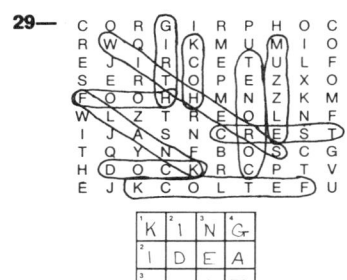

30—
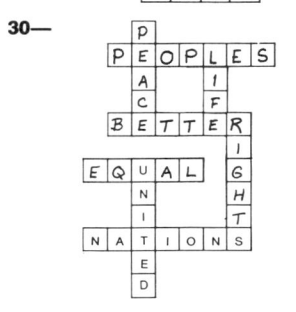
Sweden, Soviet Union, Argentina, Australia, India, Egypt, Great Britain, Canada, China, United States, World Peace

31—

32—

bell, dog, two, yarn, fish; Liberty enlightening the world

33—
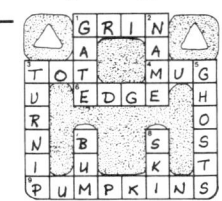
cut, cup, cop, top; pick, peck, peek, seek, seed, face, fare, care, core, corn

187

34— You are bootiful; A new scare-do; It didn't have the guts; A witch watch; Because they're both always a-gobblin

35—

cat, catch, cattle, catalog, category, cathedral, caterpillar

36— Handcuffs, ropes, chains, prison cell; hat, bat, bet, bee; card, care, bare, bore, bone; wand, hand, hard, herd, hero.

37—

float, flat, fat, at, a

38— _____ blazed a trail from Virginia into Kentucky; he was adopted as a member of the Shawnee Indian tribe; he founded Boonesboro on the Kentucky River

39—
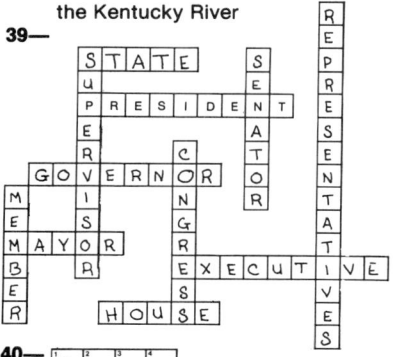

40—

B	E	S	T
E	C	H	O
S	H	O	W
T	O	W	N

stones, stone (tones), tone, ton (one), to (on), 0

41— Here rests in honored glory a soldier known but to God; veer, vet, vest, vent, era, ere, ear, eat, east, ever, eve, even, tea, ten, tan, teen, tern, tear, tee, tar, tease, terse, tense, rat, rest, rate, ran, rent, rant, rave, are, ant, art, ate, near, neat, nest, net, steer, snare, star, stare, sane, sat, set, seat, seen, save, starve, see

42—
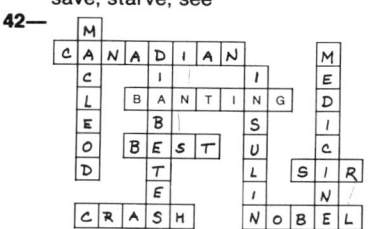

me, mine, men, mind, dime, din, den, deem, dine, need

43— _____ more books in the home; books, booked, booklet, bookends, bookstore, bookkeeper

44—
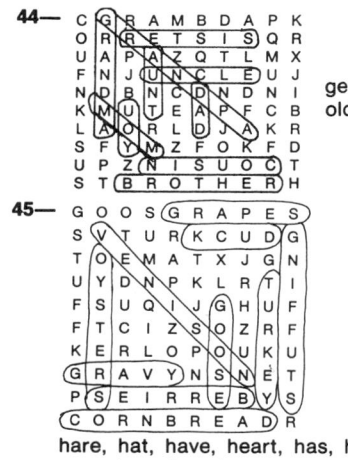

getting older

45—
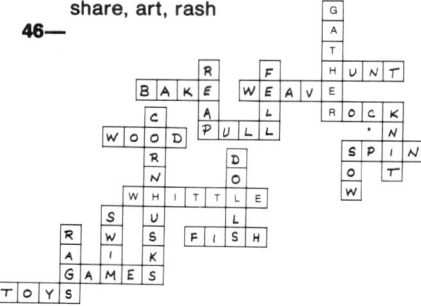

hare, hat, have, heart, has, hate, are, ate, ash, rat, rave, rest, vest, vat, vet, hear, ear, eat, east, star, save, sear, sea, starve, shave, stare, sat, set, seat, tar, tea, tear, share, art, rash

46—
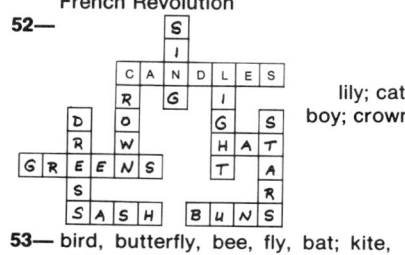

47— a, an (at, ah, as), tan (hat, sat, has), tank (sank, hats), thank (tanks, hanks), thanks; wheat, corn, grapes, rice

48— Samuel Clemens; Tom Sawyer; Huckleberry Finn

49— raisins, flour, butter, sugar, spices, walnuts, cherries, orange rind, bake, eggs; a fruitcake; wreath, wheat, heat, tea, at

50—

H	A	T		C	A	P	E		N	I	C	K
A	T	E		A	R	E	A		I	D	E	A
T	E	A		P	E	A	R		C	E	N	T
E	A	R	S						K	A	T	E

candy, doll, puzzle, train, orange, ball, storybook

51— Magna Carta; Boston Tea Party; French Revolution

52—

lily; cat; boy; crown

53— bird, butterfly, bee, fly, bat; kite, glider, airplane, jet, rocket

54—
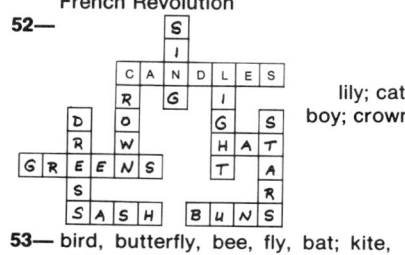

55— bobsled, skis, ice skates; snowy, snow, now, no, n; they sleigh it.

56— snow, sow, slow, snake, saw, safe, sake, now, new, news, oak, owl, own, oaf, won, wake, wan, wane, flake, flow, flew, fan, fake, folks, foal, flaw, lake, low, less, lean, loan, lass, lane, law, leak, lone, loaf, leaf, elf, eon, sea, self, sane, sale, son, sew, seal, soak, slew, season

57—
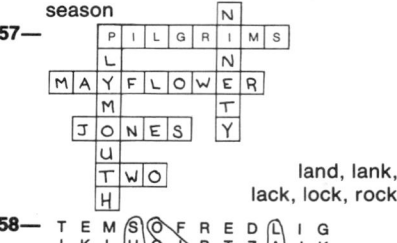

land, lank, lack, lock, rock

58—
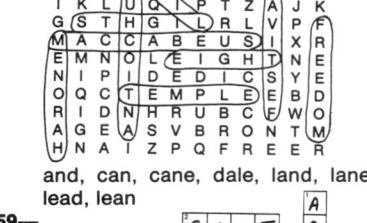

and, can, cane, dale, land, lane, lead, lean

59—
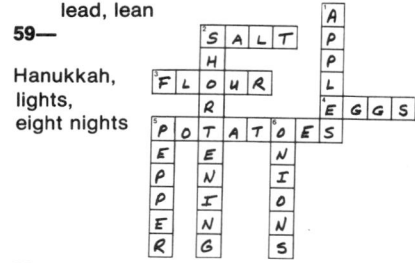

Hanukkah, lights, eight nights

60— eyes, roses, cherry, mouth, bow, beard, snow, pipe, teeth, smoke, wreath, bowl, jelly; Missile toe

61— ox, donkey, cow, sheep, horse; starts (stares), start (stare), star, tar, rat, at, a

62— ore, one, omen, oats, rent, ram, roan, roam, ream, reason, rat, rot, rest, rose, nor, nest, name, not, amen, meat, men, mare, more, man, mean, moan, mat, mate, tame, toes, ten, ton, tan, tone, sent, seam, sear, seat, son, same, some, stare, stone, steam, star, store, soar, sort, set, sat

63—
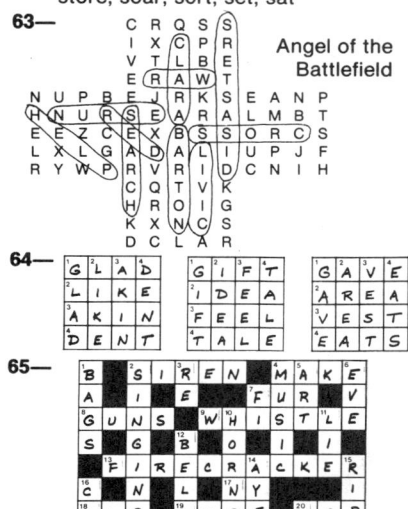

Angel of the Battlefield

64—

G	L	A	D		G	I	F	T		G	A	V	E
L	I	K	E		I	D	E	A		A	R	E	A
A	K	I	N		F	E	E	L		V	E	S	T
D	E	N	T		T	A	L	E		E	A	T	S

65—
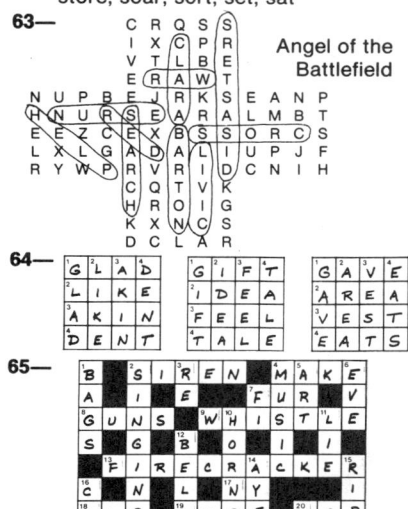

188

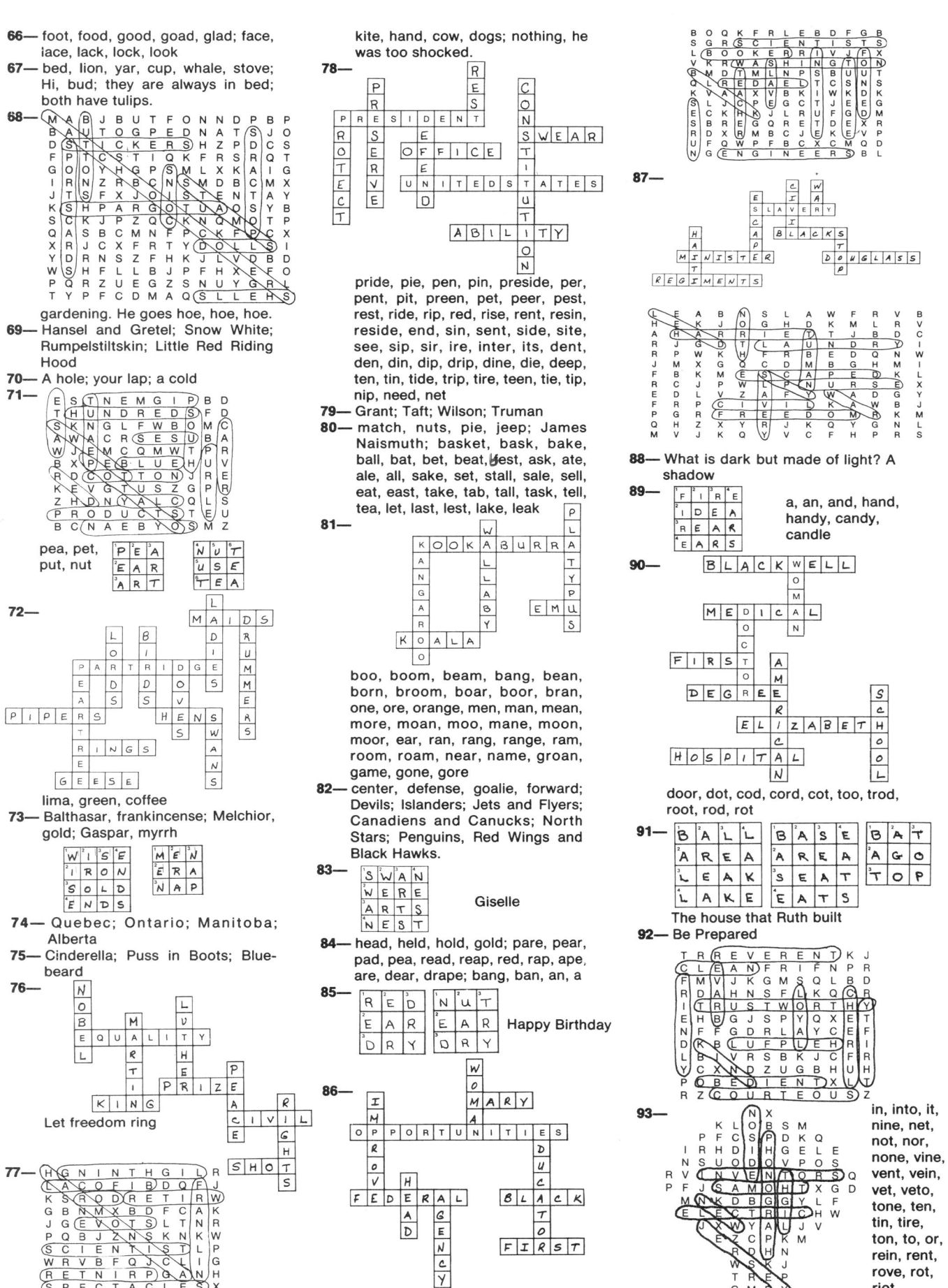

66— foot, food, good, goad, glad; face, iace, lack, lock, look

67— bed, lion, yar, cup, whale, stove; Hi, bud; they are always in bed; both have tulips.

68— gardening. He goes hoe, hoe, hoe.

69— Hansel and Gretel; Snow White; Rumpelstiltskin; Little Red Riding Hood

70— A hole; your lap; a cold

71— pea, pet, put, nut

lima, green, coffee

72—

73— Balthasar, frankincense; Melchior, gold; Gaspar, myrrh

74— Quebec; Ontario; Manitoba; Alberta

75— Cinderella; Puss in Boots; Bluebeard

76— Let freedom ring

77—

kite, hand, cow, dogs; nothing, he was too shocked.

78—

pride, pie, pen, pin, preside, per, pent, pit, preen, pet, peer, pest, rest, ride, rip, red, rise, rent, resin, reside, end, sin, sent, side, site, see, sip, sir, ire, inter, its, dent, den, din, dip, drip, dine, die, deep, ten, tin, tide, trip, tire, teen, tie, tip, nip, need, net

79— Grant; Taft; Wilson; Truman

80— match, nuts, pie, jeep; James Naismuth; basket, bask, bake, ball, bat, bet, beat, best, ask, ate, ale, all, sake, set, stall, sale, sell, eat, east, take, tab, tall, task, tell, tea, let, last, lest, lake, leak

81—

boo, boom, beam, bang, bean, born, broom, boar, boor, bran, one, ore, orange, men, man, mean, more, moan, moo, mane, moon, moor, ear, ran, rang, range, ram, room, roam, near, name, groan, game, gone, gore

82— center, defense, goalie, forward; Devils; Islanders; Jets and Flyers; Canadiens and Canucks; North Stars; Penguins, Red Wings and Black Hawks.

83— Giselle

84— head, held, hold, gold; pare, pear, pad, pea, read, reap, red, rap, ape, are, dear, drape; bang, ban, an, a

85— Happy Birthday

86—

87—

88— What is dark but made of light? A shadow

89— a, an, and, hand, handy, candy, candle

90— door, dot, cod, cord, cot, too, trod, root, rod, rot

91— The house that Ruth built

92— Be Prepared

93— in, into, it, nine, net, not, nor, none, vine, vent, vein, vet, veto, tone, ten, tin, tire, ton, to, or, rein, rent, rove, rot, riot

189

94—

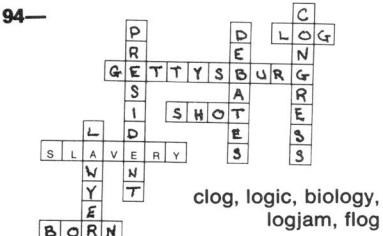

clog, logic, biology, logjam, flog

95— was the sixteenth president of the United States; center; highway; tunnel; university; memorial

96— Freckle Juice; Super Fudge; Iggie's House

97—

bow, low, law, lad; fell, fill, gill, girl

98— vale, veil, vain, vain, vein, vent, vine, vile, vane, vat; valet, vet, ale, ate, ail, ant, lane, late, lain, lean, lent, lie, line, leave, eat, eel, nine, nile, nail, net, tea, tale, tan, ten, tie, teen, tail, tile, entail, even; I don't give a hoot about you.

99— Think of me and remember our friendship; rose and daffodil; thyme and rue.

100—

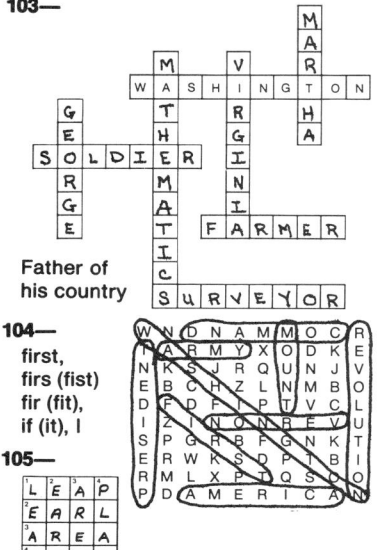

101— flag, flat, feat, beat, best; leaf, lean, loan, loin, coin

102— her, hate, heat, hat, hit, hag, hear, eat, ear, rat, rate, rag, rite, rage, it, ire, tar, tear, tag, there, their, tire, the, tie, tee, tree, age, ate, are, air, agree, ah, at, get, gather, gate, gear, grit, great, grate; flower; hair; pale; here; rain (reign)

103—

(crossword grid with WASHINGTON, SOLDIER, FARMER, SURVEYOR, MATHEMATICIAN, GEOGRAPHER)

Father of his country

104—

first, firs (fist) fir (fit), if (it), I

105—

(grid: LEAP, EARL, AREA, PLAY)

106— Hot cross-buns, hot cross-buns. One a penny, two a penny, hot cross-buns. If you have no daughters, then give them to your sons.

107—

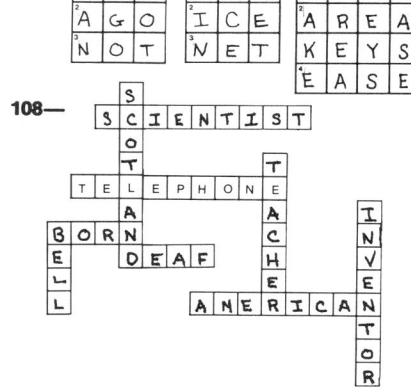

108—

(crossword grid with SCIENTIST, TELEPHONE, BORN, DEAF, AMERICAN, inventor)

Watson, Come here. I want you.

109— dolls, doll, old, do, o; pea, pace, each, ape, ache, ace, chap, cheap, cape, cap; peacefulness

110— ball, bill, mill, mile, mine; touch, too, two, ton, out, own, chow, cot, cow, hot, hoot, how, hood, dot, down, don't, wood, ouch, now, not, notch

111— Do a good turn daily

112— giraffe, lion, elephant, zebra, rhinoceros; rabbits, woodchuck, owl, fox

113— Why is it hard to hide a leopard? It is always spotted.

114— snakes, sneak, sank, ans., an, a; spat, path, patch, patron, pattern, spatula, patriot

115—

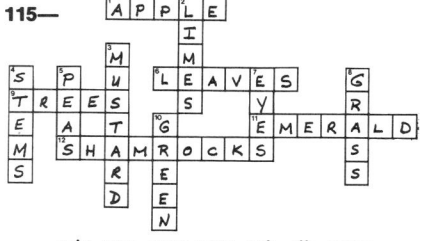

(crossword grid with APPLE, TREES, LEAVES, SHAMROCKS, EMERALD)

rain, ran, raw, row, rob, rib, roan, nab, now, nor, bow, bin, boar, born, ban, bar, oar, win, war, won

116— plot, sloth, lotion, clothes, lottery

117— cold, cord, card, ward, warm; foal; lamb; gosling; chick; calf

118—

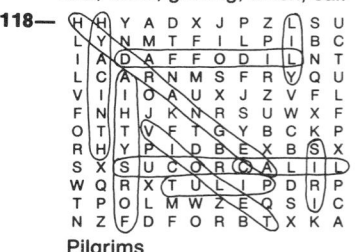

Pilgrims

119—

120—

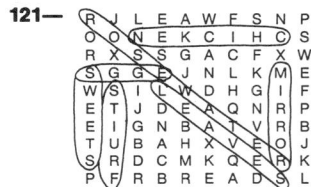

(grids: WATER, METALS, CROP, SAVE, AREA, VEER, EARS)

121—

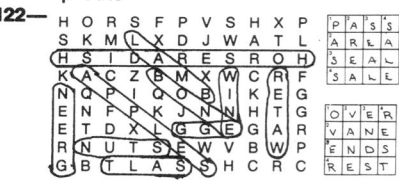

to, pot, pout, spout, spouts, sprouts

122—

(word search grid with HORSE, IDA, RESROH, NUTS, GLASS, etc.)

(grids: PASS, AREA, SEAL, SALE; OVER, VANE, ENDS, REST)

123— bread, bead, bad, ad, a; fail, fly, flay, aim, am, ail, may, may, if, yam

124—

(grids: LILY, IDEA, LEAK, YAKS; RING, IDEA, NEST, GATE; FLY, LIE, YES)

eggs

125— red, blue, green, yellow, orange, pink, lavendar, brown; Use hare spray

126—

(grids: TOP, ONE, PET; HAT, ARE, TEA; CAP, APE, PEA; TAM, AGE, MEN)

127— Smiles. There is a mile between the beginning and end.

128— What is red with purple spots and has one hundred legs? I don't know, but it's crawling on your back.

129— You just had a march of thirty-one days.

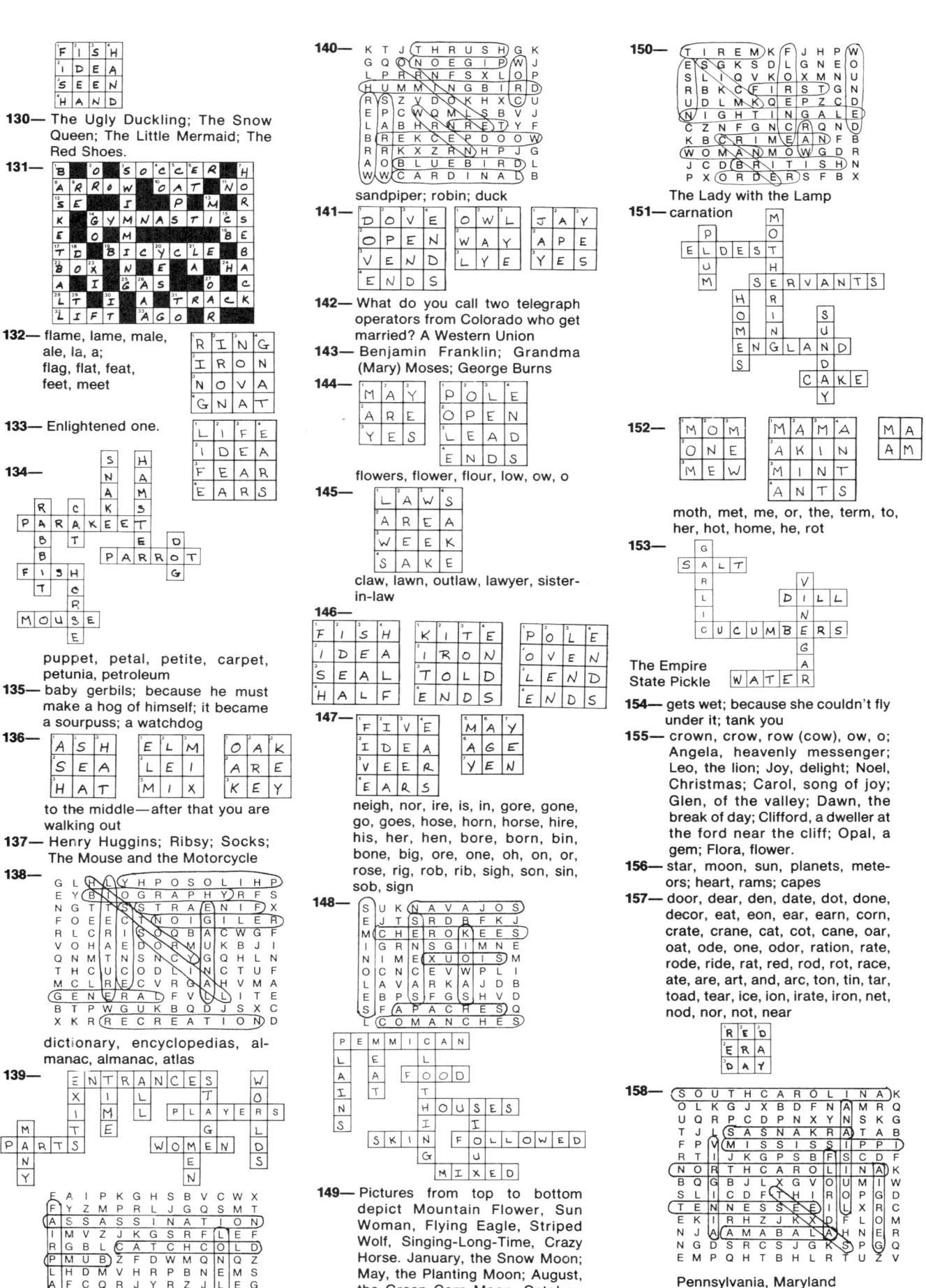

130— The Ugly Duckling; The Snow Queen; The Little Mermaid; The Red Shoes.

131—

132— flame, lame, male, ale, la, a; flag, flat, feat, feet, meet

133— Enlightened one.

134— puppet, petal, petite, carpet, petunia, petroleum

135— baby gerbils; because he must make a hog of himself; it became a sourpuss; a watchdog

136— to the middle—after that you are walking out

137— Henry Huggins; Ribsy; Socks; The Mouse and the Motorcycle

138— dictionary, encyclopedias, almanac, almanac, atlas

139—

140— sandpiper; robin; duck

141—

142— What do you call two telegraph operators from Colorado who get married? A Western Union

143— Benjamin Franklin; Grandma (Mary) Moses; George Burns

144— flowers, flower, flour, low, ow, o

145— claw, lawn, outlaw, lawyer, sister-in-law

146—

147— neigh, nor, ire, is, in, gore, gone, go, goes, hose, horn, horse, hire, his, her, hen, bore, born, bin, bone, big, ore, one, oh, on, or, rose, rig, rob, rib, sigh, son, sin, sob, sign

148—

149— Pictures from top to bottom depict Mountain Flower, Sun Woman, Flying Eagle, Striped Wolf, Singing-Long-Time, Crazy Horse. January, the Snow Moon; May, the Planting Moon; August, the Green Corn Moon; October, the Falling Leaf Moon

150— The Lady with the Lamp

151— carnation

152— moth, met, me, or, the, term, to, her, hot, home, he, rot

153— The Empire State Pickle

154— gets wet; because she couldn't fly under it; tank you

155— crown, crow, row (cow), ow, o; Angela, heavenly messenger; Leo, the lion; Joy, delight; Noel, Christmas; Carol, song of joy; Glen, of the valley; Dawn, the break of day; Clifford, a dweller at the ford near the cliff; Opal, a gem; Flora, flower.

156— star, moon, sun, planets, meteors; heart, rams; capes

157— door, dear, den, date, dot, done, decor, eat, eon, ear, earn, corn, crate, crane, cat, cot, cane, oar, oat, ode, one, odor, ration, rate, rode, ride, rat, red, rod, rot, race, ate, are, art, and, arc, ton, tin, tar, toad, tear, ice, ion, irate, iron, net, nod, nor, not, near

158— Pennsylvania, Maryland

191

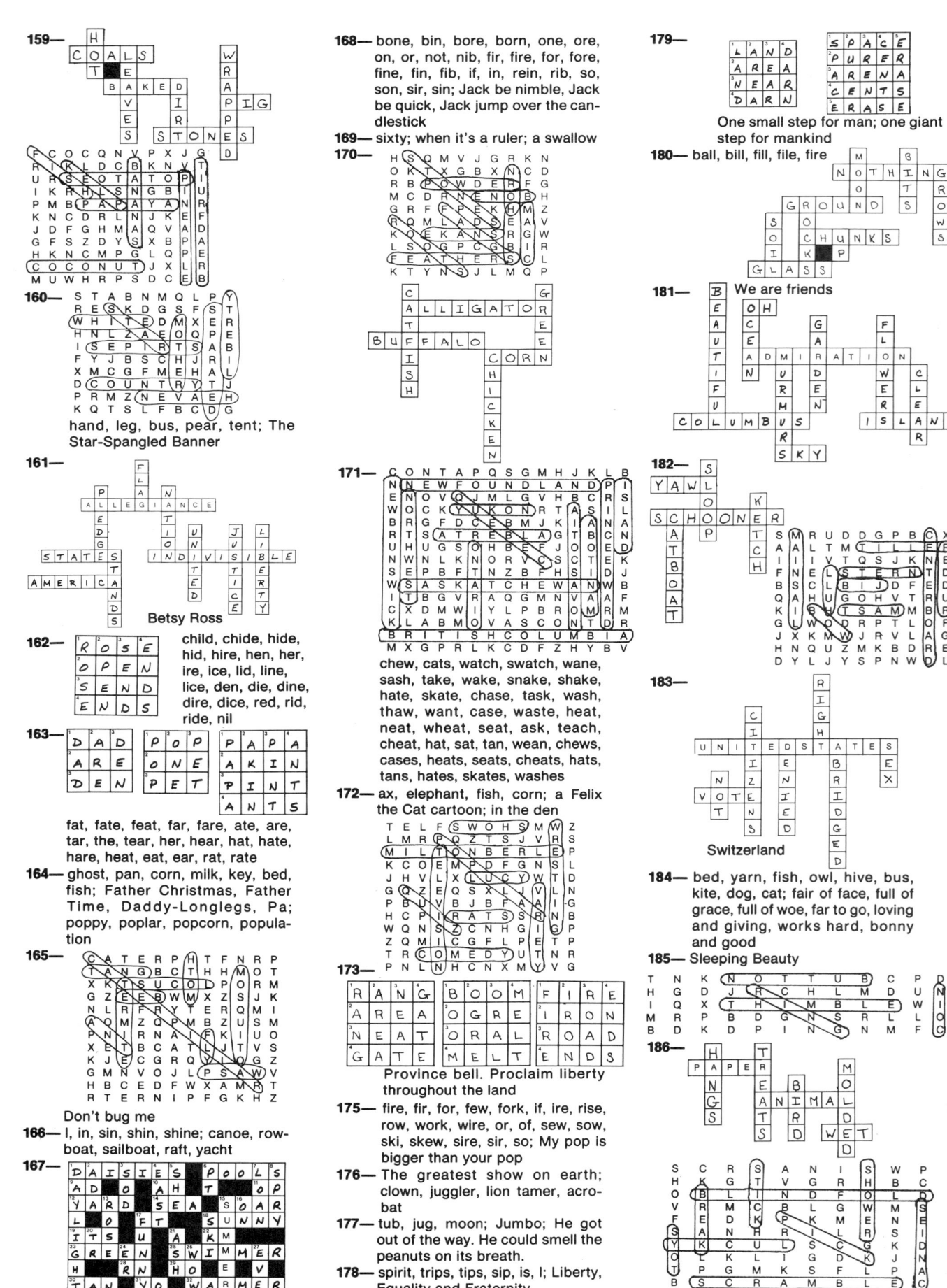

159—

168— bone, bin, bore, born, one, ore, on, or, not, nib, fir, fire, for, fore, fine, fin, fib, if, in, rein, rib, so, son, sir, sin; Jack be nimble, Jack be quick, Jack jump over the candlestick

169— sixty; when it's a ruler; a swallow

170—

179—

One small step for man; one giant step for mankind

180— ball, bill, fill, file, fire

160—

hand, leg, bus, pear, tent; The Star-Spangled Banner

161—

Betsy Ross

162— child, chide, hide, hid, hire, hen, her, ire, ice, lid, line, lice, den, die, dine, dire, dice, red, rid, ride, nil

163—

fat, fate, feat, far, fare, ate, are, tar, the, tear, her, hear, hat, hate, hare, heat, eat, ear, rat, rate

164— ghost, pan, corn, milk, key, bed, fish; Father Christmas, Father Time, Daddy-Longlegs, Pa; poppy, poplar, popcorn, population

165—

Don't bug me

166— I, in, sin, shin, shine; canoe, rowboat, sailboat, raft, yacht

167—

171—

chew, cats, watch, swatch, wane, sash, take, wake, snake, shake, hate, skate, chase, task, wash, thaw, want, case, waste, heat, neat, wheat, seat, ask, teach, cheat, hat, sat, tan, wean, chews, cases, heats, seats, cheats, hats, tans, hates, skates, washes

172— ax, elephant, fish, corn; a Felix the Cat cartoon; in the den

173—

Province bell. Proclaim liberty throughout the land

175— fire, fir, for, few, fork, if, ire, rise, row, work, wire, or, of, sew, sow, ski, skew, sire, sir, so; My pop is bigger than your pop

176— The greatest show on earth; clown, juggler, lion tamer, acrobat

177— tub, jug, moon; Jumbo; He got out of the way. He could smell the peanuts on its breath.

178— spirit, trips, tips, sip, is, I; Liberty, Equality and Fraternity

181— We are friends

182—

183—

Switzerland

184— bed, yarn, fish, owl, hive, bus, kite, dog, cat; fair of face, full of grace, full of woe, far to go, loving and giving, works hard, bonny and good

185— Sleeping Beauty

186—